PENGUIN BOOKS

Aprons and Silver Spoons

Born in 1916, Mollie Moran is now ninety-six and lives on Bourne-mouth seafront. She regularly hosts Scrabble parties and cooks for up to twenty-five people. Mollie grew up in Norfolk, and was sent to London as a scullery maid at the age of fourteen. She remains friends with the kitchen maid, Flo, from the first household she worked in, more than eighty years later.

Aprons and Silver Spoons

The Heartwarming Memoirs of a 1930s Kitchen Maid

MOLLIE MORAN

PENGUIN BOOKS

PENGUIN BOOKS

Published by the Penguin Group
Penguin Books Ltd, 80 Strand, London WC2R ORL, England
Penguin Group (USA) Inc., 375 Hudson Street, New York, New York 10014, USA
Penguin Group (Canada), 90 Eglinton Avenue East, Suite 700, Toronto, Ontario, Canada M4P 2Y3
(a division of Pearson Penguin Canada Inc.)
Penguin Ireland, 25 St Stephen's Green, Dublin 2, Ireland
(a division of Penguin Books Ltd)
Penguin Group (Australia), 707 Collins Street, Melbourne, Victoria 3008, Australia
(a division of Pearson Australia Group Pty Ltd)
Penguin Books India Pvt Ltd, 11 Community Centre,
Panchsheel Park, New Delhi – 110 017, India
Penguin Group (NZ), 67 Apollo Drive, Rosedale, Auckland 0632, New Zealand
(a division of Pearson New Zealand Ltd)
Penguin Books (South Africa) (Pty) Ltd, Block D, Rosebank Office Park, 181 Jan Smuts Avenue,
Parktown North, Gauteng 2193, South Africa

Penguin Books Ltd, Registered Offices: 80 Strand, London WC2R ORL, England

www.penguin.com

First published 2013
001

Typeset in Garamond MT Std 12.5/14.75pt by Palimpsest Book Production Ltd,
Falkirk, Stirlingshire
Printed in Great Britain by Clays Ltd, St Ives plc

ISBN: 978–0–718–15999–3

www.greenpenguin.co.uk

Penguin Books is committed to a sustainable
future for our business, our readers and our planet.
This book is made from Forest Stewardship
Council™ certified paper.

ALWAYS LEARNING   **PEARSON**

I dedicate this book to my late mother, Mabel, and all my family.

Contents

1 An Idyllic Childhood 1
Tips From a 1930s Kitchen –
Mollie's Famous Sausage Rolls 24

2 London Calling 25
Tips From a 1930s Kitchen – Bread and Butter Pudding 44

3 Tears in the Scullery 45
Tips From a 1930s Kitchen – The Perfect Roast Beef 75

4 Soulmates 77
Tips From a 1930s Kitchen – Soup to Scrub Floors On 112

5 To the Country 113
Tips From a 1930s Kitchen – Old-fashioned Irish Stew 152

6 Mop Caps and Mischief 154
Tips From a 1930s Kitchen – Christmas Pudding 190

7 Passion With the Footman 192
Tips From a 1930s Kitchen – Trifle and Brandy Snaps 233

8 Scandal Below Stairs 235
Tips From a 1930s Kitchen – Proper Fish and Chips 266

9 Castles in Spain 268
Tips From a 1930s Kitchen – Lemonade 296

10 A Cook at Last 297
Tips From a 1930s Kitchen – Steamed Suet Pudding 355

Afterword   357
List of Photographs   369

Acknowledgements   373

An Idyllic Childhood

Sweet was the walk along the narrow lane
At noon, the bank and hedge-rows all the way
Shagged with wild pale green tufts of fragrant hay,
Caught by the hawthorns from the loaded wain,
Which Age with many a slow stoop strove to gain;
And childhood, seeming still most busy, took
His little rake; with cunning side-long look,
Sauntering to pluck the strawberries wild, unseen.
William Wordsworth

Inching higher and higher, I used every fibre of my being to pull my body further up the tree trunk. Just one more foot and I'd be there. The prize was in sight and it was worth its weight in gold.

Come on, Mollie Browne, you can do it.

With a superhuman show of strength and a grunt I swung my leg over the branch and sat gasping for breath.

I'd climbed to the very top of the tallest oak tree in the village.

It started as a tingle in my chest and soon spread to the

tips of my fingers. Joy flooded my body. I'd done it. I'd only gone and done it. No one had climbed this tree, not even the bravest lads in our village.

'Sissies,' I chuckled to myself. I may only have been a ten-year-old girl, but I was more of a man than any of them.

My mother Mabel's warning, issued just before I left the house that morning, rang in my ears: 'Come straight home from school and don't be scuffing your shoes or ripping your dress climbing trees on the way. And don't you be nicking all them eggs out the nests again. I mean it, Mollie Browne, any more trouble and I'll swing for you, I will.'

I looked down at my ripped cotton dress. Oops, too late. And by the way the sun was dipping down below the spire of the church I could tell dusk was gathering.

I hesitated. What were rules for if they weren't to be broken?

The thought of the telling-off I was going to get melted away when I realized I could see for miles around the tranquil landscape. What a thrill. It was like discovering a secret magic world; just me and the birds in the twilight. Fields dotted with ancient flint churches stretched out as far as the eye could see. In the distance I could make out the town of Downham Market and just beyond that the sun glittered off the River Great Ouse.

The year was 1926. Coal miners were striking, John Logie Baird had just given the first public demonstration of the television and Gertrude Ederle had become the first woman to swim the Channel. These were exciting times. London was in the grip of the 'Roaring Twenties'.

Bright young socialites wore their hair in bobs, their skirts short, and were dancing up a storm in jazz clubs. Their louche and provocative behaviour was blazing a trail across the front pages.

Here in gentle Norfolk it was a different story.

A tractor rumbled in the middle distance, ploughing straight lines through the soil. Fields of wheat and barley rustled gently in the breeze. All was still, quiet and timeless.

This was my world. Mollie Browne's world. One giant playground full of adventures just waiting to be had. But even as I surveyed the peaceful landscape I felt the strangest sensation grip my heart. My destiny didn't lie here in the sleepy villages, forced into a dull apprenticeship before being married off to the local farmhand. No, thank you. There had to be more to life. I wasn't sure what yet but – sure as eggs is eggs – I would find a way to make it happen.

At the thought of eggs, I suddenly remembered the reason why I was up this big old tree in the first place. Wiping the sweat off my brow, I forced myself not to look down and edged along the gnarled branch to claim my prize. Two perfect brown speckled eggs were sitting in the nest within touching distance, still warm from when the crow had hatched them.

I wasn't daft. I'd never pocket a wren's or robin's egg. Everyone knew bad luck would come your way if you nicked those and your hands would fall off. Happen there be no harm in a crow's egg, though.

Just then a sharp whistle sounded from below.

My partners in crime!

I could just make out the faces of Jack and Bernard.

'It's the bobby,' Jack hissed. 'Get down afore he sees ya.'

Oh heck. There was no time to pocket either of the shiny brown eggs. Instead I shimmied down that tree faster than a rat down a drainpipe. With a loud thud I landed slap bang in front of the black laced-up leather boots of one PC Risebrough. My nemesis. I swear that man spent his whole time roaming the countryside looking for me. He always seemed to know just where to find me!

'Mollie Browne again,' he said in his thick Norfolk accent. Slowly he shook his head. 'If there's trouble to be found it's always you in the thick of it, ainch ya? When will yer learn?'

Last summer he'd caught me with handfuls of stolen strawberries. There'd not been a soul about, until the sight of his tall hat bobbed past over the top of the hedge. He'd clouted me so hard round the lugholes that my ears had been ringing for weeks.

I shook my head as I saw Jack and Bernard turn on their heels and leg it. 'I was just mucking about,' I said, shaking my red curls vigorously. ''Avin' a gorp from the tree.'

He peered down at me, narrowed his eyes and slowly and deliberately peeled off his gloves. 'Tha's a lotta ol' squit,' he said. 'Stealing eggs you was. I oughta box your chops.'

Two minutes later, and with my ears ringing from another clip, I ran for home.

'Any more trouble and I'll be letting your father know,' PC Risebrough shouted after me. 'Now git orf wiv yer.'

My heart sank as I raced off down the fields. Not again.

He was forever catching me doing things I shouldn't and my father was forever telling me off. I didn't want to trouble Father, not in his condition, but trouble just seemed to seek me out.

I ran so quickly across the fields and lanes that the bushes became a blur of green. I could run in them days. I was so strong and fast it wasn't true. So fast that at times I felt I could have flown clean over the hedgerows like a swallow, swooping and soaring.

At the end of the lane that led to our tumbledown cottage I paused and looked back over the fields. Dusk was sneaking gently over the village and soon the fields would be cloaked in a velvety darkness. Smoke curled gently from the chimney pots and suddenly my tummy rumbled. I thought of bread and dripping by the fire, or if I was lucky we might have a bit of meat in a steak and kidney pudding. Machine-gunning my way up the lane that led to our smallholding, I startled a blackbird that flew chattering from the hedgerow. My heart soared as I ducked through the hedge and crept down the back garden. It was Monday, washing day. Mother would be too busy to notice I was late for tea.

Picking my way through the sea of linen drying in the back garden, I giggled to myself. I dodged past a pair of combis, ducked under a pair of Mother's wool stockings and nipped past an old clothesline prop before landing at the back door. With a creak I pushed it open and, quiet as a church mouse, tiptoed through the scullery and into a steaming hot kitchen. Mother's back was turned to me as she prodded the vast old copper that creaked and groaned as it furiously boiled up a week's worth of dirty washing.

I'd just made it to the stairs when a voice piped up from the kitchen table.

'Mollie's 'ere, Mum.'

I whirled round to face my little brother, James.

'Hello, carrot,' he said, smiling smugly. 'Happen you're late. And you've got twigs in your carrot top.'

'Why, you little . . .' I gasped. If there was one thing I hated more than anything it was being called 'carrot'. My face flushed as bright red as my curly hair.

Mother stared at me and, wiping the soapsuds off her hands, she shook her head. 'Oh, Mollie, bird's-nesting . . . not again. What'll your father say?'

'I'll give ya a fourpenny one so as I will!' I yelled, making a lunge for my little brother.

'Oh, will you keep yer trap shut, Mollie Browne?' Mother sighed, flinging herself between us.

Two minutes later I was rewarded with a second clip round the ear and sent to my bedroom with not so much as a skerrick of bread. No matter. I didn't care tuppence for a telling-off in them days. I'd be the hero of the town.

Born Mollie Browne on 21 September 1916, I'm now ninety-six years old, but my idyllic childhood is etched into my soul and I remember it clear as yesterday.

We was poor growing up. Really poor. I'm not talking not being able to afford to pay the bills or go on holidays. I'm talking grinding poverty where every day for my poor parents was a challenge to feed me and my brother James. We didn't have a penny to our name, see. But we never starved, not like the poor folk in the cities. Out in the countryside, with an iron will and a healthy disregard for the rules, you could always find food for the table.

Money might have been scarce, but love, laughter and adventures by the bucketload never were. And a child-

Here's me at the ripe old age of ninety-six. My face may be wrinkled and my hair faded to silver, but I think you can tell by the twinkle in my eye that I still find the fun in life.

hood spent running free in the beautiful Norfolk countryside gave me a spirit as wild as the hawthorns that grew in the hedgerows.

I credit the fresh air, healthy living of my childhood and ten years of back-breaking work in domestic service for my good health. Do you know, I've not had a single day's illness in my life? I've outlived every single one of the gentry that I scrubbed, shopped and cooked for all those years. Perhaps my childhood and the poverty we experienced bred in me a will to survive. Or maybe it's the characters from whose loins I sprung.

If home is where the heart is then at the heart of my home was my mother, Mabel. When she weren't trying to belt me round the head for getting into another scrape, she was a fiercely loyal, loving and hard-working woman. I never saw my mother at rest. Ever. She was always working. Either slaving away over an open fire, cooking, scrubbing the house or flushed with steam as she spent a whole day washing, wringing clothes out through a giant mangle or wrestling with a flat iron. If she wasn't in the house she was working outside, tending to the fruit and vegetables in the garden. The women of my mother's generation were grafters and tough as old boots too.

Mother met and fell in love with my father, Sydney Easter Browne – so called because he was born on Easter Monday 1892.

I wasn't even born when my father went off to fight in the First World War in 1914. I was conceived when he came home on leave. He was there at my birth in 1916 before he was packed off back to the trenches of France, so I don't remember much of him in the early years. When he was posted back to France, Mother and I moved in with her mother, Granny Esther, in a small village called Wereham, some five miles east of Downham Market.

They broke the mould when they made Granny Esther. Five foot nothing with a fiery halo of thick auburn red hair, she was every bit as tough as the hobnail boots she wore. Granny was a familiar sight around the village. She owned and ran the local village store and she stocked everything from butter to paraffin, which she often served without washing her hands in between. People didn't give two hoots for health and safety in them days.

With a complexion like double cream, her thick red hair and a proud face, she was a handsome woman and drew many an admiring glance from the villagers as she trotted about the village on her horse and trap. She must have been a beauty in her day. When she was seventeen her red hair and shapely curves certainly caught the eye of the local squire's son. The squire owned half the lands and buildings in and around Wereham and so it seemed his son thought he also owned the right to bed whichever local ladies took his roving eye.

The story of Granny Esther's illegitimate child was something of a local legend and I can't remember a time when I wasn't aware of it.

She was seventeen when the squire's son got her pregnant and she gave birth to a little girl called Kate. An illegitimate child in those days was a huge scandal. As she cradled the little baby in her arms, even she was aware that keeping her wasn't an option. The shame her illicit liaison would have brought on her father's house would have been too much. And so she was forced to give her baby up.

Kate was raised by an aunt in a neighbouring village, only coming home occasionally years later after Granny met and married my grandfather, Wick, and had my mother and her brother, Cecil.

Ignorance and fear of pregnancy was everything in them days and no doubt Granny Esther didn't have the faintest clue what went where. The squire's son should have known better, but it was Granny who earned the bad reputation, Granny's family name that would have been tarnished, Granny seen as the morally degenerate one, leading him astray with her wanton behaviour. Load of old balderdash, of course, but such was the narrow-minded thinking of the day.

How does it shape a woman, to be forced to give up a child at seventeen? Did she weep long into the night, her arms aching to hold her forbidden baby, her breasts gorged with unused milk? Her heart must surely have hardened for I know she grew a brittle outer shell that meant we never really dared question her or Kate on their forced separation.

As for the squire's son with the lusty loins and the roving eye? I'm pleased to say that he didn't get away with it scot-free. Granny's father, my great-grandfather Pilgrim, went round and horsewhipped that wretch. He deserved a sound thrashing.

Forced to grow up too soon, Granny Esther developed a steely inner core, which meant she never suffered fools gladly. 'Gerrorf wiv yer, yer old rascal,' she'd cackle if someone asked for something on tick, 'or you'll feel the toe of my boot.' And if any of the local farmhands dared come into her shop straight from the farms without wiping their muddy feet? 'Wipe ya dutty feet afore yew come inta my clean scull'ry!' she'd holler.

Granny could only see out of one eye, but I swear that woman had eyes in the back of her head. She knew in a flash if someone was giving her cheek and if I dared to pull a face, thinking she couldn't see me, I'd soon know about it.

Me as a baby being held by my indomitable Granny Esther. I was always her favourite.

But she could never stay mad at me for long. For when it came to me, her granddaughter, she had a heart as soft as butter. I was the apple of her eye and I knew it. I loved helping her in the shop, especially when she let me sit on the counter, weigh out the sweets and take the money.

Wereham itself was a tiny little village. The population was just a few hundred, but it had a bustling high street that throbbed with life. The high street was the hub of the community and was lined with countless businesses, many of which had been in the same family for generations. Aside from Granny's village shop, there was a butcher, a greengrocer, two bakers, a market garden, a blacksmith and a post office. Can you imagine all those shops? You'd struggle to get just one of those in a village high street these days.

I loved wandering amongst the village characters, taking in the noise, hustle and bustle of village life. Granny and Mother never worried about me. What harm could come to me? There was just one car in the village and apart from one odd sort who liked to slap young girls' bottoms and the occasional bit of horse rustling, crime was non-existent.

The smell of the bakers' freshly baked cottage loaves drifted up the street to the accompaniment of the fruiterer shouting out the quality of his wares. Big fat sugared doughnuts from the bakery, oozing with raspberry jam and thick with sugar, were my favourite.

There were pubs in the village, of course. Three, in fact – the Crown, the George and Dragon, and the Nag's Head – which mostly served to shelter old boys nursing a pint of Norfolk Ale and hiding out from the missus.

'She's always mobbun about suffun,' they'd grumble.

I always used to roam about on my own, right from when I was a tiny nipper. When you're little you're invisible to everyone. Most days I hung out by the Gospel tree, the biggest tree in the village, and watched the world go by. I liked to stop here a bit because right behind it was a big, grand house. Every day young lads would hang out of the windows and sing to me as I peered curiously up at them. Good-looking blond boys they were, who sang in a funny accent that I recognized wasn't a Norfolk one.

It wasn't until two officers came into Granny's shop one day that I realized who they were.

'Here you go, Esther, pigswill from our prisoners of war,' said one, a Mr Lucks. 'Reckon your pigs'll love it.'

Turns out the big house in the village had been commandeered by the army and housed German POWs.

'Poor souls,' muttered Granny darkly. 'No older than schoolboys, they ain't.'

That was the only inkling I ever had that a war was going on. Until, that is, it ended and finally, in 1920, Father returned. Thanks to the war, he was a stranger to me. I don't even remember his homecoming as such. Just that he was not a well man and I was under strict instructions not to trouble him.

I'd heard the muttered whispers in darkened corridors between Granny and Mother, though.

'He's been gassed in Ypres, Mum,' my mother had sobbed. 'His lungs'll never be the same.'

Ypres, or 'Wipers' to the British troops, was under constant bombardment, and fighting between German and British troops was continuous for four years. The conditions there sound nothing short of hell. My father would have been packed cheek-by-jowl with his comrades in cold, waterlogged trenches. Trench foot – rotting of the skin caused by fungal infection – was common, as too were the millions of lice, which sucked off the rotting flesh of soldiers. There was little by way of sanitation, running water or hot food. But the real horrors began when the Germans unleashed a new and shattering weapon – poisonous gas. Gas as a silent enemy became more terrifying than the machine-gun fire that usually followed it, as German infantry attacked the vulnerable gassed soldiers.

Chlorine gas, which is heavier than air, sank and settled in the trenches.

My father never breathed a word about how he came to be gassed or what happened, but reading accounts of it later in life turned the blood in my veins to ice. Many accounts talk of a greenish cloud seeping into the trenches and of the soldiers choking and suffocating or running in all directions, blinded. The gas only lasted short periods until it dissipated and troops quickly learnt to use rags soaked in mud and water to breathe through, which absorbed the vapour. But many soldiers found it hard to resist removing the cloths and tried to gulp in air as they choked, which of course left them with no defence against the gas. Towards the end of the war the Germans also unleashed mustard gas, which seeped into the soil, remaining active for weeks and causing dreadful infections in burnt skin.

Relatively few soldiers died of gas poisoning. Most, like my father, were condemned to a slow death after they returned home. Poor Father. No wonder he suffered and seemed withdrawn. They called him, and thousands like him, the 'Lost Generation' as they never really recovered from their experiences.

Millions of boys died for their country during that dreadful war. Those poor young men – if they had known at the start what they would be facing, would they ever have signed up?

Father never spoke about his role in the war. He was typical of the men of his era and kept his feelings locked away deep inside. His body betrayed him, though. The terrifying coughing fits that turned my mother's face as white as flour were a dreadful legacy of his battle. Every now and again I'd wander into the kitchen to see him coughing so much that his face would turn purple. I'd stay rooted to the spot as he gasped for breath, his whole body shuddering with every gasp.

'I feel a bit queer,' he'd rasp and, with that, his body would convulse into more spasms of coughing.

Mother would rush past me with rags and a bowl of hot water. Slowly the white rags would turn crimson red as Father gasped and coughed up blood.

'Sit yerself forrards, my love,' she'd smile, gently rubbing his back. 'You'll be right in no time.' But I could tell by the way her bottom lip wobbled when she spoke that she didn't really believe it.

After each attack he'd disappear for a few days, off to a sanatorium in Hastings, where it was believed the fresh sea air would revive him back to health. His spells in the sanatorium never worked, though, and he'd return as fragile as he left.

From 1930 onwards the government issued wooden huts for all ex-servicemen with failing health to sleep in. It was believed that sleeping out in the fresh air, away from coal fires, would be better for their lungs. Once you've been gassed, though, I don't expect there's much would help.

Still, my father had his issued and it was duly set up in the back garden. The hut was on an iron swivel axis so it could be turned round to face away from the freezing Norfolk wind that whipped in off the fens or positioned to face the sun, depending on the weather. Sounds crazy, doesn't it, him sleeping in a hut in the garden when he was so fragile, but that was the thinking of the day.

'You need the fresh air, it'll do ya lungs good,' Mother would say, hustling him out to the garden.

He weren't the only one. Loads of men, poorly from the war, slept outside in huts to get their daily constitutional blast of country air.

But despite this, and his failing health, my father was an optimistic man who never dwelt on his misfortune. 'I'm the lucky one awight,' he used to say. 'Least I can still provide for my family.'

And in many ways he was lucky. He had survived – unlike the countless other young men who'd had their brains spattered out and were left to rot in the thick mud around the trenches of France. Back here in the UK the countryside around Downham Market was littered with the 'Lost Generation'. Them as fought and were left able came home and tried to pick up their lives, but if you weren't able to work through illness, what was your destiny? There was no army pension or support. If you were lucky enough to survive you were out on your own.

Injured officers were well cared for, but for non-commissioned soldiers it was more hit and miss. Many developed alcohol problems and mental illness and were left destitute, forced to sleep in barns or ditches and beg for food. Shell shock is now a recognized condition, but there was less sympathy for those with mental scars back then, they were just seen as sissies. It was an absolute scandal, it was.

Often they would come knocking on our door for handouts.

'Hot water, Miss, if you please,' they'd croak.

Mother, like most of the villagers, always took pity on them and would fill their cans with hot water or tea and give them what little bread we could spare.

'They made a sacrifice for their country,' she would say. 'It's our duty to help.'

They were known as 'tramps' locally. Many would go off and do the rounds for months at a time, trudging from village to village for lodgings and food. They all wore the same haunted expression and often had missing hands or feet. Amputated limbs poked out from underneath the rags they wore. Others had faces that were a patchwork of scars. At times, when we walked into Downham Market, we'd see them selling matchsticks by the side of the road. They stared at me with black, soulless eyes and I wondered what hell those eyes had witnessed.

'Don't be giving them no sauce, Mollie,' Mother would hiss in my ear, gripping my hand that bit tighter.

She didn't say it but we all thought it. It could so easily have been my father.

In the winter, when it was too cold to sleep in the freezing ditches, many spent the night in the workhouse in Downham Market, where they chopped wood to earn their keep. The 250-bed workhouse was a dark place and we grew up in the shadow of this institution. I didn't know much about what went on inside but I knew on pain of death you didn't want to end up there. The fear of the workhouse and such poverty was only a heartbeat away for many.

So I suppose, compared to them, Father *was* blessed. He eked out a living from our smallholding, which he rented off the local squire for ten shillings a week. No one, apart from the gentry, owned their own homes then. We kept chickens and a pig and grew fruit and vegetables on the few acres of land we had and we sold what produce we could to make a few shillings.

Father's two older brothers were postmen and when he was well enough he even helped them out on their deliveries in exchange for a little money. And I knew Granny Esther helped us with handouts of cash. She was reasonably well off, what with her shop, and she had a real business head on her. She'd never see us short. Family was everything in them days and as long as ours had breath in their bodies they'd not see us destitute. The house was always full of aunts and uncles, dropping off a gift of a bit of dripping in exchange for some eggs. That's the way it was in those days. You looked after your own.

The only black sheep of the family was my granny's brother, Horace. He'd been in the army, then had a broken love affair and lost his way. I never knew too much about Horace as he was never really spoken of, but I sensed it was always a big embarrassment that we had a tramp in the family. I'd hear dark mutterings from Mother that Uncle Horace was 'on the road again'.

Thankfully, fate had different ideas for us than it did for poor old Uncle Horace and we didn't really want for anything. Mother made all our clothes and we grew our own fruit and vegetables to eat or sell. Father's double-barrel shotgun stood by the fire in the kitchen and every now and again he'd go out and get us a rabbit or pigeon for tea. If we were really lucky we'd have pheasant. Everyone knew you could be prosecuted if you killed and ate the local squire's pheasants, but if one happened to stray on to our land, well then, it was fair game, wasn't it? All the same, Father would pluck it outside by a fire in an old outhouse so any stray feathers would be burnt to cinders, leaving no trace of his harmless crime.

'Don't you be talking of this to no one, Mollie,' he'd order if he caught me watching him plucking fast and steadily in the dark.

And if I ever dared touch that gun, I'd get a savage cut across the backside faster than you can say ''ands orf'.

Father must have been well enough on occasion though, as when I turned six my younger brother, James William Browne, made an appearance. It was a dark, stormy night just before fireworks night, and the birth was no less explosive.

I remember lying huddled in the dark in my bedroom, hearing Mother's wretched screams ring round the cottage. Her cries were at times pitiful, pleading, then at other times so ferocious in their intensity they were almost feral.

'What's happening?' I cried, alarmed, to my father.

'Go to sleep, child,' he ordered.

I covered my ears with the sheets, but still I could hear her bloodcurdling cries. My father slept in with me, well out of the way, as the local doctor thumped up and down the stairs, helped by the neighbours. In 1922 there was no such thing as hospital care and the NHS was twenty-six years away from its conception. Women always gave birth at home with the help of a doctor or midwife if they were lucky, and what friends and neighbours were around. The Midwives Act had only become law twenty years prior to that, in 1902, after a group of visionary women fought to have midwifery recognized as a profession. Before that, anyone, and I mean anyone, could deliver a baby. Most of the time it was whoever happened to be around and, in some drastic cases, prostitutes paid in gin could act as midwives. Fortunately the Act became law, the Royal College of Midwives was born and birthing standards improved.

The next morning I crept into the bedroom where Mother would have the customary two-week lying-in period. It was then that I saw the reason for her blood-curdling screams. She lay back against the pillow, her face ashen with exhaustion. In her arms lay a healthy little baby boy, but her legs were tied roughly together with rope!

Poor Mother had had a breech birth. James had come out feet first. In those days, breech births were complicated, painful and – without modern medicine – a major cause of death in mother and baby. They were incredibly lucky to have survived, but so torn and damaged was she internally, the doctor had bound her legs together to stop her moving and encourage her body to heal.

A rope! Can you ever imagine such a thing today?

'Meet your baby brother,' she said, smiling weakly.

But my mother was nothing if not tough and within two weeks she insisted the rope was untied and she was back scrubbing the kitchen, blackleading the stove, baking, washing and completing the countless other tasks that consumed her life.

As James grew up I longed to have a little boisterous playmate to get into scrapes with, but it soon became obvious that he was a quiet child who preferred to sit by my mother's side. 'You're the boy and he's the girl all right,' Mother used to cackle as we grew older and the differences in our personalities became obvious.

She was right. Tide nor time could pin me down as I roamed the land looking for adventures and trying to avoid the clutches of PC Risebrough.

The countryside was beyond beautiful. The hedgerows, trees and dykes were alive with kingfishers, yellowhammers and blue tits and on a summer day you could catch the tantalizing whiff of salt in the air off the Wash. I'm sure that today there just aren't the same number of birds about. Back then the skies were black with birds and the noise of 'em all going off during the dawn chorus could deafen you. I loved it though, it made me feel glad just to be alive.

In the summer months the grass verges were filled with rows of old brightly painted caravans belonging to the Romany gypsies who came to hawk their wares in town. I'd gaze, intrigued, at the older ladies, with their waist-length silver hair and faces as wrinkled as walnut shells. They wandered door to door selling hazel-wood clothes pegs. I'd sit on my bike and spy on them through the bushes. Gypsy folk fascinated me. Where had they come from and where would they go to next? They washed up like tides on the River Great Ouse and the next morning they'd be gone on the winds.

Father never liked them and always locked up his chickens when they were in the area, but I had no problem with them. They belonged in the countryside as much as any of us.

In and amongst all this rural splendour, me and my friends, Jack and Bernard, ran wild. While my mother busied herself with the endless washing, cooking, baking and cleaning that keeping house involved in the days before modern appliances, I had incredible freedom. Every day was filled with magic, promise and excitement. Because our time wasn't taken up with computers and televisions, we learnt to use our imagination. The Norfolk fields were one giant adventure playground. If there was a tree to climb or a ditch to poke around in, you could bet I'd be in the thick of it, spattered with mud, my face stained purple from gorging on blackberries and my pockets stuffed with nuts, birds' eggs and feathers. And if the ever-present PC Risebrough happened to catch us, well, that just added to the adventure.

We played rounders, hopscotch and skipping races in the summer. Come winter, when temperatures plunged and the Norfolk ponds froze over, we tied blades to our boots with string and skated over the ice. It was ever so deep and dangerous but what did we care? Often we'd land, helpless with laughter, in an icy scrummage of arms and legs. Only the promise of bread and dripping by the fire would have us limping for home with aching limbs and grazed knees. Actually, in my whole childhood, I don't ever remember a time when my knees weren't grazed!

The only two rules my mother would ever issue before I ran to the door of a morning? 'Don't cheek the tramps,

Mollie Browne, that mouth of yours'll get you in trouble one of these days,' and 'Stay away from the sluice. People have drowned swimming there.'

'Yes, Mum,' I'd promise.

Denver Sluice, one mile out of Downham on the River Great Ouse, was built to drain the vast wetlands of the fens and create fertile farmland. But to us kids it was like a magnet and the perfect place to take a cooling dip on a hot summer's day. Mother's words would be lost on the wind as I pedalled like crazy to the sluice with my dress tucked into my knickers.

What did she know? I was twelve, I knew better.

But a mother's wisdom should always be observed, as I was about to find out, to my great peril . . .

TIPS FROM A 1930S KITCHEN

...

Mollie's Famous Sausage Rolls

I used to run wild through the Norfolk countryside as a child, but nothing had me haring for home faster than the smell of my mother's home-baked sausage rolls drifting out over the fields. I can't remember a time when I didn't know how to bake them.

8 oz (225 g) self-raising flour
4 oz (110 g) butter
8 oz (225 g) sausage meat
1 egg for glazing

Rub the flour and butter together, adding a few drops of water, until it forms the consistency of a firm dough. Roll it out on a floured pastry board until it's a quarter of an inch (6 mm) thick. Cut the pastry into four-inch (10 cm) squares. Wet them round the edges with a dab of water. Add a teaspoon of sausage meat in the middle and then fold the pastry over the top and nip the edges to close it together. Brush the tops with beaten egg and bake for half an hour at 180 degrees or until golden brown.

Household Tip

If your fridge or kitchen is full of overpowering cooking smells, simply slice an onion, pop it in a bowl of water and leave it on the table or in the fridge, and all nasty niffs vanish.

2

London Calling

Every woman is a rebel.
Oscar Wilde

'Dare you to jump in from there,' said Jack, pointing to the highest bank of the sluice. A slippery wall of crumbly soil was all that stood between me and the dark swirling waters below.

'All right then,' I said, rising to the challenge.

Everyone that knew me knew I couldn't resist a dare. Too competitive by half, that was my problem. Even blacking out after choking on a hot-cross bun during the hot-cross bun races at school sports day hadn't curbed my ferociously competitive edge.

'It's pootrud, yer knows,' he added, wrinkling his nose. 'There's cowshit and everything in that bit, so there is.'

What did I care? The dare had been issued. I could no more back out now than I could walk to the moon. 'So what?' I said, boldly ripping off my dress and stripping down to my knickers and vest.

Here goes nothing. Taking a deep breath, I launched

myself into the unknown. 'Woohooo!' I hollered. A rush of sheer adrenalin filled my body. I was flying! I was actually flying!

You could have heard the smacking noise of my belly hitting the water five villages along.

Struggling to breathe, I floundered about until I managed to grab on to a soggy clod of mud by the bank. Cow poo and mud was plastered over my knickers and face as I hauled myself, sopping wet and gasping for air, on to the bank. Shaking myself like a wet dog, I scrabbled back up the slippery bank. At the top I paused to wipe my snotty nose on my dripping vest.

'Now your tur . . .' I said, my voice trailing off to nothing.

For who should be ready to greet me? Not the impressed audience I was hoping for, but PC Risebrough!

His beefy hand reached down to grab my sopping wet vest.

Uh-oh.

'Mollie Browne!' he yelled, his face growing as red as a tomato as I legged it to my bike and frantically started to peddle. 'You want your arse leathering.'

By the time I reached home I'd decided not to say a word to Mother.

'Mollie,' she gasped. 'You're soaked through.'

'I fell off my bike,' I lied. 'Right into a ditch.'

'Best sit by the fire and warm up,' she said, pressing a mug of steaming hot tea into my hand.

Sniffing the air, I realized it was Friday, the best day of the week, for it was Mother's baking day. The kitchen was filled with the smell of warm, rich baking. On the side lay rack upon rack of jam tarts, flaky sausage rolls, cottage pies, bread and butter puddings, boiled suet pudding with apples or jam, all piled up and cooling on the countertop.

'I might feel better if I have something to eat,' I said, shivering for dramatic effect.

'Get away with you,' she chuckled. 'Put this in your trap.' With that, she slipped me a baking-hot sausage roll.

'Fanks,' I mumbled through mouthfuls of buttery, light

That's me on the far right, aged ten, being awarded first prize at school sports day in 1926. I was the fastest runner and the highest jumper in the whole area – I always thought I was better than anyone else back then!

pastry. I closed my eyes and munched. Pure heaven. Food never tastes as good to anyone as to a hungry child.

I sniggered to myself as I pictured PC Risebrough's flaming red face as he'd puffed after me. Daresay he'd love one of Mum's home-cooked sausage rolls after his energetic morning.

Once I'd dried off we headed into Downham, for Friday afternoons were market day, another highlight of the week.

Men would stand around chatting outside pubs while women shopped, haggled and nattered with neighbours and friends. It was the social highlight of the week and gave women a break from the endless drudgery of keeping house. Gossip was a currency to be exchanged just as much as shillings and pence. Not that it mattered, mind, as everyone pretty much knew everyone else's business. It was a close-knit community and a stranger's face always stuck out.

I used to love trawling the market with Mother. Everywhere you looked there were stallholders shouting their wares.

'Thirteen herrings for a shilling,' drawled the coster to a crowd of housewives. 'Pound a prawns, fished straight out the sea this morning while you were still abed. Nice and fresh and lovely.'

Before the war this had been the site of a famous horse market where many thousands of horses were shipped off to France. Now it was full of housewives battling to get their pick of the best fish. My mother could get in there with the best of 'em and we always had fish for tea on a Friday. Carts were piled high with glistening kippers and Yarmouth bloaters and her eyes darted this way and that as she sized up the best of the lot to serve up to my father that evening.

'Let's be having you,' shouted the fishmonger, his mutton-chop whiskers quivering. 'What about this 'ere plaice?' he said to Mother, holding up a fish as big as my head. 'Come on then. Hoooge it is, a proper booty.'

'It's a great ole fish yew've got there, bor,' she laughed. 'But I'll settle for some herring.'

'All right,' he said, chucking the fish down with a slap. 'Get yer hand off yer ha'penny.'

While he wrapped up the fish in brown paper Mother slipped me a penny for some sweets. Hours I could spend drooling through the sweet-shop window in the market, carefully working out what to spend my money on. Every temptation you can imagine danced in front of my eyes: pineapple chunks, lollipops, liquorice bootlaces, gobstoppers, peanut brittle, toffees, walnut whips, cherry lips, coconut mushrooms and Uncle Joe's mint balls. I settled for a gobstopper and sucked it happily all the way back to the cottage as Mother strode beside me, swinging her bag of fish and humming to herself.

Friday had to be the best day of the week, easy. Home baking, the market, sweets and freshly cooked fish for tea. But it was also time for our weekly bath. After tea, Mother would drag an old tin bath in from outside and place it in front of the roaring fire. It'd take an age to fill up with pails of water from the copper. Finally, when it was ready, my brother and I would jump in. Helpless laughter filled the smoky kitchen as we flicked soapy suds in the flickering firelight and Mother tried to stop the cats and dogs from leaping in with us.

Father would sit by the fireside watching us, a gentle smile playing on his weary face. I often wonder if he envied us our carefree lives after everything he'd witnessed. Our heads were filled with nothing but the pursuit of fun in them days, while who knows what demons chased through his mind.

Soon the water would be thick with dirt.

'Reckon you've brought half the countryside in with yer, Mollie,' exclaimed Mother.

Poor Mother and Father. They had to bathe in that water after us, not that you ever heard a mutter of complaint pass their lips, mind you.

While I was enjoying a glorious childhood full of mud-spattered adventures, just ten miles away from my house a little girl was visiting a slightly more impressive house than our own rundown cottage.

The royal residence of Sandringham was not far from Downham and had been home to royalty since 1862. In 1928, as I was dragging myself out of sluices and falling out of trees, Princess Elizabeth, just two years old, was paying a visit there to her grandparents, King George V and Queen Mary, for a no doubt rather different childhood experience.

The sight of the royal family travelling to Sandringham was always a remarkable one. Remarkable in how many people seemed to know when it would happen and also in how little security they had. The Lynn Road in Downham Market would buzz with news that the royals were on their way. Even as young as five or six I remember clutching Mother's hand and watching as a big stately car slid by, carrying a funny-looking elderly lady gazing imperiously ahead. 'That's Queen Alexandra,' Mother whispered reverently. 'On her way to Sandringham. Calls it the big house, she does.' At such a young age I didn't understand who she was, but I picked up on the ripple of excitement that passed through the small crowd.

After her death in 1925, King George V and Queen

Mary continued to live in the much smaller York Cottage on the estate whenever they visited. You can't keep much from Norfolk folk and thanks to the bush telegraph we were always there waiting with a friendly smile and a wave to greet them home to Norfolk.

I remember one day in particular, can't have been long after the sluice incident, when someone rapped on the door.

'King and queen's on their way,' rang out a voice.

'Hop to it, Mollie,' said Mother and soon we had joined the assembled crowd on the grass verge.

Presently their black car came into view.

Straining my neck, I could just make out King George V's bushy moustache and, sitting next to him, ramrod straight with a funny little hat perched on her head, was his wife, Queen Mary. I was so close I could have reached out and touched their car window. There were no security outreach riders like they have nowadays. I waved furiously and smiled. I was desperate for the king to glance sideways and reward me with just a little smile or even a nod. Not so much as a flicker passed his poker-straight steely face. The queen didn't acknowledge our greetings either; they both just stared straight ahead. It was a little ironic that at a time when the king had been adopting a more democratic stance, attempting to bring himself closer to the working-class public, he and the queen could not spare a glance for any of us in the watching crowd.

Oh well. It didn't dent our affection for them and they were held in high esteem. The king had done himself no end of good by visiting the front line, factories and hospitals during the war, and people felt genuine loyalty to him.

'There,' declared Mother, uncrossing her arms. 'That was a little thrill. Back to work now.' With that, she went off to scrub the kitchen floor and the crowd dispersed.

As I watched their car vanish off up the Lynn Road, I found myself gripped with a funny little excited feeling that I'd not felt since that time I'd clung to the top of the tallest oak tree in the village. I could only imagine what world they inhabited, the lives they led in comparison to ours.

More emotions bubbled to the surface. Jealousy? No. Intrigue and excitement? Perhaps. But it was a defining moment. Seeing our king and queen up close and personal like that made me realize there was more to life than Downham Market. More to life than Norfolk. But the big question was – what? I could virtually taste the freedom I so much wanted to have. But options to girls my age were limited: shop work, apprenticeship or marriage. None of these were particularly appealing to my young mind.

I was pretty good at school, according to my teacher, but Mother had already set me straight on that score. 'There's no money to buy you books, Mollie,' she'd warned. 'You'll have to work when you leave school.' They couldn't afford to keep me or pay for me to go on to higher education. There were no government grants in those days.

I was twelve years old, in that funny place straddling childhood and adolescence. I couldn't keep on running wild and battling with the local bobby forever, could I?

Perhaps Mother wanted me out from under her feet or maybe she was worried I might perish in the ditches or sluices, but not long after this it was decided that I would be allowed to stay with my illegitimate aunt Kate and her husband up in London for a holiday.

'Really?' I said, bursting with excitement when Mother told me. 'I can go to London . . . on my own?'

'Well, the train guard'll keep an eye on you right enough and Kate'll be there to pick you up from Liverpool Street Station.'

I hopped from foot to foot. 'Now, now, can I go now?'

She shook her head and laughed as my brother skulked behind her. 'Get away with ya, Mollie Browne. Tomorrow.'

'She'll only stop an' mardle with strangers, Mum,' he said. I silenced him with a whack.

'No talking to any rum sorts, you hear,' Mother warned.

The day dawned bright and clear and I leapt out of bed like a spring lamb.

What a thing! Mollie Browne, off to London, on her own.

I clambered on to the steam train at Downham and wrestled with the heavy door.

'Best give it a good thack, Mollie, it's a bit stiff,' said the elderly porter.

The doors clattered shut, the whistle let out a deafening shriek and then we were off, puffing our way across the Norfolk fens like a giant steam-blowing monster.

The gentle clattering of the train soon lulled me into a deep sleep, but when I woke it was to a different world. The smoke cleared and I witnessed scenes the like of which I'd never before seen.

'Oh my,' I gasped, my eyes growing as wide and shiny

as gobstoppers. Pure exhilaration pumped through my veins as I jumped down on to the platform.

Smartly dressed porters rushed about the place like busy bees, hauling great leather trunks on to barrows. Steam trains slid majestically into the station and great clouds of smoke swirled and hung dramatically over the platforms.

Aunt Kate and her husband, Uncle Arthur, picked me up and drove me through the crowded streets. The place was teeming with life and noise, dirt and chaos. Everyone seemed to scurry about their business with meaning and direction. No dawdling to chew the cud over a hedgerow here.

Excitement drummed in my chest. The biggest town I'd ever been to was Downham or King's Lynn and even they didn't have many cars on the road. Here, there was traffic belching out smoke everywhere. A great greenish fog hung over the city and cars, trams and buses slid out of the gloom from all directions.

Smart-suited city gents in pinstripes and bowler hats strode purposefully alongside ladies in feminine tailored suits that emphasized their figures. The ladies wore little hats at an angle, with feathers or fake flowers that wiggled like calling cards when they walked.

Lady Chatterley's Lover had recently been published abroad and was causing shockwaves and everyone knew London was the place for racy behaviour.

This was the place for me.

Uncle Arthur used to be a river policeman and he and Aunt Kate lived in a terraced police house in Chapter Street in Victoria in the City of Westminster. They were reasonably well off, but now Uncle Arthur was retired he worked as a doorman at the Victoria and Albert museum.

'Would you like to go and have a look tomorrow?' he asked.

'Not half,' I grinned. I'd never been to a museum before.

In 1928 the V&A was one of the world's leading museums of style and art. Ever since art deco had come on the scene, people had become obsessed with style and London's rich and fashionable elite flocked to the place. It was also the scene of many a big fancy-dress ball attended by thousands of socialites.

'You should see 'em, Mollie,' chuckled Uncle Arthur as he drove us there the next day. 'Them aristos know how to have a party. Swing bands, champagne and cocktails flowing, and the outfits . . .' He grimaced. 'Make your eyes water. Ladies in them French fashions in next to nothing.'

'I'd like to go to a ball like that one day,' I piped up. Big ambitions, seeing as I hadn't even made it to a village dance in Downham.

'Can't see your father liking that, Mollie,' he snorted. 'Besides, I'm there to keep the undesirables out. You have to have blue blood in your veins to get a ticket to one of them balls.'

I closed my eyes as I imagined the ladies in their silky bias-cut dresses, the dances, the handsome men. What a world.

When we pulled up at the V&A I gasped. What an incredible building. The stone archway seemed to soar into the sky. It was the most majestic place I'd ever been to.

Uncle Arthur showed me round and with each exhibit room we walked into my jaw dropped further to the floor. The first floor of the museum was groaning with room after room of exquisite artefacts. Watercolours and famous cartoons by Raphael jostled for space with tapestries, glassware and statues. We climbed a floor and there were more treasures: rare books, lace and tiles from Turkey and Egypt, Ancient Greek and Roman bronzes and Oriental Chinese jade carvings. With each room I walked through I grew dizzy from trying to take it all in. I had literally never set eyes on such beautiful things. In the cottage where I grew up we had the most basic furniture, no paintings on the walls, no splashes of colour, except outside in the countryside. This was just unimagined beauty to my sheltered young mind.

'Aladdin's cave, ain't it?' smiled Uncle Arthur when he saw my face.

I didn't know who Aladdin was, but I sure as hell would have loved to live in his cave. The rest of the trip was just as mind-boggling. I stared into the windows of Harrods, gazed longingly at the pretty ladies parading around in their dresses and even went to see a Charlie Chaplin flick at the cinema. I was totally dazzled.

A fortnight later, as Aunt Kate put me back on the train, I felt like a changed person.

'I'm going to live here one day, Aunt Kate,' I chirruped. 'It's like the centre of the whole universe.'

'I'm sure you will, Mollie,' she said with a smile, slamming shut the train door and waving at me through the steam.

*

My time spent in London left a huge impression on me. Back in Norfolk, things felt flat and dull in comparison. Fortunately, I soon had other, more pressing things, on my mind –

Boys!

Up until now boys had just been irritating little brothers or potential playmates. But all at once a new interest stirred inside me. And when the fair rolled into town for its annual Michaelmas visit there suddenly seemed to be boys everywhere.

The heavy fair wagons had rumbled into the marketplace during the first week of October. 'The Statty's here!' I'd cried when I'd spotted the choking grey smoke billowing from the black oily monsters of the fairground chugging up the Lynn Road.

The Statty always brought the villagers out in their droves. The mothers would stand chatting on one side, the fathers would disappear into the nearby pubs and the kids would descend on the rides.

The fair was an excellent opportunity for both the sexes to posture and preen in front of each other like a load of hormonal peacocks. The clanging of the bells on the rides, the mirror mazes and the sight of the helter-skelter, combined with the whiff of teenage testosterone and toffee apples, made for a heady combination. Girls screamed with mock terror as they whizzed round the merry-go-round and the boys pitted their muscle power against each other on the punchball machines. I stared, intrigued at the way their tiny Adam's apples bobbed up and down, and I shrieked with laughter as they wrestled in play fights and mock ribaldry.

'Come on, Mollie Browne,' shouted one local lad. 'Let's see ya on the catwalk.'

'All right then,' I said with a grin, fluffing out my hair and putting my hand on my hips like I'd seen them film stars do at the cinema in London. With that, I took to the oscillating catwalk. It juddered up and down and your aim was to get to the end without falling off.

Not two yards in I was helpless with laughter. I wasn't strutting now, just struggling to stay upright.

'Look!' I yelled to the crowd of admiring boys. 'No hands.' I bumped and lurched along before being spat off in a heap at the end.

'What a spectacle, Mollie,' said my mother, waiting nearby. 'When will you learn?'

'She's just showing off to the boys,' deadpanned my little brother.

Poking my tongue out at him, I headed to the rock stall. This stall, run by Mr King, was the one I loved more than anything. The rock stall always drew an admiring crowd as we watched him make the rock by hand. He was a giant of a man with hands like trowels and hairy arms shaped like legs of mutton.

'Stick of rock for a penny, please?' I asked.

Fascinated, I watched as he tossed a band of pink-and-white-coloured mixture over a hook in the wall, then stretched it out. When satisfied it was the right texture and temperature he'd slap it down on the table and snip it up with scissors. He sold it in lumps bagged up to buy by the quarter or as an individual rock.

Sucking my rock, I wandered happily around the rest

of the fair, taking in the sights, smells and sounds. Soon I overheard some boys talking.

'There's a dance on next week, who you got your eye on then?'

A dance. Now that sounded interesting. Our usual entertainment round these parts was going to the cinema on a Saturday afternoon. These were the days of silent black-and-white films, before colour films and talkies. We'd queue up and pay tuppence ha'penny to watch Charlie Chaplin, Mary Pickford and Douglas Fairbanks. It was marvellous escapism and all the children from the area would flock to the cinema. The soundtrack came from old Mrs Long from Downham, who sat bolt upright and banged away on an ancient piano to provide a suitable musical backdrop.

Laughable, ain't it? You can't imagine it now with all this surround sound and 3D business.

But much as I loved the films, I was thirteen now and I wanted to be at village dances, not frantically trying to eye some fella up in the gloom of a cinema.

Surely I was old enough to make my own decisions?

'Out the question,' snapped Mother when I brought the subject up back at home.

'But, Mother,' I protested, 'there's only one every three months. Besides, I'm not daft, you know I won't get myself in trouble. Please?' I begged.

'I forbid it,' said my father, his dark eyes flashing.

I looked at his double-barrel shotgun sitting by the kitchen door and winced.

Could I sneak out?

'You'll feel the cut of my hand across your backside if you so much as try and sneak out,' he added.

'Do I need to remind you about Granny Esther?' added Mother ominously.

I shook my head and for once found nothing to say. It was absolutely unthinkable to get pregnant out of wedlock back in them days. All girls were brought up with the fear of God drilled into them at the prospect of having an illegitimate child. You would never dream of bringing such shame on your house. Besides which, everyone knew everyone else's business in the country so if you put a foot wrong it would be round the Friday market before you could say 'family way'.

There was a local girl who'd managed to get herself pregnant. She was dismissed from her job and turned out of her home. Where she went we never knew; the streets maybe, or the workhouse with the tramps perhaps? More than likely she ended up at the workhouse, where she would have had her hair shaved and been separated from her bastard child and forced into a life of mind-numbing work, like picking the tar out of old ships' rope.

Like I say, this place was frightening and fascinating in equal measure. The tiny windows were so high off the ground you couldn't see in and it was sealed off in any case behind high black wrought-iron gates.

Nowadays I see young girls round Bournemouth where I live with prams full of kids and they're so young and you know they've got a nice warm council flat and food for the table. Well, you're virtually encouraging it, aren't you? But, back then, the fear of the workhouse meant you kept your drawers pulled up. A bit of slap and tickle was fine, as long as you knew where to draw the line. Not that I knew much about any of that, aged thirteen.

'You need to drag your head out the clouds, my girl,' added Mother. 'And start thinking about what yer gonna do when you leave school next year. When I was a young girl I worked on the Mayfair telephone exchange all the hours and good work it was too. Hard work never killed anyone,' she added.

With that, my heart plummeted like a stone in the Denver sluice. I didn't need reminding that soon I would be turning fourteen and it would be time to face up to my responsibilities.

Downham Market Baptist Church members on a day out in the 1920s. I'm in the middle, behind the boy in the white shorts.

I was tall for my age and, after years of cycling, running and roaming the countryside, I had a strapping physique. This made me an excellent candidate for an apprentice-ship. Nobody wanted to employ some weakling who couldn't pull their weight and work hard, or was forever fainting or calling in sick.

As my fourteenth birthday loomed into sight, Mother came to a decision. 'A girl like you'll get work easy. Do you want to work with your grandmother in the shop?' she asked.

My stomach tightened. As much as I loved Granny Esther I didn't want to spend the rest of my life working under her.

'Oh no, don't make me,' I pleaded. 'I'll forever be under her control.'

I had my sights fixed further than a village shop. My mind wandered back to the bustling streets of London where royals and high society mixed. Why couldn't I find work there?

'All right, Miss Fussy, my friend runs a dressmaker's and a draper's in Downham and she's looking for starting girls. I'll go and talk to her.'

By the time she returned she was full of it.

'She'll take you on, Mollie,' she beamed, pleased as punch with herself. 'You can start Monday. They're charging five shillings for the apprenticeship, but I'm sure your gran'll foot the cost.'

I smiled weakly, but inside a feeling of doom gathered and I couldn't shake it all weekend.

On Monday morning at seven a.m. Mother marched me to the dressmaker's. The bell on the door clanged as we entered. It was like the sound of a jailer's key signalling the condemned man to go and meet his fate.

The room was small, dark and smelt of mothballs. A wizened old woman, who looked like a proper harridan, sat behind a wooden counter. Her shrew-like eyes sized me up.

'Follow me,' she muttered, leading us to an even smaller room out the back.

I felt like a carthorse in the poky room. The dark space was dominated by one big table covered in calico, cloth and ticking. I thought longingly of the dazzling beauty of the V&A, of all the riches and everything looking so fine and opulent. Then to this room, which was as dry and dusty as its owner. The V&A was a place of intrigue and beauty. This was a place you came to die.

A clock ticked slowly on the wall and as the woman began to run through my hours and duties I wanted to run out of that shop and never stop running. Panic and desperation pumped through my veins. I felt like a caged animal.

Can you imagine? I couldn't spend my life sitting on a chair doing fiddly sewing in a dark, airless room with a stuffy seamstress. Day after day, month after suffocating month. I would shrivel up and die. I couldn't. I just couldn't.

The walls started to close in on me. Suddenly even the air in the shop felt thin.

'NO!' I blurted out. Mother and the seamstress stared at me in surprise. 'I can't stay here. I won't.'

I knew my outburst would earn me a proper raggin' but I didn't care.

There had to be more to life than this, surely. There *was* more to life than this . . .

TIPS FROM A 1930S KITCHEN

...

Bread and Butter Pudding

If my childhood could be summed up by a recipe, then bread and butter pudding would be it. Comforting, sweet and sticky. Try it out.

> *6 thin slices bread and butter*
> *1 pint (570 ml) full fat milk*
> *4 eggs*
> *1 dessertspoonful each: sugar, sultanas,*
> *currants and candied lemon*

Cut off the crusts and divide each slice of bread into four squares, arrange them in layers in a well-buttered pie dish and sprinkle each layer with sultanas, currants and candied lemon. Beat the eggs, add the sugar, stir until dissolved, then mix in the milk and pour gently over the bread, which should only half fill the dish. Let it stand for an hour to let the bread soak up the milk then bake in a moderate oven, standing in a tin of water, for nearly an hour. If you're feeling flash, serve with cream.

Household Tip

Save a fortune on expensive leather-cleaning products. Simply run the inside of a banana skin over your bag or shoes then polish with a soft dry cloth. Sparkling in seconds.

3

Tears in the Scullery

We are all in the gutter, but some of us
are looking at the stars.
Oscar Wilde

Back at home it was hard to say who was more cross,
Mother or Father.

'What do you mean, Mollie, making a fine show of me
in front of my friend?' Mother snapped. On and on she
went as I stared dully at the flickering flames dancing
about in the grate.

'*I go to all this trouble to line you up work . . .*'

I wished I was a flame and could just dance where the
breeze took me.

'*. . . and work you will, my girl, make no mistake.*'

I didn't mean to upset my mother, really I didn't. I took
no joy from it. Girls of my generation always did what our
mothers told us. Their word was the law. But in this case I
just couldn't. I couldn't have gone to that shop and fossil-
ized into the woman who worked there.

For weeks I moped about like a wet Sunday in Yarmouth.

Even the promise of bird's-nesting didn't sound as enticing as usual. Everything felt tedious and flat and I was fed up with my little brother needling me. It was all right for him. When he left school he had many more choices open to him. He could learn any one of a dozen trades and more likely as not be out in the fresh air at the same time.

One day I came home for lunch to find a strange man sitting in the kitchen sipping at a mug of tea.

'Aye,' he chuckled as his eyes roamed over my body. 'She's a strapping lass, reckon she'll do.'

I eyed him suspiciously.

'They always prefer Norfolk lasses,' he went on. 'Reckons they last longer and work harder, so as they do.'

My eyes went out on stalks. Who were *they* and what did *they* want with me?

'This is Mr Llewelyn,' explained Mother. 'He used to be a chauffeur for old Mr Stocks up at Woodhall. He's retired now, but he's still in touch with Mr Stocks.'

I'd heard of Mr Stocks. He was a member of the gentry, a bona fide blue-blooded gentleman who owned a vast Tudor pile called Woodhall in Hilgay, two miles from Downham.

'Mr Stocks is looking for a scullery maid to start immediately.'

I stared blankly and Mother shook her head.

'Do you want to be a scullery maid, Mollie?' she asked.

I paused. Me? Be a domestic servant?

'You'll have to start up in London,' said Mr Llewelyn, setting down his tea and eyeing up a tray of Mother's sausage rolls. 'It's the London season now and Mr Stocks is up in 'is Knightsbridge home. Fine place it is too, the very last word in grandeur, like.' He placed much significance on the word *grandeur* and smacked his lips as he said it, while reaching out to grab a couple of sausage rolls.

London.

With that one word it was like a light bulb had pinged on in my head. I'd be free. I'd get to go to London! It was impossibly perfect, as if all my dreams were slotting into place in an instant.

'You'll get five shillings a week and all your food and keep,' he said through mouthfuls. 'Scullery maids work hard,' he warned. 'The bottom of the heap. You'll have to do everything the cook tells you. You're not afraid of hard work, are you, Mollie?' he asked.

'No, not at all,' I said, vigorously shaking my head.

'Well then,' he said, heaving himself to his feet and brushing off the crumbs. 'I'll tell Mr Stocks you're suitable and get your train ticket sent in the post.'

And just like that I had a job as a scullery maid!

After he'd left, Mother had to scrape me off the ceiling, I was that excited.

'Are you sure you want to go to London, Mollie?' she asked. 'You're only fourteen. It's a big, dangerous place, you know.'

'Oh, please!' I said, flicking my hand nonchalantly. 'I'll be fine.'

Father, when he heard, was just as surprised.

'You?' he snorted. 'Do as what others tell you to? That'll be the day. Suppose you'll get all your food and lodgings free though.'

One less mouth to feed would be a blessing to my parents.

Later on, lying in my bed, staring out of the window at the thick blanket of stars that stretched across the dark Norfolk skies, I could scarcely sleep for the excitement bubbling up in my chest. My parents may have been worried, but I wasn't. This was the beginning of the rest of my new life. Old people, what do they know? I laugh now. My parents can only have been in their early thirties, but when you're young everyone seems ancient.

I suppose, looking back, the only reason my parents let me go to London at such a young age was because they knew the chauffeur and Mr Stocks had a good reputation locally. He wasn't like some of these flighty young aristos setting London alight. He was well into his seventies and looked upon with a mixture of respect and sympathy. His wife had long since died, at the time leaving just him and his two sons, Captain Eric and Captain Michael.

Years back, before the war, to celebrate Michael's twenty-first birthday, Mr Stocks had ordered mountains of meat from a relative of ours who was a butcher at the time. They had an enormous bash by all rights, with the wine flowing and enough roasted meat to sink a battleship. The music, dancing and gaiety could be heard drifting over the Norfolk fields. Then a year to the day after the party, in 1914, Michael was killed in the war at Zillebeke while serving with the Grenadier Guards. Now it was just Mr Stocks and his youngest son, Captain Eric, rattling around that big old house on their own. People felt for him like they would their own, for the aristocracy lost a whole generation of sons just like the working-class poor did. Mr Stocks was left heartbroken and Captain Eric, like Father, was never the same again and suffered with consumption, though I'd heard tell that when he went to recuperate it was not to the sanatoriums of Hastings but Switzerland!

Now I was to be their scullery maid.

It may seem odd that I got the job without being interviewed, but in those days references were more important than anything. The upper class didn't want any old sort coming into their house and seeing where all the family silver was. People were terrified that you might steal things or have a boyfriend who worked in a gang. But Mr Llewelyn had been their Norfolk chauffeur for years and they trusted him. If he said I was a good honest Norfolk girl from a decent family then that was good enough for them. Besides, Norfolk girls were generally considered to be hale, hearty, strapping and hard-working and what else did you need in a scullery maid? Perhaps that's why a lot of the servants I came across in the next ten years were from Norfolk.

'I don't know why you don't wanna come and work with me in the shop,' tutted Granny Esther when she heard. 'You'll have to set an alarum clock you know. The hours are long and they won't care you're just a nipper. You'll have to scrub everything in sight. You'll be a skivvy. Servants get treated awful.'

'Oh, Granny,' I sighed. 'Maybe in the twenties, but not now. Times have changed. They're better looked after. Loads of young girls are doing it.'

It was true. I wouldn't have been alone. By 1930 there were countless young women leaving home for the first time in search of work, money, food or just the chance to better themselves, and taking a job in service was seen as a good way of doing this.

Most people think that the First World War was the end of domestic service in the UK, but that's not the case. From the end of the nineteenth century to 1911, 13 per cent of the female working-age population in England were employed as domestic servants. It's true that the First World War saw a steep decline in the numbers of servants, but there was a marked increase in the numbers employed in domestic service during the 1920s. By 1931 the percentage had dropped to 8 per cent. Despite this, domestic service remained the most common entry-level job available to young women like myself.

I doubted there was a single girl more excited than me in all the land. Granny Esther could have told me I'd have to scrub all night long and I'd still have gone. It's crazy, isn't it? You'd think I was going off to shop and party, not skivvy, but like I say, back then nothing daunted me.

My head wasn't going to be turned by nothing and nobody.

So, in May 1931, on a sunny Sunday morning, aged four-teen, I found myself bound for Cadogan Square in London's Knightsbridge. Mother had packed my bag with a few clothes, some clean underwear and some ham sand-wiches, and she and father walked me the three miles to Downham Station, along the Lynn Road. There were only two buses a week so it wouldn't do any good to wait at the bus stop.

As we trudged along I thought of how the king and queen used this same road to travel between London and Norfolk. *Now I was following in their footsteps!*

Last week Mother had taken me to Tyler's, the draper's

shop in town, and got me kitted out with my service uniform. In my bag was a green dress that, to my delight, sat just above the knee. It makes me laugh, you know. Whenever people ask me about *Downton Abbey* and whether it's true to life, I always say it's exactly the same, except that in reality the skirts were much shorter.

Aside from that I also had a white apron, a white mop cap, black wool stockings and black leather lace-up shoes. Talk about proud of my new uniform. I'd got it out that many times, Mother had had to press it with the flat iron again.

For the journey I was wearing a new cream cotton dress that Mother had made, as she didn't want me shaming myself by turning up for service looking shabby. My leather shoes shone so much you could see my freckled face reflected in them. Didn't I feel superior!

Once at the station, Mother dissolved into tears. 'You can come home if you don't like it,' she sobbed, enveloping me into her bosom. 'You don't have to stay.'

It must have been an emotional time for her, waving her young daughter off to work in the big smoke. Not that I gave two hoots for emotion back then. Tears and hugs? Load of old tripe.

Father was less sentimental. 'Don't answer back and don't get above your station,' he said gruffly.

In a flurry of tears and hugs I finally managed to make my escape from Mother's slightly soggy embrace.

'Don't fuss so,' I grinned, boarding the steam train.

I squeezed myself into a space on the train carriage seat, next to a cage of chickens and a farmhand, and with that I bid farewell to the Norfolk countryside.

*

It took some time to get to London and when I eventually arrived at Liverpool Street Station I was tired and sticky from travelling. But as soon as I disembarked, my senses were assaulted. The intense noise, the steam and the babble of sophisticated voices hit my weary head like a shower of cold water.

I was a country girl at heart and apart from my one brief trip to the city two years ago, this was my first real experience. I was fourteen and all on my own. Did I feel fear or regret? Not one little bit. I felt more alive than I had ever done in my whole life. Ready for whatever experience life had to offer me. Excitement drummed through me. What an adventure.

'Mollie Browne?' asked a voice.

The smoke cleared and standing in front of me was a most peculiar-looking man. He was wearing dove-grey knee breeches, matching grey jacket, boots so shiny they made mine look dull in comparison and white gloves, with the whole ensemble topped off with a peaked cap. A fine sight he made.

'Mr Thornton,' he said. 'I'm Mr Stocks's London chauffeur come to collect you.'

'Ooh, 'ello,' I gushed. 'Pleased to meet you. Nice of you to come and collect me.' And with that I stuck out my sticky hand.

Looking at me a little strangely, he ignored my outstretched hand and took my bag instead. Next he ushered me to where a black shiny Daimler was waiting.

'Get in,' he said, opening the back door.

Didn't I feel grand sliding into the cool, black leather seats? No one had ever held a door open for me and nor had I ever sat in such a grand motor car before. Cars were a rare sight where I came from and here I was sitting in the grandest of the lot. I could get used to this.

'This beats sitting next to a chicken,' I chattered on.

He smiled coolly as he slid the Daimler out into the road. They say the streets of London are paved with gold, but back in them days they were filled with cars, trams, buses, errand boys, buskers, traders and a million other forms of life and transport. It seemed even busier than when I'd visited two years ago.

I gazed out of the window as London in all its glory unfolded. Soon my head was spinning at the sights. In Downham Market there weren't that many cars on the road – lots of men on bikes or horses, and lugging barrows and ladders about, but not much in the way of cars. Here in London they were everywhere; not like you see today, of course, but to my eyes it was still a lot of traffic. By 1931 elegant motor cars had replaced most horse-drawn carriages. It would be another two years before the London Passenger Transport Board was established to bring all of London's transport providers together, but there were still many different ways to get about London if you had the knowhow.

Red double-decker buses and trams whizzed past, belching out clouds of smoke. The 20 mph speed limit had been abolished the previous year and drivers were bombing about at speeds that made my eyes water. Amazing when you think about it, isn't it? Driving tests weren't established until 1934 so any old lunatic could get behind the wheel.

Soon we passed an underground station, which I'd heard so much about.

'Train every ninety seconds,' informed Mr Thornton.

Unimaginable.

We paused briefly at some large poles with strange moving lights inside.

'Why are we stopping?' I asked.

'They're traffic lights,' replied Mr Thornton. 'Bloomin' nuisance they are, going up all over London.'

Traffic lights were just one of the many changes sweeping 1930s London.

Organizations were popping up to deal with the city's existing problems and make it a cleaner, more efficient place. There were slum clearances and council-house building programmes, and electric lighting was being installed across the city. The telephone exchange in Mayfair where Mother had worked when she was my age was now automated. To me, all this heralded an amazing new era of sophistication.

Charlie Chaplin's latest flick was on at the pictures and, outside, street traders sold you pretty much anything you wanted, from roast nuts for a penny a bag to chestnuts and baked potatoes. The streets were teeming with people plying their trade from the back of horse-drawn carts to simple barrows. Wounded old soldiers still wearing their medals and uniforms sold matches from trays slung round their necks with string and elderly ladies selling lavender from wicker baskets sat huddled under umbrellas. Rag-and-bone men clattered up the streets past our car calling out for 'any old iron'. Newspaper boys cried out 'Post!' to compete with the noise of car horns and 'muffin' men strode along ringing large bells and carrying trays of hot buns and butter on their heads. The noise was deafening.

'I can hardly hear myself think in London,' grumbled Mr Thornton.

The Depression may have destroyed large parts of Britain, but London had largely escaped and, driving through it now, I saw no sign of it. The new 'sunrise' industries, such as producing electrical equipment and consumer goods, helped to offset unemployment in more traditional industries. And there were many jobs created in engineering – manufacturing of clothes and shoes, food and drink production, furniture and printing to name but a few.

My mouth dropped open at this spectacle of noise and colour. It was as far removed from Norfolk as it was possible to get. Craning my neck up, I stared at the highest buildings I'd ever seen in my life, thrilled to be in London again. Norfolk is flat in all directions, but here in London, round every street corner, amazing red-brick buildings soared into the skyline. This was pre-Blitz and the streets were a jumble of eighteenth- and nineteenth-century terraced buildings. And shops, so many, many shops! Girls in uniforms and whistling errand boys on bikes zipped around like busy little worker ants laden down with brown paper packages.

Sensing, perhaps, that I was a little dazzled by my surroundings, Mr Thornton frowned. 'Now, you are going to behave yourself, aren't you?' he mumbled, staring at me hard in the rear mirror.

'Course, Mr Thornton,' I grinned as I gazed out of the window and waved at some boys hopping on to a tram.

Gradually the hustle and bustle gave way to a different

and, even to my untrained eye, more well-to-do neighbour-hood. Crowded cobbled streets turned to wider pavements and smart leafy squares. This was the Royal Borough of Kensington and Chelsea in the 1930s, and a more stylish place I'd never before seen. The air seemed cleaner and more refined somehow. Elegant, stuccoed houses looked out on a slow-moving world. The traffic thinned out and even the people looked more expensive. Smart gentlemen in wide-legged suits with large turned-up hems and creases, thin moustaches and oiled-back hair, strolled arm in arm with the most beautiful ladies imaginable. They all looked groomed, dapper and suave. From the hems of the smartly tailored wool suits to their shoulder pads and fox-fur stoles, these women oozed money, class and privilege. Their shiny hair had been sculpted into perfect finger waves and many wore jaunty little hats at an angle. I pushed back a lock of my thick red hair and nervously twisted the hemline of my loose cotton skirt.

These women looked like they'd been carved from marble. Even the children looked immaculate as they trot-ted alongside their nannies in smart sailor suits or pretty smock dresses.

Suddenly I felt exactly what I was – a knock-kneed fourteen-year-old up from the sticks. 'Ooh, my stomach's like a bag of ferrets,' I said nervously.

Mr Thornton said nothing. Instead, he pulled the Daim-ler to a stop outside the biggest house I'd seen in my life.

I literally gasped.

Number 24 Cadogan Square looked like a giant iced wedding cake and towered into the blue skies above. It was at least six storeys high. Every other house in the genteel square was just as impressive and the centrepiece was the beautiful leafy green garden in the middle, surrounded by black railings. Nannies and children sat on the

Number 24 Cadogan Square, Knightsbridge, Mr Stocks's London house. We'd come up here every year for the London season.

grass playing in the sunshine and instinct told me that wasn't a place I'd be spending a lot of time in climbing trees.

I clambered out of the car and started to ascend the six white steps that led up to the mansion.

'Ahem,' coughed Mr Thornton. 'This way.' With that,

he gestured to the 'area' steps that led downstairs to the basement. 'We're downstairs.'

'Of course,' I blustered. How could I have been so stupid?

If London's Knightsbridge seemed quiet and tranquil outside and upstairs, well, downstairs it was certainly a different story. In a way the house was like a swan – all serene up above and effortlessly gliding along, while down below there was frantic activity and constant motion to keep it staying afloat.

A long hall ran the length of the basement of the house with rooms opening off it. 'Housekeeper's sitting room, servants' halls, toilet and butler's bedroom,' said Mr Thornton, gesturing to the rooms that ran off to the right. 'This side is the footman and hallboy's bedroom. Out of bounds to you,' he muttered. 'Hallboys, footmen and butlers sleep downstairs and kitchen maids, cooks and housemaids sleep upstairs.'

On the walls of the passage ran a long line of brass bells with room names above them.

'Service bells,' he explained. 'You won't need to bother much with them. They're for the butler, footman and housemaids.'

As we clattered up the echoey corridor and into a vast kitchen at the end, Mr Thornton called out: 'New girl's here, Mrs Jones!'

A short, dumpy woman was drying her pudgy hands on her white apron. She had flour smeared on her forehead and a hot flush had spread over her from her morning's efforts. Her little dark eyes peered out suspiciously from her red face as she sized me up.

'You'll do,' she said in a strong Welsh accent. 'Right, I've just finished getting the boss's lunch ready. We sit down to ours now and when we've finished I'll talk you through the rules, all right?'

'All right,' I nodded eagerly. I wanted this woman to like me.

In the servants' hall everyone sat down to eat. No one introduced me to anyone and I hadn't the faintest clue who anyone was and where I was in the pecking order, though I guessed as I was easily the youngest person in the room, it would be me at the bottom. Trying to blend in, I took a seat at the end of the long wooden table.

A young girl, a bit older than me, started bringing in trays piled high with food. And what a feast. After my long journey my stomach was grumbling. Sunday lunch in this household was obviously a big deal.

I waited for everyone else to finish serving, then helped myself.

Dishes were piled high with piping hot crispy roast potatoes, hunks of smooth brown Yorkshire puddings and steaming vats of peas and carrots glistening in butter. The centrepiece was a giant sirloin of beef, cut so thinly the rare pink beef looked like it might melt in your mouth. Mrs Jones had quickly cast aside the paper doily and fancifully cut carrot and parsley it had been garnished with for Mr Stocks's benefit and the two eldest members of the household had helped themselves first.

A young, good-looking lad opposite me must have clocked my expression, because he laughed. 'You'll not starve in this house,' he said with a grin. 'Always beef on a

Sunday, never any different. The boss has two slices off the fillet then he sends down the sirloin to us.'

Without saying a word, I loaded my plate up, smothered it all in a lake of piping hot gravy and tucked in.

If it looked mouth-watering, it tasted beyond heaven. I'd never tasted meat quite like it afore. The meat was so tender it melted like ice cream in your mouth and the sizzling hot potatoes were fluffy and light as clouds, but with a wonderful chewy skin from being roasted in duck fat. The flavour was out of this world.

My father tried his hardest, but the odd dry pigeon and poached pheasant couldn't compete with this sirloin.

It was gone in a heartbeat and I mopped up the last of the unctuous gravy juices with a hunk of bread and sat back happily in my chair. Everyone chattered about their business and ignored me, but I guess as the new scullery maid I was pretty invisible.

Next came the puddings. Peach tart, laced with a generous jug of double cream, and spotted dick groaning with big fat currants and smothered in vanilla custard. I had landed on my feet here all right. How lucky could I possibly be? I stifled a smile. All them doomsayers telling me how hard domestic service was, what did they know?

The fella opposite me, who I later learnt was Alan, the footman, winked at me as he spooned in a mouthful of pudding.

'I love a tart,' he winked. 'Don't you?'

I grinned back. I could deal with a cheeky sort like him, no trouble.

A thin older man next to him shot him a sour look from over his wire-rimmed spectacles.

Swallowing back the last of my spotted dick, I started to feel warm, comfortably full and a little drowsy. I was just stifling a yawn when suddenly the room was full of the sound of scraping chairs and everyone leapt to their feet. Lunch was over.

'Get your uniform on and report for duty,' barked Mrs Jones. 'Servants' bedrooms are that way,' she said, gesturing to a separate stairway that led off from the kitchen. 'Never ever use front stairs, boss don't want to see you climbing 'em. Back steps are for us.'

I climbed the linoleum steps, and climbed, and climbed – the roast beef and pudding sloshing about in my tummy as I dragged myself to the very top of the cavernous house.

'I've never been up so many steps,' I huffed.

'Just keep on and stop your yakking,' Mrs Jones puffed behind me. By the time we reached the top she was the colour of beetroot. 'That's your room. You'll share it with the new kitchen maid who's starting soon,' she wheezed.

The tiny room was in the attic and was stifling hot. Throwing open the window, I could just about see over the jumbled rooftops of West London. The room was bare apart from a single iron bed, a chair and a small chest of drawers for my clothes. The walls smelt of distemper (a kind of paint mixed with glue) and were bare of any pictures.

'Bathroom and toilet's at the end of the hall,' barked Mrs Jones. 'Make the most of it, as when we go back to Norfolk there's no such luxury and you'll have to use a chamber pot and hip bath in your room.'

I daresay the room might have looked sparse and the

idea of doing your bodily functions in a pot back in Norfolk depressing to some, but I was used to a basic way of life so to me it was just fine.

'Come on then,' said Mrs Jones impatiently as she bustled out of the room. 'Get yourself dressed. Chop-chop!'

Changing into my outfit, I smoothed down the apron and teased my red curls into the mop cap. 'Don't you look the bee's knees,' I murmured to myself. Even at fourteen I had a cracking figure. A big bum and breasts but a tiny waist accentuated by the cut of the waist of my apron.

Scurrying downstairs, I presented myself to the cook, who was making a big meal of sitting down with a heavy sigh.

'Right, my girl,' she said, glaring at me suspiciously. 'You can start by tucking that hair back.'

A stray red curl was defiantly poking out from under my mop cap and I swiftly tucked it in.

She fixed her beady eyes on me. 'I know what you young girls are like,' she snapped. 'Boys, dresses and dancing is all that fills your little heads. But while you're in my kitchen you follow my rules, you hear. Your day starts at six thirty a.m. You come downstairs, blacklead the grate, polish the hearth and light the range fire. Woe betide if it's not done to my standards.' She paused. 'Put the kettles on for staff teas and bring me a nice cup. Strong, brown and sweet's how I like it.

'Then you clean the steel fender and the fire irons, clean the brass on the front door and scrub the front steps. We ain't got one here, but in the country you'll need to clean out the fireplace. Then you'll need to scrub and polish the kitchen floor and passageways.

'Then you and the kitchen maid need to start on staff breakfasts and laying the table in servants' hall so we can eat at eight a.m. At eight I will come down and make the boss's breakfast for nine a.m.'

My head started to swim as she carried on. I could see her mouth moving up and down but the words were starting to blur in my mind. Fourteen-year-olds don't have the biggest attention span in the world. Forcing myself to listen, I tuned back in.

'After breakfast, wash up and clear down, then you need to scrub down and prepare my table.'

I glanced at the vast oak table that dominated the entire room. It must have weighed a ton and was scrubbed to within an inch of its life.

'Then we start prepping the lunch and there will be all the veggies for you to prepare . . .'

On and on she went, the rest of the fifteen-hour day broken down into multitudes of repetitive and back-breaking tasks until my day finally finished at nine thirty p.m.

'You don't date the staff,' she said, glaring at Alan as he passed by and winked. 'That way only leads to trouble and keeps your mind off your work. You don't go into parts of the house that aren't your own. If you do see Mr Stocks or young Captain Eric, don't speak unless spoken to and always refer to them as "sir". The bosses are always "sir". You treat the upper servants with respect – in your case, that's everybody. You get a half-day off a week and every other Sunday. And remember,' she added finally, her eyes glittering dangerously as she leant back and crossed her beefy arms – they were so muscly from years of beating, whipping and stirring that they were like legs of mutton and I could barely take me eyes off them, but eventually I forced myself to meet her steely gaze – 'remember that in this kitchen, Mollie, I am queen. Now hop to that pile of washing-up.'

Queen? More like an old ogre. But I said nothing, just smiled sweetly.

I wasn't smiling five minutes later.

Stacked up in a vast stone sink in a cold, airless scullery was the debris of everybody's lunch. Filthy dirty plates towered over every available surface. It was piled up in the sink and even in buckets on the floor. There must have been nearly fifty plates and bowls, saucepans, jugs, pots and pans, not to mention cutlery, all smeared with cold, greasy gravy and congealed custard.

There was no washing-up liquid in them days. I had to scrub each one with soft soap that you whisked up in the water, or soap crystals, until it shone like a new pin. Each piece then had to be rinsed in an enormous enamel bowl of hot water before being dried up and put away in the wooden racks above the range. There were no gloves or barrier cream either. My lunch sat like lead in my tummy and pretty soon my hands were red raw and numb.

Wiping back a curl that was by now plastered to my forehead with sweat, I stifled a yawn. Oh well. No point moaning. Best crack on.

And with that I was sucked into the regime of a big upper-class house. That day marked the end of my child-hood and the start of a gruelling new decade of work that would see me work harder than I'd ever done in my entire life.

When people think of domestic servants they often think of butlers and housemaids and imagine it to be hard work. No one ever thinks of the poor scullery maid. A scullery maid, otherwise known as a skivvy, was the lowest position possible in a house. The very lowest of the low. You're the youngest, the lowest paid, you work the longest hours and you spend the most time on your hands and knees scrubbing. You're even a skivvy for the servants. You are literally the bottom of the heap and regarded as such by everyone else above you.

No one bothered to come and introduce themselves to me, apart from Alan, the randy footman. As a scullery maid I wasn't really worth the effort. I had to learn who was who and what was what as I went along.

But I was young and nothing if not optimistic.

I wasn't daft either and I had my wits about me. I knew, even at fourteen, that I had the worst possible job in the house, I would have to work harder than anyone else and wait on the servants. But with all the arrogance of youth I knew I'd rise through the ranks – saw it as my right almost. As I finally got to the bottom of the mountain of dirty dishes, my spirit remained as intact as ever. When you're at the bottom, the only way to go is up, after all!

I muttered to myself as I cleaned and stacked the dishes: *I'll have the best job in the house one day. You wait and see. I'll make cook. I'll show 'em all.*

Next morning I was downstairs by six thirty a.m. I'd only had a brief wash – no point any more, I'd be wringing with sweat and dirt before the day was out anyhow. Granny's words rang in my head: *You'll be a skivvy, my girl.*

First I had to light the monstrosity of a stove, which was a job in itself.

'Come on, you wretched thing,' I muttered.

You needed just the right amount of kindling and to have the knack of pulling the drawers out to give enough draught to get it to catch light. I didn't know Mrs Jones well, but I knew enough to know that surly old trout would be down on me like a ton of bricks if she didn't get her morning cup of tea.

Next I had to blacklead the grate with blacklead from a tin with zebra stripes on it. By the time I'd finished painting it on with a brush and then polished it until it gleamed the colour of the boss's black Daimler, I had hands like a black man. But there was no time to worry about that. The clock on the kitchen wall said seven and I hadn't even started on the steps.

Rushing up the area steps, I gratefully gulped in the spring air.

At that time of the morning I'd half-expected it to be like a mausoleum outside, but the smart square was a hive of activity. Not with the gentry. Oh no. They'd still be fast asleep upstairs in their starched cotton sheets, heavy velvet curtains blocking out the intrusive morning light. No, it was full of kitchen maids shaking out dusters and scullery maids like me scrubbing the front steps. Errand boys whistled as they cycled round on bikes loaded up with goods to drop at the back of the house. Paperboys dropped off thick bundles of papers at each house and chimney sweeps cycled past, laden down with brushes.

Everyone was cheerful, whistling as they worked or exchanging a fruity joke. Maids flirted with errand boys and shrieked with laughter at their ribaldry. When you get a load of youngsters together who don't mind being up with the sparrows it's inevitable they're going to lark about together.

'Morning,' I said, smiling at the scullery maid on her hands and knees on the next set of steps along from me. She didn't look much older than me.

'Morning,' she grinned back. 'You new, ainch ya? My

A very desirable postcode – all the gentry had a London house for the season.

boss has guests today so I daresay I'll be back here before the day is out. Bloomin' bane of my life these things are.' She dropped her voice to a whisper. 'Wouldn't mind, but her upstairs sees dirt where they ain't none. She's still fast asleep now, mind you, she won't raise her pretty head off the pillow for a good couple of hours, lazy cow. We gotta do these chores and get 'em out the way before they see us. They must think the cleaning fairies fly over Cadogan Square each morning at dawn.'

I smiled to show I was one of them but, ever mindful of Mrs Jones, I got on with the task in hand. I scrubbed away with my hearthstone until my arms were aching and numb. I started at the bottom and worked my way up but quickly realized that was pointless as I was only making each step dirty again by treading on it. No, I'd have to start at the top and work me way down. Unfortunately this made my bum poke further out into the square and I was aware of it jiggling as I scrubbed heartily.

At that point I hadn't realized I was allowed, on strictly those occasions only, to enter the house via the front door no less, so as not to muddy the steps.

Suddenly I felt an almighty whack round my rear end.

What on earth?

I whirled round to find myself face to face with an errand boy. He had a teasing face made for mischief and his blue eyes twinkled as they lingered on my legs.

'Lovely view,' he winked, tugging the edge of his flat cap. 'You're better than the last. She had a face like the back of a bus. And a redhead too. I love redheads. You look like Clara Bow.'

With my hair plastered under a mop cap, my hands thick with dirt and without a trace of make-up, I daresay I looked more like orphan Annie than a big Hollywood film star, but I was willing to believe him.

'Get away, you rascal,' I cackled, secretly delighted at his attention.

'Come and see me when you get some time off,' he said, hopping on to his bike. 'I work at Harrods. Come round the back entrance, Trevor Square, and ask for Billy.'

Errand boys, I quickly discovered, were the worst flirts of the lot, and the Harrods boys were the most handsome. Nipping about Knightsbridge on their natty little green bikes gave them a certain prestige amongst the local domestics.

My cloud of hormonal oestrogen was popped as I heard a familiar voice drift up the area steps. 'Mollie!' cried out Mrs Jones. 'I said MOLLIE!' Oh blimey, I hadn't even got her tea or started sweeping the passage yet.

'Got to go,' I panted, frantically gathering up my brushes and hearthstone.

'See you around, carrot,' he winked. Then he was gone, whistling his way up towards Sloane Square without a care in the world.

Down in the gloom of the kitchen Mrs Jones was not, I discovered, a morning person and nor did she like being kept waiting for her morning cup of tea. I also discovered that each morning she would come down in a different mood. She had one for each day of the week from surly to grumpy to moderately cheerful to downright foul. And on this particular morning her mood was as black as the stove I'd been scrubbing.

It was like a dark cloud had drifted into the kitchen. Her beefy hands were planted on her hips and she shot me a look so sour it could have curdled milk from fifty paces.

'I knew it,' she spat. 'Boys – is that all you young girls think about?'

I stared at her face and wondered how she got to be so bitter. Looking back now, the poor woman had probably been plagued by a long stream of giggly scullery maids, who she'd spend months training up to her standards only to have them disappear when they got something better. But back then, in my eyes she was just an old maid left on the shelf. We only called her 'Mrs' as a courtesy; there wasn't so much as a whiff of a man on the scene. I wasn't going to end up like her, oh no. To a young girl that was the worst fate in the world.

I decided to follow my mother's advice, 'keep my trap shut' and humour the surly old trout. The rest of the day her mood didn't improve and she worked me flat out. Every few minutes her thick Welsh accent rang out: *That's not up to my standards. You better learn to scrub better than that or you won't last long. You missed a bit there. Scrub that table over again. I want to see my face in it. These potatoes aren't peeled proper. Young girls these days. Don't work like they did in my day.* On and on she tutted and puffed like an old steam train.

People think they know about hygiene in kitchens now but they don't have a clue. Most people's idea of cleaning is a once-over with some cleaning spray and that's it. That would never do back then. Oh no. Nothing could ever be clean enough and what most people do once a month, back then, we did daily.

This was an age of appearances and it wouldn't do to have dirty steps, an unpolished doorknob, dusty kitchen drawers, floors or anything else for that matter. My life revolved around cleaning everything and everywhere.

The heavy kitchen table had to be scrubbed twice a day,

after lunch and dinner, and everywhere, even the legs, had to have a good scrub down with soap and soda until it all gleamed.

Next I had to clean and scrub the dresser and kitchen cupboards, inside and out.

Once a week the entire dinner service, including plates, bowls, platters, sauce boats, vegetable dishes and soup tureens had to be got down and washed, the shelves dusted and scrubbed, then the whole lot replaced.

The range was the thing that made my fingers ache the most. You had to light it each morning. There were no luxuries like gas and electric back then. The range was itself a little like the cook – large, cumbersome, temperamental and forever going off. There was a real art to getting the fire going strong enough to cook a meal on it and keep the kettles that were constantly bubbling on top of the stove hot enough to make tea with or fill up the giant saucepans.

Every morning I had to blacklead it with a thick brush and then buff it until it gleamed like marble.

Next I had to polish the steel fender, shovel, tongs and poker and steel range handles. 'I want to see my face in it,' was Mrs Jones's usual quip. 'It needs to shine like it's been varnished.'

In front of the fire was a hearth and that had to be scrubbed every day too with the hearthstone.

Once a week I had to turn out the servants' hall and housekeeper's room. And I mean turn out. You couldn't just mop it. Oh no, every bit of furniture had to be moved out and the rooms scrubbed from top to bottom.

I also had to scrub the passageway floors and kitchen

floor every day. Most people assume these floors would have been lovely old original flagstone tiles. Oh no. The floors were concrete and they had to be polished once a week on a Friday after lunch with red cardinal floor polish. No one uses that any more but it's a little like shoe polish and I had to smother the kitchen and pantry floors in it and then buff it up to a gleaming rich red shine. God, it was a mess.

After the floor, once a week, I had to polish all the vast copper pans that hung from the walls with a mixture of silver sand, vinegar and lemon juice. You rubbed it on with a rag, washed and then buffed the pans until they gleamed. And all this before I'd even started on steps, hallways, the washing-up and day-to-day activities like prepping the veggies and washing the pots and pans as Mrs Jones used them.

Before long I realized I would be spending most of my time on my hands and knees in a hessian apron, scrubbing!

And everything had to be done in a particular order too. You couldn't just get to it when you fancied. Each hour of each day was strictly accounted for and the routines of kitchens in the old days wouldn't be out of place in Her Majesty's army. I certainly worked like a soldier, that's for sure. And if I was the soldier, Mrs Jones was the culinary equivalent of a drill sergeant.

By the end of that first week reality had come and slapped me round the face like a ten-day-old wet kipper. I was just fourteen and had worked like a slave, up to my elbows in grease and muck, for fifteen hours a day.

Nothing was ever good enough for Mrs Jones. Either I

was too fast or too slow. Her tongue was so sharp she could have cut herself and nothing escaped her critical eye. Too much sand in the pan mix and you'd soon know about it.

'Dull as dishwater,' she'd snap.

Couldn't see your face in the stove? 'Polish it again.'

At the end of my first week I was filthy, not to mention so dizzy and exhausted, my head seemed to fall through the pillow. It was Friday night. If I'd been at home I would have helped Mother shop in the market, scoffed sweets and been licking my salty lips from the fresh kippers we'd have eaten for tea. My brother would be splashing about in the tin bath in front of the fire now.

I pictured Mother's face, sitting down for the first time all week in front of the crackling fire in our cosy cottage. I missed it so much I could almost hear their laughter, taste the smoky warm kitchen.

I was just a young girl alone in a strange new world.

Here in this big old house the warm London smog was stifling. What I wouldn't have done to be breathing in the fresh, clean Norfolk air. I was so homesick it hurt. I even missed PC Risebrough. Not even the prospect of a weekly bath the next morning to wash away the grime that seemed painted on to my skin could raise a smile. My spirits sank lower than the mud at the bottom of the sluice.

What did tomorrow bring? More scrubbing, I'd be bound.

As my body throbbed with exhaustion I started to sob. *Had I made a terrible, terrible mistake?*

I couldn't possibly go home now. Mother had paid for my uniform and I'd get a reputation for being flaky if I packed it in so soon. Besides, I was fourteen. My childhood was officially over. I had to work, be it here or back in that depressing shop.

How was it possible to feel this wretched?

TIPS FROM A 1930S KITCHEN
...
The Perfect Roast Beef

She may have had a temperament as sour as five-day-old milk pudding, but Mrs Jones couldn't half cook. She never went in for any of this low-fat style cooking either. Like Mrs Beeton, whose recipes she loved, it was full-fat butter, milk and cream all the way. It was full-on flavour too. I'm not saying you should cook this way all the time like I used to, but once in a while can't hurt.

Try this Mrs Beeton recipe for roast fillet of beef that Mrs Jones adapted and used. Tying it in a bag seals in the flavour and keeps the meat incredibly moist and tender.

Fillet of beef
⅓ pint (190 ml) beef gravy
For the marinade: 3 tablespoonfuls oil, 1 tablespoonful
lemon juice, 1 teaspoonful chopped onion and
1 teaspoonful chopped parsley, pinch of mixed herbs,
pepper and a pinch of ground cloves

Place the meat on a dish, pour over the marinade and let it remain for three hours, turning and basting frequently. Have ready a sheet of well-greased baking paper, drain away half the liquid of the marinade, fold the remainder of the marinade and the meat in the paper and fasten the ends securely. Roast or bake for 45 minutes, basting frequently with butter or dripping. Fifteen minutes before serving, remove the paper and when the meat is nicely brown brush it over with butter and place it in a hot dish.

Serve the remaining liquid from the bag as gravy. Just heat it through with butter, red wine and seasoning. When cooled slightly, stir through with cream.

Household Tip

Try this inexpensive treat for tired feet.

Place some glass marbles in the bottom of a large foot bowl, just enough to cover the base. Top up with warm water and Epsom salts. Plunge your feet in and gently slide your feet over the marbles. Foot soak and massage in one!

4

Soulmates

To get the full value of a joy you must have
somebody to divide it with.
Mark Twain

My homesickness followed me round all week like a dirty
black cloud. I must have been living in cloud cuckoo land
to think it would all come easy. Worst of all, Mrs Jones
weren't even the strangest of the staff. I quickly realized
there were some funnier sorts than her in the house.

Besides Mrs Jones, the cook-housekeeper, there was
Mabel, the head housemaid. She oversaw all the female
servants and took care of catering, accounts, recruitment,
linen and stores. Under her was a nice girl called Irene, the
housemaid, and another housemaid whose name escapes
me. They cleaned, dusted, tended fires, cleaned silver, laid
and tended table and generally assisted other staff.

Mr Orchard, the butler, was responsible for waiting at
table, food and drink, answering the door and overall
supervision of all the male servants in the house. Alan,
the frisky footman, was under him and attended the door

and carriages, helped at table, cleaned silver and valeted. John, the hallboy, was their dogsbody. There was also Mr Thornton, the London chauffeur, and his son Louis, the second chauffeur, and Mr and Mrs Brown, the caretakers, who lived in the mews house behind the big house and looked after the property when it was vacant.

Mrs Stocks, when she'd been alive, had had a lady's maid, and Captain Eric had a valet, Mr Bratton. Mr Orchard acted as Mr Stocks's valet. Then there was me and we were soon to be joined by another kitchen maid.

In total there were fourteen staff to look after two men. Fourteen!

I learnt the rules fast. A strict hierarchy governed us all downstairs and was way more rigid and enforced than upstairs. Mabel, the head housemaid, and Mr Orchard, the butler, were obsessed with class and were more conservative and opposed to change than any of the gentry. They were the ones I came to fear, not Mr Stocks. Just one look from them told you whether you were in line for a roasting or not.

Everyone was obsessed with bettering themselves and climbing to the top spot, either as butler, housemaid or cook, and, as is often the way with life in cities, people looked after number one.

As the days passed I quickly realized that Mabel, all buttoned up in black, was another old maid and lived for bossing us about, and Mr Orchard was downright peculiar and a proper fussy old snob. Mrs Jones and Mr Orchard ate breakfast and lunch with us, but when it came to dinner they always dined together separately in the housekeeper's drawing room with the door firmly shut.

It was a couple of days before Mr Orchard deigned to speak to someone of my level. 'And how are we finding it, Mollie?' he asked one morning over breakfast, peering at me over the top of his wire-rimmed specs. He used to drink his coffee just so, with one little finger cocked out. His jet-black hair was always perfectly greased down either side of an immaculate centre parting. The parting was so straight you could have used it as a runway. He was tall and spindly and the waistline of his smart black trousers seemed to creep higher and higher each day. He can only have been in his thirties, but his snooty demeanour made him seem ancient to me.

'Are we listening and learning all we can?' he continued. *Silly old picky knickers.*

He really thought he was the gentry and not their butler! Still, I suppose everyone likes someone to lord it over. I expect he thought I should be thankful he was bestowing me with his attention, but I didn't need his company to feed my ego.

'Oh yes, thanks,' I said, working my way through a plate of bacon, eggs and sausage. Thankfully the food here was excellent and breakfast was always eggs and bacon, which was just as well as come eight a.m. I would be ravenously hungry. It wasn't a patch on what Mr Stocks would be tucking into shortly. He had kedgeree, bacon, eggs, sausages, black pudding and porridge. He didn't even eat it all and sometimes the food came down with just a couple of mouthfuls gone. More fool him. Total waste if you asked me. Rest assured there wouldn't even be a crumb left on my plate.

As I wolfed it down like a woman possessed, Mr

Orchard narrowed his eyes like a cat and his pinched face took on a supercilious air.

'You know, Mollie,' he said, smiling imperiously and delicately placing his coffee cup back in the saucer, 'we're not common servants here. We don't work for middle-class doctors or bank managers.' At the mere mention of the middle classes he wrinkled his nose as if a dog had just come and defecated on the pavement of Cadogan Square and he'd trodden in it. 'Places such as that just have a maid of all work. We are domestic servants to the gentry and you would do well to remember that.'

'What's Mr Stocks like?' I asked, wiping my bread round the plate to get the last drips of egg off. So far he was just a shadowy mystery figure and I'd yet to even catch a glimpse of him.

Mr Orchard's face suddenly lit up.

'Oh, Mr Stocks is a fine gentleman through and through,' he gushed. 'He has breeding and class we can never imagine. He is a most refined and educated man.'

'But what's he really like?' I urged. 'What's he talk about?'

Mr Orchard looked down at me through his wire-rimmed spectacles. 'The butler hears nothing,' he said through thin lips.

As he wittered on I realized that, to him, Mr Stocks was a god and his role on earth was to serve him. He genuinely believed the upper classes were morally and culturally superior. It was so different in them days. Proper rules of behaviour were dictated by the upper class, who led society in understanding the rules of manners, such as table manners, appropriate ways to dress, the correct way to speak, including the words to use and their pronunciation. Even the rules of courtship and marriage came from the upper class. The vast majority of people in powerful positions were privately educated members of the upper classes. They saw themselves as rulers and keepers of British culture, and were not to be challenged by those below them. This rigid social order was overwhelmingly accepted and rarely questioned.

It certainly wasn't here in the basement of Number 24 Cadogan Square. Mabel and Mr Orchard had it engrained in them so deep that if you cut them in two, Mr Stocks's name would run through them.

I said nothing and, heeding my mother's advice, for once managed to 'keep my trap shut'.

Mr Stocks, as it later transpired, was indeed a nice old boy, a real gentleman, but in any case he didn't intimidate me. Why should I have been intimidated? I wasn't inferior to him. You may find it hard to believe that a fourteen-year-old scullery maid from the sticks would really not feel intimidated, but I genuinely didn't. Maybe the blood that flowed in my veins was the same as feisty Granny Esther's, but to me, humans are all just humans. Underneath the clothing, be it apron or double-breasted suit, we're all just two legs, two arms, a head and a heart.

As a scullery maid, I may have been at the opposite end of the social class to Mr Stocks and even five rungs below Mr Orchard, but we all still had the same bodily functions at the end of the day.

You have to wonder. The intricacies, the work, the etiquette that surrounded this small, privileged enclave of London – it would seem preposterous today. Fourteen of us all there to serve two men, I ask you! The butler, the footman and the hallboy didn't have that much to do in my opinion. They just hung about all day, cleaning silver and opening doors. In a way, the servants made work for each other. The housemaids had to clean our bedrooms, the staff ate most of the food that was cooked and we created most of the mess. In their own right, Mr Stocks and Captain Eric didn't require much looking after, but what else did they have to do? They didn't work, after all, and it was all about social standing. Looking back, of course, it was unfair. They were only considered bright because they had the money and time to further their education and make themselves more refined. I daresay I could have formed a whole load more opinions had I been given the opportunity to carry on at school or go to university, but by nature of birth I was born into the working class and that was that.

My grandfather had owned the local village shop; Mr Stocks's grandfather had bought this house in Cadogan Square, Woodhall in Norfolk and a number of other large country properties including Shibden Head brewery and Shibden Hall in Halifax. The Stocks family had made their money from coal-mining and, later, brewing. Mr Stocks, educated at Eton and then Cambridge, would never, ever have to sleep in a hut like my father or scavenge the countryside for pigeons for the pot.

But what good would it do moaning about it? Besides, what could I, a fourteen-year-old scullery maid, do about it any case? Relegated to the basement and hidden away behind a green baize door, I was just there to make Mr Stocks's and Captain Eric's lives as comfortable as possible. Thanks to a separate entrance and back stairs, they never actually had to even see me. I could lead a totally parallel existence to them. Myself and everyone else were there to anticipate his and Captain Eric's every need. Meals appeared on tables, fires were miraculously lit, beds warmed, covers turned and front steps left gleaming. Not that I begrudged him. He was only living the life expected of the gentry.

But times were changing outside on the rarefied streets of Kensington and Chelsea. A seismic shift of a magnitude that few of us could even imagine was on its way. Little did I, Mollie, sniffy Mr Orchard, cantankerous Mrs Jones or blue-blooded Mr Stocks upstairs, delicately picking at his kedgeree, know, but this little world of ours was about to be blown apart. Soon it wouldn't matter if the front doorstep was sparkling or what staircase you used. Dark forces were brewing. Forces that were to irrevocably alter our way of life forever.

British fascist supporters and the anti-fascist opposition were clashing across the East End and in the centre of London. Large numbers of Jews fleeing persecution elsewhere in Europe were arriving in the UK and were settling in London. Hitler had taken control of the German Workers' Party, which he renamed as the Nationalist Socialist German Workers' Party, and bestowed on himself the title of Führer. His speeches, in which he condemned Jews, Communists, democrats and capitalists, were arousing people's injured national pride. By 1931 he was gaining in power and popularity. Even here in London a local Nazi group had been established and its membership was growing rapidly.

These powerful events in Germany were to shape all our lives in ways none of us could have foreseen. But for now a new change, albeit on a smaller scale, was coming my way.

My homesickness was cured in an instant with the arrival to Cadogan Square of a lovely lass by the name of Flo Wadlow. Friendships formed between women are some of the most magical on earth. They are lasting, meaningful and can sustain us through the longest hours. We all need a woman in our life, someone we can gossip long into the night with, spill out our hopes, dreams and ambitions to. Someone to giggle over first kisses with and confide our darkest fears in. And so it was with lovely Flo and myself.

We had no idea back then, when she nervously pushed open the bedroom door, what a wonderful journey we would go on together. The friendship we formed when I was just a lowly scullery maid at Cadogan Square and she a kitchen maid has lasted eighty years. Who would have thought it? Eighty years! We still chat regularly on the phone and Flo, now a hundred years old, is planning a visit from Norfolk, where she still lives, to Bournemouth. I can't wait. We still giggle and laugh like we did back in the old days and we both still have all our marbles and relatively healthy bodies. Not bad for a couple of old scullery maids, eh?

We've lived through so much that I'd say we're a part of history. We were both in the crowds in London, cheering at the Silver Jubilee of King George V and Queen Mary, we gawped at the fascist MPs on their soapboxes in Hyde Park, admired Wallis Simpson when we saw her in London, waved off King George VI's coffin and between us cooked for royalty and politicians.

Back then we never dreamt we'd live to ninety-six and one hundred years old. In 1931 we had rather different preoccupations than we do today. We're more likely to discuss Scrabble moves than moves on cute errand boys, but the laughter and the friendship remains as strong as it ever was. The blood, sweat and toil we shared in domestic service bonded us forever.

Mrs Jones was right in one respect, though – all we did care about was boys, dresses and dancing, and I recognized a kindred spirit the minute she timidly opened the bedroom door one evening after dinner service. Flo had a kind face, with intelligent blue eyes, framed by clouds of soft dark hair.

'Hello,' she said. 'I'm the new kitchen maid. Looks like I'm sharing with you then.' Her soft Norfolk accent immediately gave her away.

'You're a sight for sore eyes,' I said with a grin. 'I'm from Downham Market. Where you from?'

'Wells-on-Sea,' she said, grinning back. 'But I moved up to London aged sixteen when I got a job as a scullery maid not far from here.'

At nineteen, Flo was five years older than me and more experienced. She'd done her dues scrubbing doorsteps and was now trying her hardest to learn all she could so she could make cook.

'What they like here then?' she asked as she unpacked her small case and sat down on the iron bed opposite me.

'Oh, they're all right really,' I said, smiling. 'Ones to

watch out for is Mr Orchard, the butler, and bossy Mabel, the head housemaid. Watch your bum when Alan the footman's about too,' I warned. 'He's got more hands than an octopus.'

Her eyes shone with glee as she giggled.

'And the cook's a bit temperamental too,' I added. 'You don't want to get on the wrong side of her.'

Flo opened her case.

'Here,' I said. 'Let me help you.'

Together we finished her unpacking. She had some beautiful dresses, even some silky evening ones like I'd seen the smart ladies wear out on the streets of Knightsbridge.

'You've got lovely clothes,' I sighed wistfully, thinking of my one good dress.

'I make them,' she said. 'I bought a sewing machine from the Brompton Road. It's easy, I can run you up a couple if you like.'

My heart soared. 'Really?' I gasped. 'You'd do that? Oh, that'd be smashing.'

Our eyes met and a current of understanding flowed between us.

'Course, Mollie,' she smiled. 'We've got to stick together, us Norfolk girls.'

Seems Flo was used to odd sorts after her four years in domestic service. 'Do you know, in my first job I wasn't allowed to be called Florence, my full name, as they already had a parlour maid called Florence, so I suggested they call me Georgina – my middle name,' she said as she tucked herself down under her eiderdown and flicked off the light.

'And did they?' I asked.

'No, the lady of the house reckoned it was too much of a mouthful and too smart for just a scullery maid in any case, so they called me Ena. Got me in no end of trouble

My dear friend Flo Wadlow, the kitchen maid I worked with at Woodhall and Cadogan Square, in her uniform in a previous job. She was my partner in crime and a gentle, kind and loyal friend. We met in 1931 and we're still friends to this day.

as they kept calling me Ena and me not being used to it thought they were talking to someone else and ignored them. They must have thought me a proper ignoramus.'

I shook my head. 'Well, I'll call you Flo if you don't mind, and I'm Mollie.'

'I'd like that, Mollie,' she giggled.

'Have you ever been to a dance before, Flo?' I whispered.

'Oh yes,' she said. I could see her eyes shining in the dark. 'In my last job the boss had a big house in the countryside in Kent and I was allowed to go to the village dances. The village boys loved girls from the big house so they taught me to dance. Not that I told my mum, Mollie. You know what mothers are like. I mean, what wicked things you can get up to at a dance.'

I nodded, even though in truth I had no idea.

'Will you teach me to dance?' I whispered.

'Course,' she said. 'I'll show you the Palais Glide if you like. It's all the rage, you know.'

'Blimey,' I laughed. 'You're a bit with it, aren't ya?'

As our giggles filled the dark, I started to feel a little less homesick. Life was looking up.

Flo quickly became my sidekick and, now that I had a confidante, there was no looking back. With Flo to giggle and lark about with, scrubbing the front steps didn't seem half so bad. I could even handle that old toad Mrs Jones now that I had Flo on my side. Every morning we went about our business, humming and whistling, and we'd take bets on what mood Mrs Jones would be in.

'I reckon black this morning,' I said one day not long after Flo's arrival.

'Oh no,' said Flo. 'Her niece is visiting this morning so she may be all sweetness and light.'

Soon after breakfast Mrs Jones came down and a look at her face told me I'd won. She was red as a beetroot and her chubby fingers were feverishly wringing a tea towel. 'Boss has a dinner party tonight so you silly girls had better stop your tittering and pull your fingers out,' she shot.

One wink from Flo and we both dissolved into fits of giggles.

'I mean it,' she blustered, slamming her fist down on her trusty tome, *Mrs Beeton's Book of Household Management*. 'It's Mrs Lavinia so it's got to be just right. No mucking about today.'

Poor Mrs Jones. She dreaded dinner parties.

Every day at ten a.m., after breakfast, Mr Stocks would come down. As soon as Mrs Jones heard the heavy thudding of his boots down the staff passage, her mouth would tighten and she'd disappear off into the housekeeper's sitting room with him to go through the day's menus. If she came out smiling and a normal colour it meant he was dining out and we were saved a job. If she came back the colour she was this morning, it meant only one thing: all hands on deck.

Usually the boss just had lunch parties – probably preferred it at his age – but every so often his late wife's sister, Mrs Lavinia, would come to stay so she could do the London season, and everything had to be just so.

Personally, I loved it when he had lunch and dinner parties as the atmosphere in the kitchen would become charged with electricity, but I daresay to Mrs Jones it made the day a whole lot harder. Dinner parties in those days weren't like dinners now. There was none of this casual cooking in front of your guests and pouring your own wine. The moment Mr Stocks's guests' cars pulled up in Cadogan Square, the footman, Alan, would appear, on his best behaviour, and with a lightness of hand and deferential manner, show them through to the drawing room for cocktails served by Mr Orchard at his most obsequious.

That morning, as I'd finished scrubbing the steps, I'd sneaked a peek up the large entrance hall. It was a hive of activity as the housemaids scrubbed, dusted and polished. Even the outfits above stairs were smarter as housemaids wore black frocks and little white aprons and the hallboy, footman and butler wore smart black livery and coats with tails and silver buttons.

The parquet flooring gleamed as fresh as morning dew and the smell of lavender polish and carbolic soap lingered sweetly in the air. Big gilt mirrors and oil paintings lined the walls and a vast glittering chandelier dominated the hallway. Opulent-looking rooms filled with antiques, rich-coloured carpets and Turkish rugs led off the hallway. Velvet curtains framed the vast rooms that looked out on Cadogan Square, and massive armchairs, so big you could curl up and sleep on them, were dotted about in every room. And there were books, beautiful leather books everywhere.

I sighed. It wasn't much like the servants' hall down below. Plain wooden furniture, no curtains, just small windows covered in bars that looked out on to a sparse well between the houses and a bare bulb hanging from the ceiling. And as for books? Forget it. We didn't have time to read, unless you counted *Mrs Beeton's Book of Household Management*. What reading material we did have below stairs was either the *Home Companion* magazine or the

News of the World, sold for tuppence an issue. The *News of the World* was beloved by the working classes like my father, but not by the gentry, who wouldn't dare be seen with it upstairs. Just as well, as when I appeared in the *News of the World* a few years on, I wouldn't have wanted Mr Stocks to see me in all my half-naked glory (but more of this later!).

The scandal rags were best left below stairs in rooms that smelt not of lavender but of damp and distemper. Everything up here in this scandal-free room spoke of money, comfort and ease.

This evening Mr Stocks's guests would be sinking their well-padded derrières into these plush chairs while Mr Orchard served them flutes of ice-cold champagne. Restrained laughter would tinkle around the room as the men gathered on one side to talk business and the ladies would talk about whatever it is posh ladies talked about. Dull as dishwater.

'Oh well, Mollie,' I said to myself. 'Back to the kitchen before Mrs Jones blows a gasket.'

The gentry thought nothing of having six courses, all with matching wines, and believe you me it took all day to prepare them. Flo and I were braced and ready. It was our job to act as a support staff to Mrs Jones. The minute she'd used a pan or a piece of equipment, I had to whisk it out from under her nose, wash it and have it back in a jiffy, gleaming for her. And while Mrs Jones flicked through her bible, *Mrs Beeton's Book of Household Management*, and began writing out the menus, we would have to lay up her table.

That in itself was a task. You think about the equipment needed to prepare a six-course menu from scratch.

You can't even imagine. We would have to lay out two chopping boards, one big and one small, two graters, several sieves including a hair sieve and wire sieve, at least five mixing bowls and a bewildering range of knives, spoons, forks and whisks. Then there was the seasoning. A flour canister, caster sugar, salt, pepper, cayenne pepper, paprika pepper, oil and vinegar all had to be ready and waiting.

At the end of the table we laid a pristine white cloth on which to place the special silver serving dishes. It wouldn't do to send them upstairs scratched. All the utensils and kitchen equipment were kept on an in-built shelf under the table, so all you had to do was reach under the table and grab them. In many ways these items and the copper saucepans were as precious to Mrs Jones as children. The copper saucepans were worth a fortune and had been in the family for years. Mrs Jones travelled with them and took them with her when she moved between Norfolk and London.

'With care, these pans outlive us,' she was fond of saying.

By the time we'd finished, the whole table was completely covered. No wonder those tables had to be so blinkin' big. Back then there was no such thing as electric whisks, blenders, microwaves or any of the labour-saving devices we take for granted nowadays. A cook was a cook in the proper sense of the word, not someone who just assembles things.

From that moment, everyone was totally switched on and the kitchen throbbed into life as we peeled, scrubbed, boiled, whisked, sautéed, chopped, blended, marinated and mashed until we felt our arms would drop off. Mrs

Jones, to give her her dues, ran that place like clockwork and she was like a conductor commanding an orchestra. She had a lightness of hand that defied her looks and she always knew just which bubbling pan contained what and what time each piece of meat or fish had gone into the range.

All morning food was delivered via the back stairs in a quantity that would seem extravagant by today's standards. Even when they weren't entertaining, the food that arrived down them stairs was mind-boggling. Whole saddles of lamb and mutton, sirloins as pink as a baby's cheeks and steaks as big as your head would all come streaming into the kitchen, delivered on pallets by a whistling errand boy.

These things never arrived frozen – no one from the butcher to the fishmonger did frozen – so the smells and tastes made your head spin they were that good. And the flavour . . . oh, the flavour. Food never tasted as good as it did back then. It makes me laugh when I hear Jamie Oliver talking about freezing to lock in the flavour. I'm a huge fan of his but I don't reckon that bor knows what real flavour tastes like – I don't suppose anyone does nowadays. Nothing was ever freeze-dried, frozen, reduced or arrived hermetically sealed. The food was eaten immediately after it was picked, slaughtered or fished. That's why people shopped or had food delivered every day. And everything was cooked with butter or oil, never margarine or half-fat this or half-fat that.

I suppose in many ways we was lucky as Mrs Jones had a wealth of ingredients at her fingertips and never had to limit herself much in anything. Mind you, she was ever so good at keeping her stores and never over-ordered anything. She knew how much she had of everything, right down to the last ounce of sugar. If she'd been wasteful she would quickly have been given her marching orders. What meat we didn't eat from the Sunday roast would be served cold on a Monday and hashed up into stew on a Tuesday. Every bone, scrap and vegetable peeling would be thrown in the stockpot and even the fish leftovers would be boiled up for fish stock for soups and sauces.

Each morning the milkman would deliver vast pats of glistening unsalted and salted butter, cream and milk. The milk wouldn't come in bottles but in great churns that the milkman would pour, frothing, straight into our kitchen jugs. If you were to take a sip of that milk today you wouldn't even recognize it. It wasn't until a few years after the Second World War that legislation was passed that meant all milk had to be pasteurized. Back then the milk was as fresh as it comes. The taste was just heavenly and it had a head of cream on it four inches thick. Skimmed milk, so healthy today, back then was regarded as the dregs and sold to the poor for a penny a pint.

Everything went into the pantry and larder, which was down a few steps to keep it several degrees cooler. We had no fridges in them days either, of course, so meat and fish was kept fresh in great big iceboxes in the larder. It was huge and lined with lead and once a week the fishmonger would bring you in a massive slab of ice. The old melted water would run off into a tray at the bottom that I had to yank out and throw away.

You put the ice in the chest and you either put things around, packed them in or placed them on top of the ice, depending on how cold you wanted them to be. Fresh meat and fish would get packed in and covered with a clean tea towel. It was my job to freeze my fingertips off getting whatever fish or meat cook wanted. I also had to store away cooked meat and butter in the larder on marble slabs. And I'd curl the butter into fancy twirls to put in a butter dish for upstairs or plain pats for cooking.

With all this food and provision on regular order, Mrs Jones would probably have got a kickback from some of the grand stores like Coopers opposite Harrods and the butchers and fishmongers. She never told me, mind you, but I know I did when I made cook years later. It was regarded as a perk of the job.

We never had to order any fruit and vegetables as all that came fresh from Mr Stocks's estate, Woodhall, back in Norfolk, twice a week. I couldn't believe my eyes the first time I saw Mr Thornton bring a giant wicker basket down the stairs into the kitchen, big as a laundry hamper, stuffed with every vegetable you can imagine. Fresh new potatoes, huge bundles of asparagus, shiny broad beans, plump tomatoes, lettuces, raspberries, peaches wrapped in paper, and anything else that was in season, was all neatly packed away in the hamper.

It was covered in mud, but was so fresh it's not true. They didn't call it organic, but back in them days everything was organic. The vegetables had travelled all the way from Woodhall on the train from Downham Market and Mr Thornton would collect them, like he had me, fresh off the train at Liverpool Street. No such thing as air miles back then! You wouldn't believe it now, would you? Chauffeur-driven vegetables! But everything had to be the best of the best for the gentry, you see.

Mr Stocks was obviously a great believer in fresh local produce as he wouldn't get his fish from Billingsgate. Oh no, only fish caught fresh from the Norfolk coastline every morning would do. It was also Mr Thornton's job to collect the fish off the train daily and bring it to Cadogan Square. Fresh fish would be loaded on the train at Norfolk, just fished out of the sea that morning, put on the train at Ryston and arrive, still flapping, at Liverpool Street.

Oh, it was beautiful: whole salmons, plaice the size of dinner platters, lemon sole, turbot and cod steaks cut lengthways. The staff would always have the cod steaks every Friday, as they only cost thruppence each, and Mr Stocks would have the more refined fish, like lemon sole. Mind you, I didn't much mind. Nothing tasted better than a great big cod steak, served with boiled eggs in a butter and parsley sauce and homemade chips cooked in dripping.

Every so often, Mr Thornton's son Louis, who acted as second chauffeur in Norfolk, came up to London to help out his father and, on the day of the dinner party, he'd come to assist him with the chauffeuring.

Louis was as handsome as they come.

At twenty-five he was a good ten years older than me, but he had eyes the colour of milk chocolate, jet-black hair and a bum you could bounce a penny off. You could keep your weedy-looking gentry; give me a solid man, a man bred from the land, any day. Louis was a real man through and through. He was as solid as the oaks that grew in the Norfolk soil.

The minute we heard his whistling come down the area steps, Flo and I nudged each other. Tummies were sucked in, breasts pushed out and hair pushed under our mop caps.

'Morning, ladies,' he grinned.

'Morning, Louis,' we giggled back. What silly girls. Honestly, I cringe, remembering it now.

'How are we all today?' he said, beaming.

On the left is Louis Thornton (in the white apron), Mr Stocks's second chauffeur. A good deal of time was spent lusting after this handsome man. On the right is Ernie Bratton, Captain Eric's valet, a lovely fella who took me to the Chelsea Arts Ball.

All the better for seeing you.

We gazed longingly at his tanned, hairy, muscular arms as he helped Mrs Jones unpack the fresh fish his father had just brought in. His hands looked as big as tractors and you could only imagine what he could do with them.

'Got a bootiful big one for you, Mollie,' he winked.

One look at those dark eyes and my pulse started to race.

'Oh, I bet you have,' I simpered, flirting outrageously.

Louis oozed charm and having him in the kitchen was the highlight of the day. Mrs Jones glowered from across the kitchen, but even her cloud of disapproval did nothing to get rid of the heady mix of teenage hormones that hung like steam over the room. With all the simmering pans and the bubbling hormones, it's a wonder nothing boiled over.

Alan skulked about in the background, cleaning silver and shooting Louis jealous looks as Flo and I hung on his every word. When it was time for him to go, we were flapping about nearly as much as the fish.

'See you all when you come back to Woodhall,' he said with a smile, and then he was gone, off to help out his father.

Flo and I gazed longingly after him as his magnificent bottom disappeared up the kitchen steps.

'Any chance you silly girls can do some work now?' shot Mrs Jones, bringing us back to earth with a bump. 'We've a dinner party to get ready, you know.'

Alan muttered something under his breath and stalked from the kitchen.

After that it was my job to prepare the veggies for Flo and Mrs Jones. Great mountains of potatoes and carrots needed peeling and chopping, and there were always piles of onions to dice.

'He's so handsome, ain't he?' Flo whispered, sidling into the pantry beside me.

'Reckon I'm in with a chance?' I whispered back.

'Doubt it, Mollie,' she replied. 'I hear he's courting a kitchen maid back in Norfolk. Anyway, you want a hand?'

She'd been there and done that and knew slicing fifty-odd onions in the cold and dark of the stone pantry was no fun.

'I'm all right, you go on, you'll get into trouble otherwise,' I said. Then I grinned wickedly. 'Afore you go,' I said, picking up a whole trout from the icebox and slapping open and shut its wet mouth, 'who's this put you in mind of?'

She snorted so loud I could hear Mrs Jones clear her throat loudly in irritation. 'Out of there, dolly daydreams,' she bellowed.

'Best go,' said Flo, flashing me a cheeky grin.

As I peeled and chopped the onions, I let my mind drift back to handsome Louis. I couldn't wait to start courting. It was all Flo and I talked about. The laughs and camaraderie that she and I shared were a tonic. We was giddy girls, high on life. Even a tower of onions couldn't dampen my spirits. Besides, I never grumbled in any case, I just put my head down and got on with it. I knew that the quicker I finished, the more I could hang out in the kitchen and watch what Mrs Jones did. Watching her at work was fascinating and, though I didn't realize it, I was picking up so much just watching.

She'd written out the menu and it sounded amazing. Clear beef consommé to start, followed by cheese soufflés. Next came the fish course. Mrs Jones was going to send up a whole dressed salmon. Meat course was poached chicken in aspic with duchesse potatoes. Next came a pudding of peaches and raspberry mousse. And just in case anyone was still hungry, Mrs Jones was going to send up savouries. No one has these any more but back then it was quite commonplace to serve small savoury dishes at the end of a meal. Things like eggs stuffed with prawns, angels on horseback (which is oysters wrapped in bacon), chicken liver on toast, curried shrimps and sweetbreads.

The meal finished with cheese and coffee and after that, for the men, port and cigars. Mrs Jones kept the cigars near the range in the kitchen to keep them nice and dry.

This sounds like a lot for one meal, and it was, but the portions were much smaller in them days. Mr Stocks would still have as many courses to eat even if it were him dining alone, apart from the savouries, but most of the dishes would come down with just a few mouthfuls gone from each plate.

A huge amount of work went into preparing these meals and Mrs Jones made everything, and I mean everything, from scratch.

Once she'd finished writing out the approved menu, she delicately slotted it into a silver frame and gave it to Mr Orchard to take up and place on the table. This wasn't a special one-off for the sake of the dinner party. Every day at lunch and dinner, even if it was Mr Stocks dining alone, she would place the menu in a silver frame and up it would go.

Mrs Jones began work on the soup and soufflés.

'Why are you doing that now?' I asked.

'A good cook always looks ahead, Mollie,' she replied.

For most of the morning she'd had a shin of beef and bones boiling away on the stove. We nearly always had a stockpot on the go. Into that went everything – beef bones, lamb bones, leftover vegetables. These scraps, when cooked, produced the most amazing flavour. She added little muslin bags filled with herbs to the beef stock along with carrots, onions and celery. While Flo grated huge piles of Parmesan for the soufflés, she tipped egg whites, egg yolks, and then finally the shells themselves, into the soup.

'Why are you putting egg shells into the soup?' I gasped.

'That's what gives it a lovely glossy sheen,' she said.

Next she whisked it all vigorously, her huge arms powering through the big copper saucepan, before adding lean beef and sherry and leaving it to simmer.

Every so often, Flo would skim off the scum and fat from the top.

Mrs Jones was right, too. When the soup was drained through a super-fine hair sieve it was as rich and glossy as a thoroughbred's mane. Flo let me sneak a taste and, oh my, I'd never tasted such a concentrated burst of flavour before.

After that, Mrs Jones made her own aspic jelly with stock and gelatine for the chicken dish, and the salmon was gently placed in a massive copper fish pan that seemed to take up half the stove and poached gently with herbs and water. Meanwhile, Flo was making fresh hollandaise sauce to go with it by dropping egg yolks one by one into a basin and mixing with olive oil, until she had a lovely glossy thick yellow sauce. All the sauces were made fresh.

Then she mixed potatoes and mashed them up with egg ready to pipe out.

Meanwhile, I scooted round the kitchen like a little busy worker ant, jumping to Mrs Jones's every command, washing pans and wiping down. I loved it. What a thrill to be part of this. Mrs Jones's energy, focus and calm as she assembled the feast was something to behold.

'Over here, Mollie, and wipe down my whisk,' she ordered. 'Muddle makes more muddle.'

There was none of the shouting and hissy fits like you get with these celebrity chefs nowadays. There wasn't time. You couldn't turn out a meal like that from scratch if you wasted your energy on shouting.

Mid-morning we got a break for an elevensy of coffee, bread and butter or dripping sprinkled with sugar. It was always a welcome breather. Mrs Jones would reach down and pour us all a coffee from the percolator that had been bubbling away all morning on the stove.

Wrapping my hands round the steaming mug, I leant back and breathed out slowly. For the first time in days I allowed my thoughts to drift back to Mother. Thanks to my new friend I was ashamed to say I was no longer missing Norfolk or even allowed it to crowd my thoughts as it once had.

Was Mother missing me? Worrying about me?

'Make us a coffee, Mollie,' grinned Alan, snapping me out of my daydream. 'My tongue's hanging out.' He'd been cleaning silver for the dinner party that evening and the green baize apron he wore over his livery reeked of silver polish. The smell of freshly brewed coffee acted like a magnet to that boy.

'I must have cleaned a mountain of silver,' he grumbled.

Behind him Flo pulled a face and I started chuckling. I knew what was coming next and I was faster than him. As I reached up to the rack over the stove to get him a warm mug, I knew he'd give my bottom a cheeky pinch. Quick as a flash I whirled round and cut him across the hand with a wet tea towel.

He whipped his hand away and I cackled.

'That'll teach you,' I snorted. 'Now keep yer hands to yerself, you filthy so-and-so.'

Our laughter was drowned out as Mr Orchard thundered into the kitchen and Alan slunk off.

'Need I remind you where you are,' he said, his mouth twisting in disgust. 'We do not want those sorts of unsavoury activities going on under Mr Stocks's roof.'

Flo pulled another face behind him and I had to use every muscle in my face to stop myself from falling apart. Didn't that man ever have fun? Rumour had it that he had a boyfriend who worked in an office, so I suppose he may have been homosexual, as were a lot of butlers back then. We never knew for sure and he certainly wouldn't have shared such personal information with me, the scullery maid, but one thing was for certain: he kept his private life very private.

It must have been hard being a gay man in the 1930s. Not that we called them gay back then. Gay was someone who was jolly or happy. Back then they were called pansies or nancy boys. Traditionalists, from the working class up to high society, frowned upon homosexuality and they were regarded as sinners as well as criminals. Homosexuals were seen as a threat to marriage, family and church. It's hard to imagine it now, but in the 1930s homosexuality was illegal and was actively sought out by the police and prosecuted by the state. The 1885 Criminal Law Amendment Act, famously used to prosecute Oscar Wilde, specifically outlawed any sex act, public or private, between two men, enshrining in law homosexuals as criminals. These acts could be punished by up to two years' imprisonment.

The number of arrests and prosecutions for these acts went up dramatically between 1919 and 1935 as police focused attention on increasing the number of raids and breaking up meetings between gay men. Evidence used was often spurious and custodial sentences were handed out more frequently. In the 1920s there was some degree of freedom, but from 1931 things became much stricter and a serious anti-homosexual backlash began. The issue of homosexuality was of such concern to the police that they held the first Conference on Homosexual Crimes in London in the same year as I started as scullery maid. Only down the road from us in Holland Park, sixty men, many working class, were arrested following a police raid at a private Holland Park ballroom. The men had been caught dancing together, with many wearing women's clothes and make-up. 'Pansy case' the papers called it.

Homosexual men had resorted to meeting in secret, at clubs, bars and houses throughout London, and a whole underground subculture had emerged. Looking back, that could have explained Mr Orchard's twitchy, repressed behaviour. He was probably terrified of being arrested, poor fella. As I said, he always kept his private life scrupulously private.

But all he was to me was just a buttoned-up old butler, hell bent on destroying my fun.

After his dressing-down, Mrs Jones glowered from over the top of her basin.

'Oh, don't carry on so, Mollie. Now, get out from under my feet and pop to Coopers and get me some more sugar. We're running low.' Coopers was a major store opposite Harrods that sold groceries and sundries and was always a place you could nip to, to top up your supplies.

This was music to my ears. I loved popping out to the shops more than anything. Any chance to get away from the house and Mr Orchard's oppressive gaze and see a bit of London was a tonic.

Outside in the spring sunshine I walked out of Cadogan Square and, humming to myself, I headed out on to Sloane Street and then hooked a left on to Brompton Road and Harrods.

I've heard of some scullery maids who were ashamed to wear their uniforms outside, for fear of being seen as a skivvy. Not me! I was proud of it and I wore my apron like a badge of honour. I had a job and was sending money home to my mother. That meant I was respectable. Why on earth some people would lie about their jobs I'll never know, but I know plenty did, whether it was because they worried they wouldn't get a boyfriend if a fella thought they worked all the hours sent, or just because they thought they'd be looked down on, I don't know. I just know I was pleased to be wearing this uniform. What did it matter? I was earning good money as a scullery maid in Knightsbridge.

What a rarefied place this area was back in the early 1930s. There was hardly any traffic on the road and what cars there were were Daimlers and Rolls-Royces. The place was crawling with gentry. Ladies and gentlemen paraded through the numerous green squares. These folks were the crème de la crème of society.

'You are lucky to be here, Mollie Browne,' I said to myself as I walked with purpose up Brompton Road.

The sun glinted off the black railings and it felt like all London society was out this season, waiting to be seen. By day it was like a scene from *Mary Poppins*. But by night, who knew what went on in the big ballrooms of the huge London hotels and nightclubs?

I paused and watched as a number of glamorous women swept past me out of a large house and disappeared into the back of a Daimler. They were dressed beautifully in long black silky backless dresses and not a hair on their heads was out of place. A footman wearing white gloves held the back door open for them. They walked like pedigree cats slinking along the pavement and they gave off a nonchalant air. There wasn't a trace of fat on them, they were stick thin. Not like me. I was rounded and curvy with an hourglass figure.

These women didn't look like demure debs off to be presented at court. They looked like racy actresses off to dance to big bands and drink champagne cocktails. As a young scullery maid I daresay I was invisible to them, but all these sights and sounds made lasting impressions on me.

After purchasing my sugar I nipped round the back of Harrods to visit the errand boys. The Trevor Square entrance on the other side of the Brompton Road was where all the deliveries left from and it was teeming with bikes and vans piled sky high with parcels and packages.

They didn't have to cross the road to reach Harrods and stock up. Oh no. There was a tunnel that went under the Brompton Road where they could pass unobtrusively and unseen. The goods were dispatched from Harrods via a freight lift operated by a driver who had to line up the lift with each floor. Once in the basement they were taken in small trains that pulled the goods in cages along the tunnel to the other side of the road. The gentry didn't want to be faced with grubby delivery boys, after all! The tunnel has been there ever since the present building was completed and apparently is still in use today. Lifts and escalators were for the Harrods customers; the back stairs and tunnel were for its employees.

I loved the idea of a secret tunnel, a whole other world beavering away underground, just like we did at Cadogan Square. In fact, London was pulsing with secret, shadowy, unseen worlds. With servants scurrying up hidden stairways, errand boys in underground tunnels and homosexuals meeting in secret clubs, the smart London I had just walked through was only the tip of the iceberg – the presentable face of the 1930s.

Just then I spotted Billy the errand boy pushing his bike out of the delivery bay.

'Hello, gorgeous,' he grinned. 'Come back to see me? Knew you would.'

Some intensive flirting followed, with Billy trying to persuade me to go out with him, before I realized the time. Oh crumbs. Mrs Jones would be wondering where her sugar was.

'Best go,' I shrieked. Fortunately all those years running wild in the Norfolk fields meant I was a good little runner and soon I was pounding up Sloane Street, my apron flapping behind me and the wind ruffling my mop cap nearly clean off my head.

Rich and spicy smells had filled the kitchen. Luckily Mrs Jones hadn't noticed I was late as she was too busy serving up the boss's lunch. On dinner-party days they would serve a light lunch of cold meat and salad.

The rest of the afternoon passed in a blur as everyone focused on his or her own tasks. Finally, by seven thirty p.m., everything was ready to go up. The sound of the silver gong chiming in the hallway signalled that the guests would be finishing their cocktails and moving to the dining room.

Shortly after, the service bell rang in the passage. It was all systems go. The gentry were ready to eat.

The piping hot consommé was poured into a vast tureen that had been warming on the rack above the stove and the light-as-air soufflés were rising gently. The salmon was really something to behold. It was the little touches that made it special. Mrs Jones served it whole on a silver platter with a head and tail made from puff pastry. The fish had been glazed with aspic and was as pink as candyfloss. Flo had cut little pieces of cucumber into the shapes of diamonds and hearts and it was garnished with parsley, quarters of egg, lettuce and carved tomatoes. It looked fit for a king.

The chicken was no less impressive. It had been poached and then brushed with a thin layer of aspic jelly until it glistened and was served with fat asparagus stalks, dripping with melted butter. Flo's duchesse potatoes, which she had spent ages mashing and passing through a sieve this morning, had been moulded into diamond-shaped pieces and baked in the range before being brushed with warm butter and garnished with finely chopped parsley. Served up on silver trays with white doilies and decorated with more aspic dots and parsley, it looked a treat.

Nothing left that kitchen without a white doily and a parsley garnish. Old habits die hard – I still serve up food like that.

My mouth weren't half watering. Imagine that being served up to you by a butler and footman in white gloves. You'd think you were the bee's knees, wouldn't you?

The raspberry mousse looked as light as gossamer, served up next to slivers of succulent white peaches. 'By! It'd melt in your mouth, wouldn't it?' Alan winked, when he noticed me gazing lustfully at the pudding. Then he was gone, taking the silver platters through to the little hatch next to the kitchen, where it would go up in a lift to the next floor. Mr Orchard would be ready and waiting to take the food into the dining room on a big butler's tray. He and Alan would then wait hand and foot on the party for the rest of the night. Every two minutes that bell seemed to tinkle and off they would scurry to tend to their masters' needs.

You never knew how the food went down. Mostly I'm sure it was appreciated by Mrs Lavinia, Mr Stocks and their cronies, as it always came back for the most part eaten. I wondered if they knew the effort and hard work that went into creating that meal, or how my father would have killed for just one mouthful of that delicate chicken dish.

After dinner service was over, Mrs Jones, quite over-come with exhaustion, retired to her bedroom, and me and Flo, still on a high, played cards on the kitchen table.

Finally, the dinner party dispersed and Alan came downstairs.

'That's that over with then. Seen 'em all off into their taxis and cars,' he said. 'Mrs Lavinia's real pretty,' he added with a sigh, shaking his head. Then he fixed his penetrating gaze on me. But not as pretty as you, Mollie,' he said.

I flushed red. 'Get away with you,' I giggled, flicking a playing card at him.

But that night, as Flo and I washed and changed into our nighties, she couldn't help but tease me.

'I reckon that footman has a thing for you, Mollie,' she said.

'Behave,' I said. 'Besides, I couldn't court him. Mrs Jones says dating other staff's not allowed, is it? I couldn't . . .'

Could I?

My mind drifted back to my carefree childhood. Since when did I give a fig for things like petty rules? I could date a footman if I wanted and it would take more than a cantankerous old cook to stop me.

'Well, we're back off to the country soon,' said Flo. Her voice was rich with mischief. 'You know all that fresh country air makes a man frisky,' she teased.

I giggled.

'Besides, plenty of haystacks to hide behind and hedge-rows to lean on,' she snorted.

'You wicked thing,' I cackled, hurling my pillow at her. 'Hah,' she laughed, hurling it back. Soon we were giggling so much, helpless tears of laughter streamed down our faces.

'Sssh,' hushed Mrs Jones crossly through the wall.

As we settled down to sleep, images of Alan's and Louis's faces danced through my mind and a shiver of excitement tingled through my body.

Countryside, here we come!

A heavy silence fell over Cadogan Square that night, each of us closeted away in our own allocated space. Mrs Jones snored softly next door. Mr Stocks sat downstairs enveloped in a cloud of expensive cigar smoke and memories of yesterday. Mr Orchard was probably still folding his clothes away just so, his head preoccupied with thoughts of his master. Goodness knows what lusty dreams chased through Alan's mind and, upstairs, in the dark of the attic, lay two young girls, dreaming of tomorrow and a world of adventures just waiting to be had . . .

TIPS FROM A 1930S KITCHEN

•••

Soup to Scrub Floors On

Consommé may not be to everyone's taste, so why not try this instead? I love this recipe for chicken, vegetable and pearl barley broth. It's cheap, healthy and has kept me going a few years.

Whole chicken
3 pints (1.7 litres) water
2 cloves garlic
1 carrot
1 onion
1 stick celery
Finely chopped parsley and tarragon too if you like the flavour
Good handful of pearl barley

Place the chicken in a stewpot with the water, garlic, vegetables and herbs and simmer gently for two hours. Remove the chicken and strain the liquor.

Now add a good handful of pearl barley to the broth and simmer until the pearl barley is cooked and the broth has thickened. Dice the chicken breast off the bird and add to the broth along with salt, pepper, more parsley and a dash of lemon. Serve piping hot with hot buttered toast.

Household Tip

To stop your kettle from furring, keep a small stone marble inside the kettle.

5

To the Country

Dearest tie of young connections,
Love's first snow-drop, virgin kiss.
Robert Burns

The stench was like nothing on earth – wave upon wave of a putrid, fetid odour so foul it filled the small, dark room like a cloud. It was as pungent and sweet as a rotten melon. A curious mix of sweet and sulphur that can only come from congealed blood and decomposing flesh.

The vapours crept into my nostrils and drifted down into my tummy, whereupon I was seized with an instant urge to be sick.

Come on, Mollie. Get a grip. You can do this.

Taking a knife, I gripped the head of the creature and, before I could chicken out, sliced a deep hole between its legs. Plunging my hand into the cavity I closed my eyes as soft, rotting intestines squelched between my fingers.

'Eurgh!' I squealed. 'That is revolting.'

As I whipped my trembling hand out, the entire contents of the bird's insides – entrails, intestines and maggots –

slithered out and landed with a soft slapping noise on to the floor of the game room. The rancid smell that rose up to meet me was so sharp I gagged and ran screaming from the room.

In the kitchen, Mrs Jones and Flo didn't bat an eyelid at the sight of a screaming scullery maid covered in blood.

'Oh, stop your fussing, child,' Mrs Jones tutted, shaking her head. 'When you gonna learn to pluck and gut them partridge? It's yer job, you know.'

Scrubbing the blood off my hands at the sink, I nodded miserably. I knew it was my job, but it didn't make it any easier.

Ever since we'd arrived at Woodhall three months ago in July 1931, I'd quickly realized that the boss's time would be devoted to stalking, shooting and hunting down pheasants, partridge, rabbits and hares. If it moved, he would shoot and eat it. Which meant that somebody had to devote a lot of their time to plucking, skinning and gutting dead animals. And who would that somebody be? Yes, you've guessed it. The scullery maid, of course.

The game room, which led off from the kitchen, was full to the brim with the rotting carcasses of dead animals that Mr Stocks and his hunting cronies had killed. Hares, partridges and pheasants all hung from iron hooks high up on the walls and pools of blood congealed on the floor. In the country they liked to hang them for a good two weeks. Apparently, it improved the flavour. I don't know about that, but it certainly made them stink a whole lot more.

Between the dead game and the gardener, whose smelly feet competed with the stench from the game room, the air around these parts weren't so fresh, after all.

Flo came up behind me at the sink.

'I'll do it,' she said with a kind smile. She was an expert at plucking and gutting birds and did it without a murmur. 'You always know how to get round me, don't you?'

'Thanks, Flo,' I grinned back. 'You're a real pal. What would I do without you?'

'I don't know,' she said, shaking her head and laughing. 'Find someone else, like as not.'

Apart from the rotting stench of the game room, Woodhall was quite the loveliest place I'd ever seen. A great fifteen-bedroom listed Tudor home set in acres of stunning countryside. It was huge; much bigger than the Cadogan Square house. Mr Stocks's father, Major Michael Stocks, had purchased it in 1895 and, as we'd bumped up the gravel drive in the back of their country car, I could quite see why he must have fallen in love with it on sight.

It was a hazy summer's afternoon when we arrived and, after the hustle and bustle of smoggy London, the sweet country air was a tonic. Mr Thornton had met us off the train at Downham and soon we were whizzing along the quiet country lanes. Mrs Jones stared resolutely ahead, clutching some of her beloved copper pans to her bosom for dear life, but Flo and I soon had the windows wound down and were gawping at the scenery as it unfolded outside.

The countryside was beyond beautiful.

Ancient mellow villages unchanged for centuries passed by as if wrapped in a time warp. The verdant green hedgerows were bursting with wild flowers and a rush of fresh country air laced with the aroma of wood smoke tingled in my nose. Every so often a gap in the hedgerow revealed a tantalizing glimpse of a windswept creek or sweeping wild views of the backwaters beyond.

Out of my bedroom window in London the only scenery had been a jumble of chimney pots. Here, the Norfolk skies seemed to stretch on forever. Fields of wheat and barley soon gave way to fertile fens, flanked by gently swaying rushes.

'This is Hilgay,' announced Mr Thornton as we drove through a picture-postcard village. 'It's quiet, all right. Daresay you girls won't be able to get up to too much mischief here.'

Mrs Jones said nothing, just raised her eyebrows half an inch and bristled. Flo and I exchanged wicked little grins.

If Constable himself had come along he couldn't have painted a prettier picture of a chocolate-box English village. Ancient flint-and-stone workers' cottages nestled in lush green gardens and in the middle of it stood a sweet little church. The village of Hilgay is on the banks of the River Wissey and fat creamy-coloured geese dozed in the sunshine. Before long a duck, followed by a line of little ducklings, waddled up the village high street, forcing Mr Thornton to slow to a halt outside the church. There wasn't another motor car in sight as he eased the car to a stop. Time seemed to have stood still, village life unchanged for centuries. An old boy, chewing on a bit of straw and hanging over a fence post, gazed curiously at the waiting car full of women.

Eventually he raised his cap.

'Hold yew hard, bor,' he said with a nod to Mr Thornton, a gap-toothed grin on his face. 'Them ducks a crossin'.'

That'll learn yer to rush about.' He looked like he moved as slowly as the mother duck and her ducklings, but then I guessed everybody moved slowly round these parts. There wasn't much to rush to.

Mr Thornton nodded towards the graveyard.

'Captain George William Manby's buried in that there

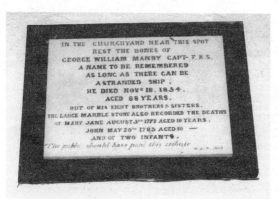

A plaque in Woodhall's church graveyard to commemorate Captain Manby, previous occupant of Woodhall and inventor of a rocket device used to save the crews of shipwrecked ships.

graveyard,' he said proudly. 'He's the one what invented the rocket device that was used to save the crews of ship-wrecked ships.' He shook his head and chuckled to himself. 'Tested it from the roof of that church tower, so he did. Must have scared the birds half to death.'

Flo and I giggled at the thought of a rocket blasting over the tranquil fields. It must have been the most excit-ing thing that had ever happened round these parts.

'He used to live in Woodhall, he did,' continued Mr Thornton. 'Except the boss is the lord of the manor now, a course.'

And what a manor to be lord of! Soon the ducklings had moved safely to the other side of the street and we were off again. In no time at all we had crunched to a halt up the gravel drive. As we disembarked from the car in a scrummage of tired, aching limbs and clanking pots, Flo and I had paused to take in our new home.

'Quite something, ain't it?' I whistled, wide-eyed.

'Very gracious,' Flo agreed.

The red brickwork of the house, mellowed over time, looked as much a part of the landscape as the pheasants that rustled in the hedgerows flanking the gardens. Great stag antlers had been attached either side of the arched stone porch and countless Tudor chimneys soared into the sky. It was magnificent, but a trifle imposing.

Then we saw a sight equal in its magnificence.

Louis was hard at work, his white shirt sleeves rolled up to reveal sun-kissed muscular arms as he polished Mr Stocks's Daimler outside the stable block. He lovingly buffed the Daimler's sleek bonnet with his strong brown hands and Flo and I watched him, mesmerized.

What a sight for sore eyes.

When Louis spotted us, his face lit up with a broad grin and he lifted his chauffeur's cap an inch.

'This is my younger brother, George,' he said, gesturing to the man beside him. 'Welcome to Woodhall.'

All traces of fatigue vanished as we spotted the handsome brother and waved and giggled frantically. Turned out George worked for a local farmer and he and his handsome brother, Louis, lived with their father on a big farmhouse on Woodhall's estate.

'Nice to meet you, George,' I purred.

'This way, girls,' said Mrs Jones firmly, hustling us inside via the back door.

'I've never seen anywhere as grand as this in all me life,' I whispered breathlessly to Flo as we made our way up the back stairs to our new shared bedroom in the attic. The servants' rooms didn't quite compete with the grandeur of the rest of the estate. Our bedroom was dusty, hot and contained just two small single beds.

'This side of the house is strictly for female servants,' Mrs Jones said, fixing her beady eyes on us. 'The other side is for male servants. There is no access to that side of the house from here, just in case you get any ideas. Now freshen up and then get yerselves down in the kitchen,' she ordered.

Interestingly enough, I only recently discovered that Mrs Jones told us a little fib. There *is* access, by means of a small secret doorway, leading to the male servants' quarters. I suppose you can't blame her for not showing it to us!

Once inside, we plonked our small cases on the lino floor and I flung open the window to let in some fresh air. 'The view's not bad, mind,' I commented when I leant out of the attic window and realized I could still see Louis, his breeches stretched tight over his magnificent bottom, as he bent over to polish the tyres.

Flo's face lit up like a sunbeam as she poked her nose out of the window next to me.

'Yep,' she giggled. 'Reckon we're gonna like it here, all right.'

I noted with interest that leading out of our window was a small ladder, which served as a fire escape. 'Hmmm,' I murmured half to myself. 'That may come in handy!'

Unfortunately, grand it may have been, but when it came to washing facilities, Woodhall was much more basic than Cadogan Square. Flo and I each had a chamber pot under our beds to do our bodily functions in and, as for a bathroom, forget it. A tiny hip bath stood in the corner of the room.

Tired and hot from our long journey, we decided to have our weekly bath and wash the grime of London off. Filling up our hip bath with water from a housemaid's cupboard on the landing, we filled it to the top. It took an age using an old enamel jug, but eventually we had it done.

'You go first,' said Flo. I'd never been naked in front of anyone before, apart from my family, and suddenly I was overcome with a rush of shyness. I had boobs now and hair in places I never used to.

Peeling off my sweat-soaked dress and knickers, I felt very exposed.

'It's all right, I won't peek,' chuckled Flo. 'Besides, we're going to have to do our business in front of one another now, so it don't matter.'

This was true, but all the same I kept both hands firmly clamped over my bits, which made it quite hard when it came to the matter of actually getting in the hip bath. Should I go in bum first so my knees came up to my chin or did I just crouch in it like an idiot? What was the knack here? The blasted thing was so damn small! Hang it all. With one hand still covering my bits, I hopped from foot to foot, then took the plunge and slid in feet first.

Flo squealed as a great tidal wave of water gushed

over the sides. 'You're flooding us, Mollie!' she screamed, falling on the bed with helpless laughter. 'It's like the *Titanic* in here.'

'Help me, then,' I spluttered.

I floundered about naked like a fish out of water, all flailing legs and arms. By the time Flo had stopped laughing enough to pull me out, there was one inch of water left in the bath and the floor was flooded.

'I'm just as grubby as when I got in,' I giggled, wrapping a towel round myself.

The wild laughter attracted the attentions of Mabel, the fusty old head housemaid. She burst in, took one look at the state of the floor and had a blue fit.

'Whatever are you girls doing?' she gasped.

'S-sorry,' I said, my teeth chattering. 'The bath over run.'

'I've a good mind to make you change your own chamber pots,' she tutted, shaking her head. 'Heads in the clouds.'

Our subsequent attempts at a bath were no more successful and I half wonder we didn't give up altogether. We must have stunk in them days. But we always made sure to give our feet a good wash in the basin every night, come what may.

Despite the lack of washing facilities, life in the country was good, albeit more pungent. Maybe it was the slower pace of life or the lack of formal lunch and dinner parties to cater for, but everyone, even Mr Orchard and Mrs Jones, seemed a bit more relaxed at Woodhall. Alan, the footman, and John, the hallboy, were just as frisky and

Alan kept up his outrageous flirting, seemingly oblivious that I only had eyes for Louis.

The vast kitchens were actually at the front of the house on the ground floor, overlooking the lawns, so a continual stream of fresh air and sunshine poured through the windows. And what with the constant presence of handsome Louis about the place, things were definitely looking up!

I still had all the usual tasks to do, like whitening the steps and scrubbing the floors, but Woodhall was a little backward compared to London. For starters, milk was delivered from a neighbouring farm on a horse-drawn cart. An old nag plodded up the drive each morning with his eyes half-closed, tossing his mane about to flick off the summer flies. Soon as we heard the clopping of hooves we'd leave out three kitchen jugs for the milkman to fill with fresh frothy milk.

Instead of a range there was an actual coal fire in the kitchen and an old boiler in the scullery, which was used to heat water for the whole house. Ooh, I hated that old thing. In the mornings the coal fire had to be raked down and then piled up with coal to the top. It took three buckets at a time and the ash had to be swept out first thing and then heaped high again. With no gloves, my face and hands would soon be black with soot and ash and, no matter how many times you washed your hands, the smell of coal dust lingered on your skin and up your nose. Like I say, I must have been filthy in them days. The coal for the fire and boiler was kept in a sort of vast open cupboard in the kitchen, so when you needed more you just reached over and grabbed a few more lumps. You can't imagine that now, can you? Coal dust floating about in the kitchen near food! Coal fires were to become obsolete during the 1960s and would largely die a death thanks to Clean Air legislation, but back then they were the best form of heating for most people.

Instead of the concrete floors of London, Woodhall's kitchen had a lovely old wooden floor, which I had to scrub once a week with a brush and some carbolic soap until it gleamed and shone like a new pin.

Two months after we arrived, the shooting season went into full swing with the arrival of partridges in September and pheasant in October. Mr Stocks had vanished for most of August, off up to Scotland for the grouse season, but in September he returned and, thanks to the open outlook of the kitchens, I got to have a good look at him properly for the first time.

As scullery maid, it was my job to get his dogs' meals ready. You've got to laugh at the gentry. Even their beloved black Labradors had to have specially prepared meals. They had three ounces of chopped raw shin of beef and two tablespoonfuls of cooked cabbage.

After his return from Scotland, Mr Stocks clumped down the passage one morning to collect his dogs' biscuits and water.

'Go on then,' blustered Mrs Jones, pushing me forwards. 'Boss wants his dogs' food. Just give him the biscuits, mind, dogs don't eat their proper meal until after the shoot at four p.m. Don't be shooting off at the mouth.'

I looked up and in strode a most peculiar-looking fella. He was an elderly gent and was wearing spacious knickerbockers, spats, leather boots, light-brown single-breasted

Harris tweed jacket, plaid shirt and a flat cap in matching check tweed. The jacket had a chamois gun pad on the right shoulder to protect the material from the gun recoil. He had a kindly, if slightly aloof face. Never mind the dogs' breakfast, he looked like a dog's dinner.

At the sight of her master 'below stairs', Mabel fell about in raptures.

'Morning, sir,' she said, virtually bowing. 'How may I help you?'

'Just come for the dogs' water,' he said.

Smiling, I handed him the enamel water bowl. 'Here you go, sir,' I said.

'You new here?' he asked, surveying me closely from under his cap.

'Yes, sir,' I replied. 'I'm the scullery maid.'

He paused. Then said, 'Good good, what.' And with that he stomped off back down the passage.

That was the extent of my dealings with Mr Stocks. More's the pity. I'd far rather have answered to him than Mrs Jones or Mr Orchard.

Unlike some of the gentry who charged for people to join their shooting parties, Mr Stocks kept his a strictly cronies-only affair. After the dogs had lapped up their water and the gentry had feasted on kedgeree, kippers, sausage, bacon, egg and porridge, they all assembled outside on the front lawns. What a sight!

Eight or so men all dressed identically, with flat-coated Labradors yapping at their heels. As well as the 'guns' as they were known, there were three beaters, whose job it was to go on ahead with large sticks to beat the undergrowth and scare out the game birds, making them an easier shot.

The dogs also used to forage through the undergrowth and help drive out the birds into the path of the guns.

I don't think Mr Stocks ever felt truly more comfortable than when he was stalking his own lands, gun in hand, blasting furry and feathered creatures. In fact, this poem, 'The Old Squire' by Wilfrid Scawen Blunt (died 1922), could have been written about Mr Stocks and his cronies.

I covet not a wider range
Than these dear manors give;
I take my pleasure without change,
And as I lived I live.

I leave my neighbours to their thought;
My choice it is, and pride.
On my own lands to find my sport,
In my own fields to ride.

Shooting was everything to these men and I mean everything. It was virtually imprinted in their DNA. Mr Stocks and Captain Eric, when he felt well enough, were shooting men through and through. His father shot, his father's father shot. The idea of not doing so was simply inconceivable. Their lives and pastimes were dictated by the seasons. Summer season was May through to July in London, where he would, when his wife was alive, attend a good many balls, including the Chelsea Arts Ball, various operas, Henley Royal Regatta and Royal Ascot Week. From September through the winter was strictly set aside for shooting. So, you see, I don't expect they had time to do much actual work.

I thought fleetingly of my father, shivering out in his hut, willing to risk prosecution for a poached pheasant, and here was Mr Stocks with more food and lands than he knew what to do with. The divide between the classes never felt so vast.

Did Flo and myself think the shooting wrong? Not in the least, it's just the way of the countryside, ain't it? It's just what they did and who were we to question it?

The fashions that went with shooting were terribly strict. Bespoke tweed suits, flannels, breeches, knicker-bockers and plus fours, all from Savile Row, for the day and the full fig for evenings. I never once knew Mr Stocks to wear anything other than full evening dress when he dined at night. Even if he was dining alone at home he would be immaculately turned out in a black dinner suit, white starched shirt and a black bow tie. Mr Orchard would prepare it all and help him to dress every evening. Seemed an awful lot of fuss and bother to go to just to sit by yourself in a big old empty dining room, but such was the etiquette of the day I suppose.

That dining room must have echoed with the ghosts of its illustrious past. Mr Stocks seated at the head of the table, the butler behind him, his wife to his right, with the footman behind her, and his eldest son seated opposite at the other end of the table. The family silver must have sparkled like jewels under the glittering chandelier and the room would have hummed with genteel chatter and life.

Now, of course, an elderly gentleman dined alone with only a silver-framed menu for company, his wife and eldest son long gone, and his only surviving son wasting away in a sanatorium. Mr Orchard still faithfully sounded the silver gong every evening at precisely seven thirty p.m. to signal the start of dinner, and he and Alan waited on Mr Stocks as he dined.

Mr Stocks, my boss and the owner of Woodhall. A finer gentleman you'd be hard-pressed to find. Unlike some of the gentry, he was kind and generous and a real old-fashioned gent. We didn't have much to do with him, mind you, but whenever I did see him he would be striding about the place in his plus fours, flat cap on his head and a Labrador trotting by his side.

The war had destroyed the lives of so many, including my father and Mr Stocks. Why, I wondered, did the boss cling to these vanishing traditions? I remember the first time I dared voice that opinion back in London.

'Why does he bother?' I'd asked, when I found out he wore a dinner suit while he was eating alone. 'He sits up there all dressed up in his Sunday best, with his menu in a silver frame, but what's the point? I mean to say, there's no one there even to see him except the servants and we don't count.'

Mr Orchard looked as if he'd been boiled alive.

'How dare you be so impertinent?' he fumed. 'Don't speak about things of which you know nothing.' His proud face stiffened as he attempted to compose himself. 'Mr Stocks is the last of a dying breed of gentlemen,' he sniffed. He looked as if I'd offended him personally, which in a way I suppose I had. With that, he had delicately picked up the silver tray containing Mr Stocks's usual afternoon tea – a pot of leaf tea, two sandwiches with the crusts off and two fairy cakes, lovingly arranged on a plate.

He'd carried that tray to his master like it contained the Crown Jewels.

That same night, all the food Mrs Jones had prepared came back down barely touched. The softest, lightest soufflé looked like it had been nibbled by a mouse, and the delicate lemon sole, a tiny portion anyway, had only a few bites missing.

Something about those half-eaten dishes had tugged at my heartstrings and I'd suddenly regretted shooting off at the mouth. He'd lost his wife, outlived his son and heir, and his other remaining son was so ill from the war he spent half his time being treated for consumption in Switzerland. It must have been a lonely life. I wouldn't have swapped places with him for anything.

If he wanted to spend his whole time shooting furry things while dressed in knickerbockers, then who was I to judge? Poor old gent.

I stared, transfixed, out of the window at him now as he prepared for the shoot.

'Mollie,' snapped Mrs Jones, slamming the window closed on my nose. 'Don't just stand there gawping, girl, we've their lunch to prepare.'

The gentry would get a huge chicken or beef casserole or Irish stew for their luncheon. Mrs Jones would have it in the range straight after breakfast, so by lunchtime it would be lovely and tender and the meat would just fall off the bone. None of this for the beaters, mind you, they'd get a baked potato, salt beef sandwich and a bottle of beer.

When the food was ready, Alan and John loaded it all in a box, then put it inside another box, then proceeded to pack in hay around the cavity.

'Keeps it warm,' explained Flo when she saw me watching.

'Where are they going?' I asked, puzzled.

'Mr Stocks eats on a farmhouse at the far end of the estate,' said Mrs Jones. 'He don't have time to come back to the house to eat.'

He had a number of large, grand, double-fronted farmhouses dotted over his lands. The chauffeur, Mr Thornton, his wife and their sons, Louis and George, occupied one; the head gardener, Mr Dickson, and his wife lived in another. The rest sat empty.

'Now come on,' Mrs Jones chided, batting away Alan and taking over. 'Pack all this hay in tighter, lad. I haven't spent all morning slaving over this for it to arrive cold.'

Next, they loaded it into the back of the country car and Louis bumped across the fields to deliver it. Talk about meals on wheels. Apparently, on fine days, Mr

Stocks and his friends even dined on long tables in the fields waited on by Alan and Mr Orchard, and watched by a herd of curious cows in a neighbouring field.

When the lads left, I chuckled to myself. What a sight they made, Alan and John clinging to the back of the car in full black livery, holding on to the haybox for dear life.

With lunch out of the way, I started scrubbing down the table and Mrs Jones and Flo went back to the soup they were preparing for that night's dinner. It was hare soup and all morning they'd been painstakingly preparing it. I'd managed to talk Flo into skinning the hare, and she'd gutted it, and Mrs Jones had made a soup from it. She'd been at it since breakfast, cooking that while simultaneously preparing the stew.

I'd watched, fascinated, as she'd wiped the hare with a clean cloth. 'Never wash game,' she'd told Flo and me. 'Washes away all the flavour.'

Next she'd chopped it up and simmered it with butter, vegetables, herbs and stock. Ever so carefully she'd lifted the carcass from the pan and set about picking the meat from the bones. Once it had all been painstakingly shredded to remove the hare's fine bones, she handed the meat to Flo who had then pounded it in a mortar and spent an age rubbing it through a fine sieve. What a job that looked and poor Flo's face had gone bright red with the effort. It had been worth it, though. For when the meat was returned to the stock and stirred through with wine and cornflour, it didn't half look lovely.

'By, that tastes good,' said Flo, sipping a spoonful.

I looked on longingly as Mrs Jones proudly stirred it through. All morning she'd been tasting it, seasoning it and lovingly tending to it, like she was nurturing a baby. The sweet aroma filled the kitchen with a rich warmth that made my mouth water.

'Perfect,' Mrs Jones declared, a rare smile crossing her pudgy face. 'Just how the boss likes it.' She breathed in and let out a sigh of satisfaction that saw her full bosom frantically try to escape from the fabric of her apron. When she relaxed and smiled she looked almost pretty. Her face softened as she gazed at her soup and I suddenly wondered what circumstances had conspired to make her an old maid. Well, rest assured, there would be no such fate for me. I wasn't ending up on the shelf, oh no. Watching her make that hare soup, I could easily imagine how years of preparing food and being a slave to the kitchen may well have robbed her of her chance at happiness.

Course, things are never that black and white, but when you're young, that's how you see things, isn't it? As far as I was concerned, if she'd channelled some of the energy that she used to make the boss's dinner into finding a husband, she wouldn't be sleeping alone night after night.

Mind you, in this case it was worth it.

It may have taken her four hours to make, but Mrs Jones had put her heart and soul into that soup. It was the soup of kings.

Just then, an almighty explosion rang out through the kitchen.

'What on earth . . .?' screeched Mrs Jones as a blur of feathers flashed past us, upending everything in its path. Pandemonium broke out. Soup splattered the walls, glass rained down and in the middle of it a scullery maid and a kitchen maid screamed like a couple of banshees.

In all the chaos it took me a couple of seconds to register what had happened. A pheasant had come crashing right through the closed kitchen window, showering the whole room in glass.

'Well, don't just stand there!' screamed Mrs Jones at us. 'Catch it!'

I don't know who looked more terrified, the pheasant or me. The poor thing flapped and scrabbled its way round the kitchen acting like a feathered wrecking ball. Flour canisters were upended, plates came crashing off the table and cutlery went flying. Flo and I darted this way and that, but pheasants are surprisingly fast runners. Soon we were joined by Alan and John and the gardener, who'd overheard the commotion. But even with so many hands that damn pheasant evaded capture, bursting high up into the air the minute anyone got near.

Suddenly, with the effort of an Olympic athlete, Flo flung herself over the kitchen table and, with a grunt, grabbed the bewildered pheasant by its tail. She hurled it out of the window and it vanished back off into the undergrowth from where it had come with an indignant croaking sound.

We stood stock-still in the debris. No one uttered a word. Then all of a sudden the hilarity of the situation hit us and one by one we fell about laughing.

'Why didn't you wring its neck, Flo lass?' croaked the gardener, with tears streaming down his ruddy cheeks.

'I don't know,' panted Flo. 'I didn't think about that.'

A muffled sob came from somewhere near the stove.

I whirled round and there stood Mrs Jones, surrounded by feathers and glass, with a droplet of her precious hare soup about to drip off the tip of her red nose.

'My soup,' she whimpered.

Poor old Mrs Jones. All she wanted was a quiet life. But between us giggly girls and a runaway pheasant she wasn't about to have it any time soon.

We spent the next hour cleaning up the mess and straining what was left of the soup through hair sieves. Well, we hadn't time to start again, so we had to improvise. Fortunately none of the gentry seemed aware how close they came to sipping on hare and glass soup.

In the afternoon Mrs Jones went to lie down and calm her frazzled nerves and, as always after lunch, Flo and I were allowed two hours off before we came back to start dinner. We tore upstairs like whirlwinds to change out of uniforms and into our casuals.

Flo loved cycling as much as me and in no time at all we were speeding down the quiet country lanes on our old bikes, with the wind flowing in our hair. The bikes were only old rattly things. Granny Esther had bought mine for me for two bob, not like the hundreds they cost now, but they got us around all right.

After the heat of the kitchen it was the most glorious feeling of freedom. Autumn was brewing and I could smell it in the air. The golden light had cloaked the fields in a misty glow and the trees were shedding their leaves, turning the landscape into a kaleidoscope of red and gold.

Even though I'd been on my feet since the crack of dawn, my legs frantically pumped the pedals faster and faster until the hedgerows were just a blur.

'Did you see Mrs Jones's face when she saw that pheasant?' shouted Flo behind me.

'Not half,' I cackled. 'I thought she was going to burst a blood vessel.'

Hilgay was only a few miles from my mother's house and before long we were jumping off our bikes and parking them up against the old stone cottage.

I sniffed the air.

'Brilliant,' I said, grinning. 'Baking day.'

I hadn't seen Mother much since I'd left for London five months ago the previous May. I couldn't wait to introduce her to my new friend and share all our adventures.

Mother fell on me like she hadn't seen me in years. Endless questions spilled out of her mouth: 'You're not working too hard, are you? You're watching your mouth, ain't you? You're learning all you can?'

'Stop fussing,' I tutted, helping myself to a couple of jam tarts. 'Make me and Flo a brew, will you, we've had a busy morning.'

As she bustled round the room preparing the tea and Flo and I settled ourselves by the crackling fire, a rush of love and familiarity settled over me. Coming into this cosy farmhouse was like having a warm hug. It felt good to be home. As I looked at my mother running around, for the first time in fifteen years I realized how hard her life was. Her feet barely touched the ground.

I suppose that's what hard work does to a girl. It gives you a perspective you lack as a carefree child. Now that I was working I suddenly truly appreciated what a remarkable woman she really was and how much she did for her family. At least I was paid for my efforts.

My mother loved us unconditionally. She may have come across as tough and had a right hook that could floor a six-foot sailor, but underneath it all she was a warm-hearted soul. I crept up behind her and tucked a few shillings in her apron pocket from my wages.

'Get away with ya, Mollie,' she said, batting away my hand. 'You keep it. I daresay you've earned it.'

Flo and I had a lovely couple of hours telling Mother about the pheasant in the soup and the bath overflowing. Her tired eyes lit up like stars and before long she was belly-laughing. At last, standing up, she dabbed at the corner of her eyes with her apron. 'I haven't laughed like that since you fell off the catwalk at the funfair, Mollie,' she chuckled. 'Now be away with you, you best be off or you'll git it orf that Mrs Jones when you get 'ome.'

At this, we shot up. We were only allowed out for two hours after lunch and it'd be more than our life was worth to be late. But just as we got to the door of the cottage, Mother called me back.

'Mollie,' she said, 'I'd like you and Flo to borrow this.' With that, she handed us her old gramophone. 'I daresay you'll get more use out of it than me and your father. Poor soul, his lungs ain't so good nowadays and he spends half his time out in that hut.'

'Thanks, Mother,' I grinned, planting a kiss on her flour-dusted cheeks.

As we sped back to Woodhall, the gramophone tucked tightly under my arm, I couldn't believe my luck.

'Now you can teach me to dance, Flo!' I yelled.

At the big house I left the gramophone in the servants' hall and it was back to the hustle and bustle of the kitchen. Suitably recovered from the pheasant incident, Mrs Jones was getting her revenge by slicing up one of his relatives with a large knife, ready to be roasted for the boss's dinner. It may have stunk to high heaven while it was hanging in the game room, but once that pheasant was roasted it smelt delicious. Mrs Jones stuffed it with beef-steak and covered the breast with lard and strips of bacon. Every so often she'd take it out and baste it with butter. When it was nearly finished she removed the bacon, lightly dredged it with flour and then basted it again before returning it to the oven. This gave it a lovely glossy sheen. By, it looked succulent.

Meanwhile, Flo was slicing the potatoes I'd peeled so finely you could have used them as wallpaper. Next, she carefully laid them out on a cloth and pressed another cloth over the top of them to dry them out. Just before Mrs Jones sent the pheasant up, she would drop these sliced potatoes into a saucepan of melted lard for just a few seconds until they were deep fried and golden brown. She'd shake them with salt and arrange them around the bird.

'Now remember, girls,' Mrs Jones said. 'Fried potato crisps is the only thing you serve with game, you hear me?

Never do potatoes in the usual way. It's the only way gentlemen like it with their game.'

Without really realizing it, just by being around Mrs Jones and Flo and by keeping my ears open, I was learning a lot. When Flo had her half-day off I would step into her shoes and for once heeded my mother's advice to listen and learn all I could. Mrs Jones was good like that, I suppose, in letting me have a go at things.

Whatever she did, from rolling pastry to filleting fish, marinating meat to garnishing the meals, she did it with such a light, deft hand and eye for detail that everything just looked mouth-watering. She seemed to know everything too. She could make three types of pastry with her eyes shut, from choux to puff to short-crust. I reckoned I could have picked any recipe from her *Mrs Beeton's Book of Household Management* and she could have made it there and then on the spot.

Her mind must have been constantly whirring, planning ahead and working out lunch and dinner menus for the days ahead.

'Here, Mollie,' she said to me now. 'Flo's doing some quenelle of rabbit. Give 'er a hand.'

Together we pounded the rabbit meat using a mortar and pestle. Watching Flo carefully and following what she did, I started to push it through the sieve raw.

'It's what gives it a lovely light texture,' explained Flo. 'You can only get the meat nice and smooth by working it through.'

It took ages putting it through that sieve and before long my arms were on fire.

'Not smooth enough,' commented Mrs Jones over

our shoulders. 'Put it through again. It has to look like pâté.'

After it was finally worked to her standards, I watched as they mixed the raw meat with egg and sauce and then lightly steamed it.

Come seven thirty p.m. everything was ready and Mrs Jones stood back and surveyed it all, her beady little eyes flicking over every aspect of the meal. The juicy pheasant was served with the feathered head on one end and the tail feathers at the other, on the ever-present white doily and garnished with watercress. The delicious-looking salty crisps were arranged around the edges. Mr Orchard had decanted some of Mr Stocks's finest claret to serve up with it. It was a treat for the eyes.

'Wait!' yelled Mrs Jones, tugging Alan back by his coat-tails. She arranged a sprig of watercress just so. 'Now you can go.'

Shaking his head, he disappeared off with the silver butler's tray.

Looking back, the food Mr Stocks enjoyed on a nightly basis was restaurant-standard food, always made to such a high quality.

'Cooking's not hard,' Mrs Jones said, time and again. 'Just follow the recipe and you can't go wrong.' But I knew the food she cooked was more than that, it had a special touch.

Later, as we all tucked into rabbit pie in the servants' hall – staff always had rabbit or hare in shooting season, never partridge or pheasant – we heard the sound of rich, garrulous laughter followed by the faint odour of cigar smoke.

'They'll be cracking open the port by now,' remarked

Alan enviously. His eyes flashed dangerously through dark lashes.

'Jealous sort, ain't ya?' I teased.

He shot me a look that turned my heart to stone. Then, just as quickly, his face changed and a sly smile spread across it. 'So, Flo, you going to teach us all to dance then?' He nodded to my mother's gramophone.

'Oh yes, Flo, do, go on,' I urged.

'All right,' she laughed.

Wolfing down our rabbit pie, we pushed back the servants' hall table and I put a record on the gramophone. Soon a lively waltz rang out round the room. Before I had a chance to object, Alan swept me into his arms and Flo partnered John, the hallboy. We all watched as Flo led us through the steps and soon the room was full of the sounds of crashes and bangs as feet were trodden on and tables bashed into.

Fortunately, if Mr Stocks or any of his cronies had happened to be passing at that moment, they would not have seen our efforts as the servants' hall floor was especially designed to be so low and the windows so high that the gentry was spared the sight of their servants 'at leisure'. Just as well as right now we looked like a load of chimps at a tea party.

'I can't get the hang of this,' grumbled Alan.

'Let's try this instead,' Flo suggested tactfully. 'This is the Palais Glide. It's all the rage in America. Start on the left foot,' she said, linking her arm in John's. 'And we dance in a row left to right. Point left heel diagonally, step left behind right, step right to side, cross left foot in front of right.'

She started to sing, her beautiful soft Norfolk voice filling the servants' hall.

'*Learn to do the Palais Glide, all together side by side, it's as easy as can be, all you've got to do is take your step from me.*'

Grinning, I picked up the beat and started dancing alongside her.

'*So come and do the Palais Glide, you'll be happy when you've tried, once you start you'll want to go on forever, swaying in the Palais Glide.*'

But Flo's tuneful voice didn't help Alan's two left feet. His limbs were all over the place and in no time he got so muddled he tripped over himself, lurched forward and slammed into the servants' hall door with a crack.

'Ha ha,' I cackled. 'You right splutterguttered into that, didn't ya?'

Alan drew himself up to his full height, his eyes narrowed to slits and his fists clenched in fury. 'I oughta slosh you one round the ear, Mollie Browne,' he raged.

'Calm down, Alan,' John gasped. 'She's only having a joke with you.'

This wasn't the first time I'd seen a flash of Alan's explosive temper and it wasn't a pretty sight. Just as quickly he recovered himself.

'I don't like dancing, that's all,' he shrugged. Suddenly, his dark eyes glinted and he made a grab for me. 'I'd far rather watch you,' he growled. With that, his hands slipped down from my waist and brushed against my buttocks. A strange tingle shot up my spine as he pressed himself against me.

'Oi!' I yelled, recovering myself. 'Keep yer hands where I can see them.'

From behind Alan's head Flo winked and before long we were all in hysterics. Suddenly the door to the housekeeper's room flew open and Mr Orchard loomed in the servants' hall doorway. He was so red of face he looked like he might suffocate with rage at any moment.

'Myself and Mrs Jones can't hear ourselves think and Mr Stocks will be wondering what on earth is going on,' he bellowed. 'Now keep that infernal noise down.' He turned on his heel and stalked down the passage.

As soon as he was out of earshot I turned to Flo. 'So much for the butler hears nothing,' I whispered. Her face crumpled into a smile. 'I bet he's only jealous,' I went on.

But despite Mr Orchard's dressing-downs, we danced each night in the servants' hall until our feet ached. Alan lost interest and spent his whole time trying to grope me or pull off my mop cap, rather than learn the steps, but to my delight I found I quickly picked up the dance moves. I even learnt the Palais Glide to perfection, thanks to Flo.

The best nights were when we were joined by Louis and George, who could both dance well. Flo and I showed off something rotten when they were in the room. And when Louis took me in his arms to dance I felt I could have melted like butter. Everything about him was so intoxicating, from the feel of his strong thighs against mine to his handsome face and chocolate-brown eyes. When he removed a stray hair from my cheek one night I swear my heart skipped a thousand beats.

Some men just smell delicious, no matter how little they bathe. Unlike the poor gardener with the smelly feet who Flo and I laughed about constantly, Louis smelt of fresh lemons and soap. His skin was as warm as toast and he could dance too! Could you ask for more in a man? He had an easy charm that brooding, intense Alan would never have. I had to keep reminding myself that he was promised to a kitchen maid. Lucky cow.

Nothing seemed to exhaust us in them days and Flo and I would whisper long into the night.

'Here, Flo,' I hissed in the dark. 'I'm going to kiss a boy soon.'

'Me too,' she whispered back.

Long hours were spent plotting how we would achieve our objective and what it would feel like.

'Do you keep your eyes open, do you reckon?' she asked.

'Only if he looks like Louis,' I sniggered. 'Otherwise keep 'em shut and hope for the best.'

'And what about the tongue?'

'Depends on where he wants to put it,' I quipped.

We laughed so much, our shoulders shaking with the force, that we had to stuff sheets in our mouths to stop anyone hearing.

When I look back now I know they were some of the happiest times of my life. I had turned fifteen at Wood-hall. I was on the brink of becoming a woman and I was so alive it wasn't true. Colours seemed brighter, smells more pungent, jokes funnier and even the sun seemed to shine every day. I suppose it was all those hormones racing round my body. I was stuffed full of them. Flo and I just lived for new experiences and were fizzing over with energy. Every spare chance we got we were out on our bikes and could cycle for miles, sometimes up to fifty miles in a go. Even when thick fog rolled in off the sea and enveloped the landscape in an eerie shroud, we'd still get on our bikes. Only out there in the fens did we feel free.

'Here, Flo,' I'd laugh. 'I can't see a hand in front of me.'

It's a wonder we never ended up in a heap of tangled metal, but the gods seemed to look down on us.

It didn't matter how many times Mrs Jones, Mr Orchard and Mabel chastised us, nothing knocked our confidence or appetite for fun. Mind you, I had noticed since we started at Woodhall a certain softening from Mrs Jones towards us. The more I learnt and the more I could show her I'd been listening to her, the more she seemed to give me a grudging respect.

Even Mabel was having more fun in the countryside.

Flo and I were just cleaning up after dinner one night when I heard a soft giggling coming from outside. Tiptoeing to the door of the kitchen, I hovered and listened.

'Lend us a lug,' I said, beckoning to Flo.

'What is it?' she said, coming over to join me by the door.

'Sssh,' I said, silencing her with a finger on the lips.

Out of the velvety darkness came a gruff man's voice, followed by high-pitched laughter. It was coming from behind the woodshed. We strained our ears to listen.

'Oh, go on Mabel, please,' groaned the man.

'It's Mabel,' I mouthed, my eyes as wide as saucers. Flo's hand flew to her mouth in shock. Then came Mabel's funny little high-pitched voice.

'Not tonight, Frank.'

Flo and I snorted and ran back into the kitchen, cackling. Later that night in bed we were beside ourselves.

'Not tonight, Frank,' I mimicked.

Who'd have thought it? Buttoned-up Mabel, the head housemaid, wasn't an old maid after all. She may have been the picture of reserve and respectability below stairs, but behind the woodshed she was a different lady!

Who could blame her for letting off steam?

But while racy Mabel was getting up to wicked stuff, poor old Mr Orchard obviously wasn't. He was still as sharp as a rattlesnake and had a sting in the tail that was just as venomous.

After we'd been at Woodhall for a few months, and after all our plotting and scheming, we finally got the chance to go to a village dance. The local village dance only came along every three months and it was Mrs Jones herself who told us about it. Apparently it all started with a whist drive to which she would go and after that they would clear away all the tables and a local band would play.

'You can go, but only because it's the local dance and I can keep an eye on yer,' she snapped. 'And you're to be home by eleven o clock, latest.'

This was music to our ears. You may as well have told us we were going to a ball at the Royal Albert Hall, not some draughty old village hall, we were that excited.

On the night itself, we cleared away dinner while Mrs Jones went to the whist drive. As I washed and stacked great piles of dirty dishes, my heart was singing. Tonight was the night. I was going to get a kiss.

Flo had run us up a lovely couple of dresses in a beautiful floral cotton. We didn't have any make-up, not that at our age we'd have been allowed it in any case, so we fluffed up our hair and pinched our cheeks to add colour.

Alan, John and Irene the housemaid were coming too and we cycled into the village in a babble of noise, the excited chatter of teenage voices filling the air.

Inside the village hall the band was warming up and Mrs Jones and all her mates from surrounding villages were just finishing up their game.

'Now remember,' she said, waggling a finger in my face. 'Not a minute after eleven and no funny business.'

Alan dug me in the ribs, but I managed to keep a straight face.

It was nothing special in that room. Wooden floors, a slightly raised stage for the band and trestle tables with a few sandwiches and an urn of tea at the side. But to my young eyes it was the height of sophistication.

The band fired into life with a lively foxtrot and Flo and I sat by the side on wooden chairs and waited ... and waited. I drained my cup of tea, but still nothing happened.

'What now?' I hissed.

'You have to wait for someone to ask you to dance,' she replied.

There were dozens of local girls just like us lining the room. On the other side of the room facing us were a dozen or so boys, all local farming lads. We eyed each other warily, no one wanting to be the one to make the first move. It was like a human cattle market. This was plain daft!

Finally there was a tap on my shoulder.

'Would you like to dance?' came a smooth voice.

I looked up and straight into the eyes of Louis.

'Yes please,' I said. Setting down my teacup, I suddenly felt very shy. My long legs wobbled as Louis led me to the centre of the room, placed one warm hand in mine and the other round my waist.

Didn't I feel like the bee's knees as he whirled me round the hall in his arms? All those hours of practice in the servants' hall paid off as people gathered round us and whistled and clapped as we foxtrotted our way round the room. Louis and I looked like a golden couple. His feet were as light as Fred Astaire's as he led me this way and that. I was like putty in his hands and gazed up adoringly into his brown eyes.

It was utterly, utterly glorious.

Dance after dance we had. The foxtrot was followed by the waltz and then the Palais Glide. My head was spinning by the end of it. Resting my forehead on Louis's shoulder while I got my breath, I suddenly realized my heart was pounding like a tennis ball in my chest.

I tilted my chin up, closed my eyes and my lips parted.

Please kiss me . . . please just kiss me.

I didn't dare open my eyes for fear it might somehow break the magic spell.

There was a long silence followed by . . .

'Best go,' he said abruptly, stepping back so that I stumbled forward. 'Promised the girl I'm courting I'd write to her this evening.'

And just like that my dreams popped like a bubble.

'Thanks for that, Mollie,' he said with a smile and then he was gone.

I glanced over at Flo, who was wrestling with a spotty village lad with two left feet, and shrugged my shoulders in misery.

She smiled sympathetically.

Suddenly the band did a Paul Jones number. This was where all the men went round the middle and the women went in the opposite direction. When the music stopped you had to dance with whoever was opposite you.

'It's a good chance to put the moves on whoever you fancy,' Flo had told me.

As the music burst into life, everyone joined in, eagerly eyeing up the one they fancied and frantically hoping the music would stop as they passed them by. I saw Alan gamely lolloping round. He hated dancing, but I knew he'd give this one a go if it led to something. He smiled and winked as he drew near to me but the music carried on. I just made out the scowl on his face as he found himself planted in front of another girl.

I smirked to myself. Looking up, I found myself opposite a nice-enough-looking lad.

'Me name's Trevor,' he told me as he took my hand. 'I work on the farm near Woodhall. I've seen you around.'

Trevor can only have been sixteen and, as I quickly discovered, didn't have much in the way of conversation. In fact, once we'd got past the mating habits of his boss's bullocks, there wasn't much else to say.

All too soon I realized Flo was frantically gesturing at me.

'Nearly eleven,' she mouthed. 'We have to go.'

Trevor and I stumbled outside into the darkness. I was perilously close to being late and God only knew what Mrs Jones would do if we missed our curfew. But it was now or never. Who knew when the next dance would come around? Trevor was never going to set the world on fire and he was no Louis, but he did have a pair of lips.

'Can I kiss you?' he squeaked, his voice cracking a little.

'All right then,' I replied.

He gulped hard, his Adam's apple shooting up his spotty neck. Then he tore on ahead into a neighbouring field like his heels were on fire and quickly found a suitable haystack to lean against. The sound of muffled laughter from the other side told us it was occupied.

Leading me further into the field, he paused by a dyke, turned in the darkness and dived in for the kill.

They say a first kiss should be a magical experience. Well, this one was wet and sloppy. I stifled a giggle as an image of one of Mr Stocks's Labradors popped into my mind. Trevor kissed me so furiously I felt like I was going to get sucked into his mouth. Suddenly I felt his hand brush my thigh.

Then it was creeping up and under my dress.

'Oh no you don't,' I snapped, slapping his hand away. I knew that way only led to trouble.

'Just a feel, Mollie, please,' he groaned. 'I know where to draw the line. I'm not stupid.'

And nor was I. It wouldn't be Trevor turned out of his job and left with the bad reputation.

'Bye, Trevor,' I said, turning on my heel and making a run for it.

Back at the village hall I grabbed Flo and we headed for Woodhall, leaving Trevor scowling after me. Mrs Jones was waiting to greet us at the back door in her nightie, wearing an expression that could curdle milk.

'In. Now,' she stormed. 'You're late.'

'Sorry, Mrs Jones,' we said meekly as we scurried up the back stairs in the dark.

Lying in our beds, Flo gave me the third degree.

'So, did he try it on?' she asked.

'Course,' I laughed. 'But I gave him a cut across the hand. What about that lad you were dancing with?'

'Just a peck,' she said. 'It was nothing to write home about. You going to see yours again?'

'Not if I can help it!'

As we gossiped long into the night I realized that talking about kissing was often better than actually doing it. Not that it mattered. I had actually kissed a boy! He wasn't a man like Louis, but everyone has to start somewhere.

The next day we skittered about the place like a couple of lambs.

'Wipe the smiles off your faces, will you, girls?' said Mrs Jones over breakfast. 'You're putting me off my sausages.'

With that, we collapsed into fits of giggles.

In the passage after breakfast Alan collared me and grabbed me by the elbow.

'When you going to kiss me, Mollie Browne?' he said. 'You can't keep me waiting, you know.'

I wrenched my arm away. 'You don't own me,' I snapped. 'I can kiss who I like.' And I waltzed back into the kitchen with Alan glowering after me.

The dance had left us so buoyed up we spent hours talking about the next one. Three months seemed like an awful long way away. But then, soon after, we got chatting to some lads from a neighbouring village. We'd met them out cycling one afternoon and stopped to chat.

'Dance is on Saturday night,' one said. 'You coming?'

'Course we are,' I lied.

'See you there,' they smiled.

'Not if we see you first,' I giggled back.

It wouldn't be a problem to go, right? Er, wrong, actually.

'Out of the question!' snapped Mrs Jones, back at Woodhall.

Sadly, our timing was right off and we'd chosen the worst possible day to ask her. Mr Stocks's sister-in-law, Mrs Lavinia, was coming to stay, which meant extra work in the kitchen.

'You're too young,' Mrs Jones went on. 'I can't have you gallivanting all over the countryside. Whatever would your mother say? Someone has to keep an eye on you young girls.'

Her tone of voice told us not to push it, but after lunch during our time off we moaned like stink.

'Who does she think she is?' grumbled Flo as we sat idly by the river, tossing stones in and watching them sink to the bottom.

'She's not our master,' I agreed.

Just then, a white feather on the opposite bank caught my eye. A cold breath of wind caught the feather and I watched it dance, float and flutter higher into the air before it vanished into the cold autumn skies. It was free to float wherever the wind took it.

Suddenly a seed of an idea took hold in my head.

'Who's anyone to tell us what to do and where we can and can't go?' I said. 'She's not our mother.' Fired up with self-righteous anger, I stood up. 'We will go to the dance,' I announced.

'But Mrs Jones said . . .' protested Flo, her voice fading away to nothing.

'Come on, Flo,' I argued. 'Where's your sense of adventure? We can't end up an old maid left on the shelf like her. We're never going to find boyfriends at this rate.' I could see I was getting through to Flo.

'But sneak out?' she gasped.

'Yes,' I said. 'Exactly. Mrs Jones is snoring the minute her head hits the pillow. She'll never know. Remember that fire escape directly outside our room? We'll climb down that.'

She hesitated.

'Do you want to end up an old maid when you're in your twenties and ancient?'

'All right,' she sighed.

'You won't regret it,' I whooped, flinging my arms round my new partner in crime. I'd known that ladder would come in handy when I spotted it!

As we cycled back to Woodhall I was brimming over with confidence at my plan. Like Cinderella, we would go to the ball – well, village dance.

After all, how hard could it possibly be to sneak out?

TIPS FROM A 1930S KITCHEN

•••

Old-fashioned Irish Stew

Eat like a lord of the manor! This is the Mrs Beeton recipe for Irish stew that I used to cook for my boss and all his landed friends after a hard morning's shooting. Enjoy yours with a great hunk of crusty bread and a glass of red wine, perfect for chilly days.

3 lb (1.35 kg) neck mutton
4 lb (1.8 kg) potatoes
1 large onion
12 button onions
1 ½ pints (845 ml) stock
Salt and pepper
Finely chopped parsley

Cut the meat into medium pieces and trim off some of the fat. Wash, peel and slice the potatoes and the large onion. Blanch the button onions and peel them. Put a layer of potatoes at the bottom of a stewpot, cover these with a layer of meat, add slices of onion and a few button onions, and season well with salt and pepper. Repeat until all ingredients are used up. Make sure the top layer is potatoes.

Add the stock and bring to the boil, skimming off the fat as it bubbles to the surface. Cover the stewpot and gently cook in the oven for one and a half hours, or until the potatoes are thoroughly cooked and the stew loses its watery appearance.

Pile in the centre of a hot dish and sprinkle on a little chopped parsley before serving.

Household Tip

Got some leftover stock, gravy or wine? Simply pour it into ice-cube trays, freeze and then pop out to add to stews or soups as and when you need it. Waste not, want not.

6

Mop Caps and Mischief

When a man is tired of London, he is tired of life;
for there is in London all that life can afford.
Samuel Johnson

Clinging to the fire escape three floors up with the icy
Norfolk wind whipping at my hair and face, I gulped hard
and tried not to look down.

'R-remind me again why we're doing this,' whimpered
Flo in the darkness. 'It's perishing up here and I don't
know how much longer I can hold on for.' She clung to
the ladder above me like a limpet, her knuckles as white as
a ghost and her blue eyes bulging with fear.

It was a fair-enough question under the circumstances.
Some girls will go to any lengths to get out, but this had to
be our most hare-brained plan yet. Ever since Mrs Jones
had banned us from going to the dance three villages
along we'd silently seethed about it, until finally we'd
decided we were going to sneak out and go anyway.

When I'd first put forward the idea, all swaggering
bravado and cocksure confidence, it had seemed so easy.

Now it seemed, well, plain daft really. But it was too late to back out now. Besides which, Flo's foot was resting on my head, which made shinning back up the slippery fire escape really quite difficult.

'Come on,' I hissed. 'We're nearly there.' With that, I loosened my grip and started to edge further down. Just then, my foot slipped off the ladder, knocking a clod of moss and mud from the stone wall. I watched it plummet to the ground beneath and land with a soft thud.

I heard someone stir inside.

'Sshh,' I hissed to Flo.

Suddenly my hands seemed to lose all strength and I whizzed down the slippery fire escape like I was on a helter-skelter. Past Mrs Jones's room I slid, faster and faster. Down I plummeted, gathering speed, until I landed in an ungainly heap on the conservatory roof.

Oh crumbs. Please don't break.

The Victorian conservatory at the back of the building, which housed Mr Stocks's rare collection of palms and orchids, was his pride and joy. Goodness knows how old the sheets of glass in the roof were. But the most important question was: would they take the combined weight of a scullery and kitchen maid?

Flattening my body out, I slid myself over the roof, commando style, breathlessly inching myself nearer to the edge.

'The scrapes you get us into, Mollie,' muttered Flo behind me.

Hardly daring to breathe and half-expecting to find myself crashing through the glass roof at any moment, I made my way to the edge of the conservatory roof. So relieved was I when I reached it intact, I immediately swung one leg over the edge and slithered down the side, before landing in a heap on the ground.

The air rushed out of my body and for a minute I saw stars.

This is the back of Woodhall. Can you see the fire-escape ladder Flo and I used to sneak out of the servants' quarters to go to the dance?

A strange gasping noise sounded above and a second later Flo landed with a thump and a tangle of limbs next to me.

'This dance better be worth it, Mollie Browne,' she groaned, shaking her head and clambering to her feet.

Once we'd brushed the mud off our knees, we tiptoed to the stables and, quiet as church mice, pulled out our old bikes. As we silently crept past the front of the house the stag antlers loomed ominously from above the doorway, casting dark shadows on the driveway. Mrs Jones would string us up on them if she caught us! Shivering, I pulled my old wool coat more tightly round myself and went to say something to Flo, but suddenly found I was too cold to talk.

We were soon rattling down the dark country lanes. The wild weather swirled over the freezing Norfolk fields and thick fog rolled in off the coast. It seemed to seep through my coat and into my very bones. Still, at least it was clean fog, not like the mucky green fog that settled like a heavy blanket over London.

Suddenly I thought longingly of my bed.

'Think how much fun we'll have!' I said in the most confident voice I could muster. 'It'll be worth it, right enough.'

Flo said nothing, just cycled stoically on with her teeth chattering.

Finally we made it to the dance. It was the usual do – a dusty village hall, a smattering of hormonal farmhands, tepid tea and foxtrots. But once inside, did Flo and I enjoy ourselves as much as we had last time? Not for a minute. The lads who'd invited us were nowhere to be seen and every time someone looked at us I convinced myself it was a friend of Mrs Jones. After one lacklustre foxtrot and a cup of tea, I was finished.

'It's no good,' I whispered to Flo. 'I'm frightened to death. I'm a bag of nerves.'

'Me too,' she said, nodding. 'What if someone recognizes us and splits on us? We'll get the sack. Why on earth did we dream this up?'

We cycled home in a state of abject terror. How we made it back into our bedroom, to this day I will never know, but I do know that incident showed us up for what we were. Timid girls. We could talk the talk, but really we lived in terror of our bosses.

We weren't really rebellious, just high-spirited and desperate to get out and see and experience life. Working fifteen hours a day in the kitchens under the stern and exacting eye of an all-controlling butler and cook made life a bit claustrophobic at times. All we wanted was a little harmless fun. I doubted very much they'd see it that way, mind. We had deliberately defied Mrs Jones's orders and in 1931 that was a crime punishable by instant dismissal.

For weeks after that we crept around and barely uttered a word. Even Mr Orchard noticed our new demure personalities.

'Glad to see you girls applying yourselves and not giving Mrs Jones cheek,' he smiled smarmily one morning. 'One learns more when one uses one's ears first and mouth second.'

I poked a tongue out at him as he retreated from the room. But still, each and every morning we convinced ourselves that today would be the day Mrs Jones would find out and we'd get the sack. And then what? Without a good reference we'd never get another job and it would be straight back to our villages and homes with our tails between our legs.

References were everything in them days. Half the time I don't think people even got much of an interview. You wouldn't get a job unless the cook or housekeeper said you were honest, straight, hard-working and from a good family. Imagine what Mrs Jones would have said had she known we expressly disobeyed her orders. Not least risked our lives scaling the side of the house! She'd have sent us packing and I daresay my mother would have given me the birch, she'd have been that furious. I'd have been packed off to work in Granny Esther's shop with a flea in my ear and no chance of escaping to London ever again.

That was the problem, you see. Nowadays young people don't have the respect for their elders that we did. Got yourself pregnant, lost your job, failed your exams, kicked off your college course? So what? What's your mother going to do about it? Kick you out? Not likely. Even if she did, someone would have to take responsibility for you. The state, like as not. But back when Flo and I were gadding about, there were no state handouts and we lived in fear, and I really mean fear, of a dressing-down from our parents.

If they were to turn us out of our homes and we had no husband to rely on or job to go to, what was our fate? No council flats or queuing up for jobseeker's allowance and unemployment benefit, that's for certain. It would have been the workhouse for us. That place was horrific – like a real-life nightmare – and the fear of it was larger than life.

We were forever treading that fine line between being typical teenagers, high on life and full of spirit, but mindful not to overstep the line for fear of where it could lead us. So we kept our heads down and worked like Trojans. We tried to behave, we really did, but teenage girls being what they are, mischief was never far away . . .

*

By the following year, with my job still intact and another London season under my belt, my mind was forever wandering back to the eternal question: *when would I get a boyfriend?*

It was simply inconceivable to me that I would end up in service for the rest of my life. Along the way I'd heard about women who'd married butlers in the same household and ended up staying in employment together under the same roof for evermore, before retiring on to a cottage on the estate. I couldn't have thought of anything worse. Why would you want to have to stare at your husband day in, day out? Or worse still, end up like Mrs Jones. Too old to have a choice and stuck working for the same employer until you probably keeled over mid-service.

'What about Alan?' said Flo one night as we cleared down after dinner.

'Good grief, no!' I gasped. 'Mr Orchard would have a blue fit if he thought we were cavorting below stairs. Can you ever imagine?'

'He's good-looking,' she added.

With his jet-black hair and chiselled features, he was handsome all right.

'No,' I said. 'He's got a terrible temper on him. He goes up like smoke in a bottle. Besides which, he can't dance neither.'

'George then?' she suggested.

George! A light bulb pinged on in my head. I'd never thought of George before. I was usually too busy lusting over his older brother to pay him much attention. But he was reasonable-looking all right. I'd seen him out there working in the fields. His body looked like it had been carved from marble and he was strong too – he tossed those hay bales about like they were kittens.

Yes, I decided, I could do far worse than George.

'I'll sort it for you,' said Flo confidently.

Sure enough, on her next half-day off, she just happened to be passing the field George was working in.

'If you ask Mollie to the local pictures, she'll go with you,' she told him.

'Really?' he said, looking up from his pitchfork in surprise. 'Right then,' he spluttered. 'I'll do that then.'

'All sorted,' said Flo when she came back to Woodhall. 'The things I do for you, Mollie.'

A few days later I was tackling a pile of dirty dishes in the scullery when Flo sidled up next to me. 'Visitor for you,' she said with a wink.

I came out, wiping my filthy hands on my apron, and who should be standing by the kitchen door, cap in hand, but George.

'H-hello, Mollie,' he stuttered, a red flush sneaking up his neck. 'Happen I'd like to take you to the pictures on your next half-day off. If you'd like to, that is.'

I smiled broadly. 'I'd really like that, George,' I said.

He twisted his cap nervously, opened his mouth to say something then obviously thought better of it. We stood there in awkward silence, until Alan stalked by.

'Make sure he has a bath first, Mollie,' he snapped. 'He'll stink the picture house out with the smell of cow dung.'

George's face fell and I turned on Alan.

'Get away with ya, he's more of a gentleman than you'll ever be.'

I turned back to George. He looked mortified and stared at the floor. Poor fella. That Alan could be plain vicious at times.

'*Frankenstein*'s on at Downham,' I said. 'Why don't we go and see that? I'm off tomorrow afternoon. I'll meet you out front on our bikes.'

The next day he was waiting for me at the end of the lane. His hair was combed down neatly and he was nervously clutching a bunch of wildflowers he'd picked for me. He'd obviously shined his shoes and was wearing his good pair of trousers. Judging by the way his face shone he'd clearly scrubbed hard to remove all traces of the farm.

Bless him.

He was a gentle, sweet man, proper Norfolk bred and born, as they say. But as I pushed my bike over to meet him, I noted with a trace of disappointment that there was no nervous flip-flop of excitement in my tummy. My heart simply didn't turn over in the same way it did when I saw his handsome older brother, Louis.

'These are for you, Mollie,' he said, thrusting the bouquet at me and blushing furiously as he stared at the ground. 'I wanted to find some flowers that matched your eyes, except yours are brown, so I couldn't find none. Quite unusual to have a redhead with brown eyes . . .' he mumbled, trailing off.

'That's all right,' I beamed. 'I'm unusual, right enough. My mum reckons we must have been descended from Vikings.'

'You're certainly brave enough to be a Viking warrior,' he said with a shy smile.

I thought back to when Flo and I climbed out of the

top-floor windows to escape to the dance and grinned. 'Perhaps you're right. Hope I don't look like a warrior, mind you.'

He looked mortified. 'Of course not, Mollie. I didn't mean that. You're pretty . . . very pretty.'

'It's all right,' I said, giving him a playful tap on the arm. 'Come on, let's get going or else we'll miss the film.'

As we cycled there I was full of it.

'I hear it's a talkie,' I babbled. 'I've never seen a talkie afore, have you?'

George shook his head slowly. I realized he was a man of few words. Not that it mattered as I kept up a constant stream of chatter.

'People speaking on films,' I laughed. 'Whatever next?'

Up until the late 1920s the only films we'd seen were silent films, but in 1932, the same picture house that I'd watched all those Charlie Chaplin films in every Saturday afternoon as a child was now starting to show talkies. Sadly, this meant old Mrs Long had to pack away her piano and was out of a job. No more bashing away on the keys to provide a dramatic backdrop.

'That's a sign of the times, eh?' I said to George as we settled into our seats to watch the film. He nodded and pulled out an old brown paper bag of slightly furry pineapple chunks. Dusting one down, he offered it to me with a broad grin.

As I nestled back into my seat, sucking on my sweet, I realized how happy I was. *I was courting. I was actually courting a fella.*

The cinema was packed to the rafters. They always was back then. I supposed it was because between the wars life was tough and at seven pence a pop (five pence on a Saturday afternoon) cinema provided an affordable form of escapism. They didn't call it the golden age of cinema for nothing. They made some marvellous films back then. Charlie Chan, Laurel and Hardy and the Marx Brothers had the cinemas packed out night after night. By 1930 there were 250 cinemas in London alone, double the number from 1911.

Humour was popular, but what everybody seemed to be lapping up most was horror and thrillers. The monster horror film *Frankenstein* had been wowing cinemagoers in London for ages, but these things always took a little while to reach the country. Now it was here in Norfolk and expectations were high.

The lights dimmed and a ripple of excitement ran through the darkened picture house. Just then, the screen flickered into life and suddenly the lead character, Edward Van Sloan, stepped from behind a red velvet curtain and spoke – *actually spoke* – in a low, sinister voice.

'*We are about to unfold the story of Frankenstein, a man of science who sought to create a man after his own image without reckoning upon God. It is one of the strangest tales ever told.*'

'It's like he's right here in the room, ain't it?' I whispered. George nodded, his eyes as wide as saucers, clearly struck dumb.

'*It deals with the two great mysteries of creation – life and death. I think it will thrill you. It may shock you. It might even horrify you. So if any of you feel that you do not care to subject your nerves to such a strain, now's your chance to – uh, well, we warned you.*'

George gulped hard. 'W-would you like to go, Mollie?' he stuttered.

'Course not,' I said gleefully. 'I can't wait, this is going to be terrifying.'

'Ah, of course,' he blustered. 'I was just thinking of your nerves.'

Poor George. He hid it well in the gloom of the cinema, but I could see he was scared by the way his feet were tapping up and down. The film cut to Frankenstein, holed up in an abandoned watchtower, which he had equipped as a laboratory. Folk must have been more naive back then as the whole audience was gripped, frozen to our seats as we watched Frankenstein assemble his monster and attempt to bring him back to life. Women screamed and men jumped out of their seats. None of us had seen anything like it in our lives before. And when Frankenstein and his hunchback assistant raised their dead creature on to the operating table, there was a collective intake of breath. There was a terrific crash of thunder; Frankenstein's electric machines crackled into life and suddenly the monster's hand began to twitch.

'*It's alive!*' yelled Frankenstein.

'Cor, blarst me!' yelled George, jumping clean out of his seat and showering the floor with pineapple chunks.

Poor George. As we exited, blinking, into the sunlight in Downham Market, he looked quite drained by the experience. Fortunately, by the time we'd had a sticky bun and a cup of tea at a nearby teashop, he'd recovered himself.

'I had a really lovely afternoon, Mollie,' he said earnestly, placing a warm hand on mine. 'I'm right keen on you.'

'I don't want anything shameful happening between us, George,' I warned.

He whipped his hand away like it had been scalded.

'My heart alive, I didn't mean that, Mollie,' he spluttered. 'I just meant I likes you. I'd never try anything to offend you.'

I was so used to fending off lecherous farmhands behind haystacks and frisky footmen that I hadn't realized some men could be decent. George was the perfect gentleman after that and when he'd cycled me home and left me at the entrance to Woodhall, he paused only to place a soft kiss on my cheek.

'Fare 'ee well, Mollie,' he smiled gently.

I could just make out Flo and Alan peeking through the kitchen window.

I'd give 'em summit to talk about.

'Thanks, George,' I grinned, taking his cheeks in both hands and planting a quick smacker on his lips. 'I had a lovely day.'

His face crumpled into a delighted smile and he pedalled off back to the farm the colour of a tomato.

I floated into the kitchen.

'Is he your new boyfriend?' Flo gushed. 'Are ya courting?'

'Maybe,' I teased.

Alan glowered from over the pile of silver he was polishing. 'He's a boy, all right,' he snapped.

'You're so green with envy you're the same colour as that apron,' I laughed, flicking his baize apron.

'OK, we've had our fun,' thundered Mrs Jones, throwing my apron at me. 'Can we get back to some work now?'

After that, George and I lived in each other's pockets and saw each other as much as our time off allowed, which wasn't much, admittedly, and true to his word he was the perfect gentleman.

There was just one snag – his older brother, Louis. Try as I might, when I was kissing George goodnight, it was Louis I was thinking of.

I confided my fears to Flo in our bedroom.

'It sounds awful, but my heart belongs to Louis,' I wailed.

'I know, Mollie, but he's promised to another,' she said softly. 'Don't go breaking George's heart. He's keener on you than you are on him. That's plain for all to see.'

I hadn't been seeing George long when Christmas rolled round. Christmas in service is much like any other day, to be honest. You work the same hours. Steps and floors still need scrubbing and the range still needs blackleading. There was no well-filled stocking waiting for Flo or me when we blearily opened our eyes at six thirty a.m., just the prospect of a mountain of work.

'There's goosebumps on my goosebumps,' I joked as I cracked the ice that had formed on the top of the jug of water we used to wash with. I splashed cold water under each armpit and doused my feet and cheeks in the freezing water for as long as I could bear before running shivering back to the bed to change into uniform.

I was just about to throw over the covers when, to my surprise, I found a small brown package neatly tied with red ribbon.

I turned to Flo. 'So Father Christmas has been!'

'It's nothing big,' she blushed. 'I . . . well, I just thought us girls have got to look after each other, haven't we?'

I ripped open the package to reveal a beautifully knitted pair of emerald-green wool gloves. I slipped my hands into them and they were as soft as kittens.

'Oh, Flo,' I sighed, throwing my arms round her. 'You didn't need to do that.'

'Oh, don't worry,' she protested. 'It's just a little something. I've been knitting them on my half-days off.'

'But I haven't got you anything,' I sighed.

'You don't need to worry about that, I weren't expecting nothing,' she said.

'Hang on,' I laughed, pulling out a package from under the bed and handing it to Flo. 'What's this?'

Flo unwrapped it to reveal a bar of milk chocolate. Her smile was like the sun coming out from behind a cloud.

'Tease,' she giggled.

'I'm sorry,' I said. 'I wanted to get you a bigger bar but that was all I could afford.'

'It's the best present I've ever had,' she said. 'In fact, you're the best friend I ever had. Even if you do make me shin down ladders from three floors up.' She smiled at me and I felt a sudden rush of warmth towards my friend. Flo was so gentle, sweet and honest, it wasn't true. She radiated sincerity and kindness. She didn't have a drop of bad blood in her body and in all the time I'd known her I hadn't heard a single nasty thing uttered from her lips.

I wasn't the least bit surprised when she snapped the bar of chocolate in two and offered half to me. Giggling, I peeled off one of my gloves and she slipped it on.

That cold and frosty Christmas morning in 1932 a

scullery maid and a kitchen maid sat on a bed in an old servants' quarters, nibbling on a bar of chocolate and wearing one green glove each. I knew from that moment on we'd be friends for life.

Downstairs there was no tree or Christmas music, but Flo and I, being young girls high on life, tried our hardest to inject some Christmas cheer into the cold, dark kitchen that morning. Even Mrs Jones coming down and grumbling about her varicose veins couldn't suck the joy out of us.

'Hark the herald angels sing,' I warbled as I piled up the stove with fresh coal.

'I'll give you hark the herald angels if you don't get that stove on and a kettle brewing, my girl,' she muttered.

In fact, if it hadn't been for mine and Flo's singing you'd barely have known it was Christmas Day. It was the same each year. Mr Orchard wafted about Woodhall without a hair out of place, looking like he had a pole up his backside, and Mrs Jones was in one of her dark moods as she prepared the boss's breakfast. It was only the youngsters – myself, Flo, Alan, John and the two housemaids – who seemed to even really care that it was Christmas. There wasn't a tree or sprig of holly about the place. I guessed that with it being Mr Stocks on his own he didn't reckon there was much point.

But after Mrs Jones had retired to her sitting room with Mr Stocks, she came out with news to finally instil everyone with a bit of Christmas spirit.

'Present from Mr Stocks,' she said, pressing half a crown into everyone's hands.

Now, I have read of other servants having a miserable

old time at Christmas and being forced to line up in order of priority, with scullery maids at the bottom of the line and butlers at the top, to receive a handout gift. 'Gift' being used in the loosest sense of the word, as more often than not it would be a new apron or something they would have to wear in service, which doesn't strike me as much of a gift. So getting actual money had to be a step up, surely?

'Half a crown,' sighed Flo happily, staring at hers like it was made of rubies and pearls. 'I've always been given a pair of scratchy old black lisle stockings. He's a proper gent, through and through.'

'I told you so,' sniffed Mr Orchard as he swept past. 'Who do you think spring-cleans this place or Cadogan Square when we're not there?' he went on, warming to his theme. 'Not us. In most households you'd have to do it and for no extra money, mind, but Mr Stocks pays the head gardener and his wife to spring-clean Woodhall when we're not here and there will be someone spring-cleaning Cadogan Square before we go there for the season. Who do you think comes in here and spring-cleans the place, the fairies?'

Flo and I found ourselves speechless for once. I knew the work involved in a spring clean. What people do for a spring clean today is what we did on a day-to-day basis. A spring clean in the 1930s involved no end of work.

All of Woodhall's Tudor chimneys would be swept and the flues cleaned out. Every single room would be turned out and scrubbed down. Every single piece of silver, china and every ornament would be brought out and polished. Curtains would be taken down and beaten, mattresses aired. No nook or cranny in the vast house would be left untouched. Even the game room would be scrubbed with carbolic soap and steaming hot water until the dark red pools of dried blood were cleaned off. It was a major operation. So I supposed we should be thankful.

The rest of the day was all about the food.

Mrs Jones cooked an amazing roast Christmas dinner. We had a beautiful big goose and a Norfolk turkey from the local farm. The enormous turkey was stuffed with veal forcemeat. It was a Mrs Beeton recipe, so of course Mrs Jones loved it.

'The king of stuffin', this is,' she said.

It would be enough to stuff anyone, mind.

She'd taken a pound of veal and minced it up so fine it was almost like a smooth pâté. Next, she'd pounded it with beef suet and smoked bacon. Then Flo had taken over and passed the whole lot through a wire sieve before mixing with onion, two eggs, mace, parsley, nutmeg and fine breadcrumbs. The whole lot was stuffed in the cavity of the bird, coated in more bacon and roasted in the range until it was golden brown. By, it looked tasty!

An even bigger goose was roasted next to it and stuffed with a rich onion forcemeat. The smells that came from all that cooking meat drove everyone near crazy, they were that delicious.

Alan and I hovered around the range like a couple of excitable puppies.

'A watched bird don't cook,' Mrs Jones scolded. 'Now can you all get away or you'll feel the toe of my boot somewhere in a minute.'

By the time it was lifted, sizzling, from the range and

171

sent up with roasted potatoes, more stuffing, gravy, apple sauce, bread sauce, cranberry sauce, sprouts with bacon and chestnuts and parsnips, we were near delirious.

The boss had just two small slices off the turkey and Alan brought the rest down.

'Happy Christmas, everyone!' he cheered. 'Boss says the rest is for us.'

The servants' hall was alive with laughter and chatter as we gorged ourselves on turkey and all the trimmings, followed by Mrs Jones's really excellent suet Christmas pudding drowned in some of the local farmer's extra-thick cream.

After I'd scraped my plate clean and sat back with a tummy full of really good food, I closed my eyes, loosened my apron strings and smiled dreamily. My limbs seemed to melt into the chair, I was that tired and full. Alan took his chance to hover over me with a sprig of mistletoe and plant a cheeky kiss on my cheek. I jumped out of my skin so high that even Mrs Jones and Mr Orchard managed to raise a smile.

As the staff chattered and played cards and the room was filled with a convivial buzz, my mind drifted to dear old Mr Stocks in his dining room. He'd be up there now, eating alone in his dinner suit, in that big old room. It seemed such a crying shame that he couldn't come and eat in here with us in the warmth of the servants' hall and have some company. Our laughter must have carried along the hall to his quarters. Did he ever long to join us – have some company, a laugh and a joke with the people who devoted their entire lives to caring for him? Who knew? But in any case, I wasn't daft. The divide was clearly marked between him and us. Even if he wanted to, he could no more cross that class divide than he could walk to the moon. His dining room was on the other side of the house, but it may as well have been 500 miles away, so apart were we. We used different doors, we ate at separate tables, and yet we all lived under the same roof. What a strange world we occupied.

Little did any of us know, but by the end of the decade a dangerous evil would be busy breaking down the great British class structure, throwing into chaos everything that the upper class held as sacred. World War Two was a great social leveller. In six years of war, Hitler's bombs were to blow apart centuries of tradition and put Mr Stocks's way of life into peril. People would finally become just that – people. For the first time, as we fought to overcome tyranny, the class divide would be put to one side. But, for now, the upstairs/downstairs divide remained resolutely in place and that Christmas we dined in blissful ignorance of the horrors that lay ahead.

Boxing Day was even more fun. After a leftover lunch of devilled turkey legs and hashed turkey there was a big dance at the village hall. Mrs Jones and Mr Orchard went to the whist drive and me, Flo, John and Irene were allowed to let our hair down at the dance that followed.

'You have to stay here and look after Mr Stocks,' Mr Orchard ordered Alan.

He had a face like thunder as we all cycled off to the village dance.

Once there, Flo and I listened to other servants from nearby grand homes moaning like mad about their bosses. They were full of it. Who was having an affair with who,

who got the stingiest present. Flo and I kept our traps shut, for once grateful we had nothing to say.

Later that evening, George took me outside and kissed me in the snow. As the flakes fluttered down and settled on our eyelashes, he wrapped me into his big warm wool coat and planted a gentle kiss on the top of my head.

'I think I'm falling for you, Mollie,' he sighed.

Magnificent Woodhall, a beautiful listed Tudor home in the stunning Norfolk countryside.

I said nothing, just snuggled down into his warm embrace and tried to push an image of Louis out of my mind.

As winter thawed it gave way to a countryside beautiful beyond comparison. The fields around Hilgay were blanketed in bluebells, snowdrops pushed their way through the soil and wildflowers burst out the hedgerows.

The sap was rising in Woodhall too.

Alan cornered me by the woodshed one afternoon.

'We'll be heading back up to London for the season soon enough, Mollie,' he said, his eyes glittering. 'You'll have to wave goodbye to that boyfriend of yours. Then you'll be able to get your hands on a real man.'

Angrily, I pushed my way past him. I hadn't really thought what would become of George and myself when we moved back to London, but how could I court him when we were eighty miles apart? I couldn't ring him and I knew neither of us were letter writers.

'He'll wait for you, I'm sure,' soothed Flo when I spilled out my fears to her later.

'But I'll miss him so,' I sighed dramatically. 'I've never really courted a man before. What will become of us?'

It was May 1933 and as the day drew ever nearer to us leaving and Mrs Jones began to pack up her beloved copper pots, a sense of sadness settled in my heart. I liked George. He was kind, considerate and treated me right.

'Don't worry, Mollie,' he said when we met briefly after lunch service. 'I'll wait for you. Old place won't be the same without your red hair bobbing through the fields.' He smoothed down a stray hair. 'Same colour as cherry-ade,' he said softly. With that, he planted a soft kiss on my lips. He smelt of fresh-cut grass and tasted as sweet as strawberry jam.

I watched his strong lean body lope off back along the fields to his father's farmhouse and I sighed deeply. I wasn't only going to miss him but the country too – the fresh air, the space, the lights of Woodhall spilling out over the fields as Flo and I cycled home for dinner service. Being here was like taking a warm bath: safe, closeted, comforting.

But, as ever, in service your time is never really your own and the London season and Cadogan Square beckoned.

The next day, as we boarded the train bound for London, even Flo couldn't raise a smile out of me and I was as low as a snake's belly by the time we reached Knightsbridge. Mabel sat and stared gloomily out of the window, obviously reflecting on how much she was going to miss her trysts behind the woodshed with the mysterious Frank. Only Mr Orchard looked pleased to be returning to London.

Once back at Cadogan Square, Flo kept up her mission to lift my spirits, as only a true friend does. 'Look,' she said, triumphantly pointing to the servant's toilet at the end of the landing by our bedroom. 'No more smelly old chamber pots. We get to use an actual toilet.'

I shrugged.

'Tell you what,' smiled Flo, putting an arm round me, 'as a treat after lunch tomorrow, what say we go to Pontings on Kensington High Street [now the site of House of Fraser] and we'll use that half a crown we got for Christmas to buy some flash material. I'll run you up a lovely dress, perhaps in emerald green. It'll go a treat with your red hair.'

I frowned.

'We can even go to Lyons Corner House at Marble Arch and treat ourselves to afternoon tea if we're quick enough. Sandwiches with the crusts off and tea from a fancy pot. Maybe even a scone, if you like?'

I nodded. I did love having a good nosy around London.

'Perhaps stop in on Harrods on the way back and have a look?' she added. 'They have the best window displays, you know.'

My mouth twitched into a smile. 'George who?' I said.

Flo burst into laughter. 'That's the Mollie I know and love,' she grinned.

Youngsters aren't half fickle. If you'd have asked me the week before back in Woodhall if there could be life after George, I'd have sworn not, but back in London with the thought of a scone on a bone-china plate and a chance to gawp at pretty, glittery Harrods and he was but a distant memory.

The next day, no sooner was the last plate dried up and put away on the rack than Flo and I were haring upstairs, tearing off our uniforms and heading out on to the teeming streets of London. Flo had made herself a lovely tailored wool coat. It was nipped in at the waist and then flowed out, giving her a wonderful hourglass figure. The sleeves stopped just above her wrists and she'd teamed it with a pair of white gloves, matching black and white court shoes and a hat that she wore at an angle. Her soft brown hair was styled in elegant finger waves and under her arm was tucked a little leather clutch bag. She looked the picture of sophistication.

'You look like one of them,' I nudged as we strode out together along Sloane Street.

'Get away,' she giggled.

But she really did.

'How did you get so good at sewing?' I asked.

'In my first job as a scullery maid in South Kensington, if I had any spare time I wasn't allowed out. I'd have to help the housemaids do the sewing and darning for the house. Trust me,' she sighed, 'we've got it good with old Mr Stocks.'

Kensington High Street was an Aladdin's cave of wonderful grand old stores. As the season was just starting, the road was full of chauffeur-driven Rolls-Royces and inside the stores glamorous ladies shopped for the perfect outfits for the multitude of balls and parties they had to attend. In Pontings we had a wonderful time, giggling as we tried on elegant hats and draping material round ourselves in the haberdashery department.

'What about this, Mollie?' Flo asked, holding up a length of beautiful green fabric.

I wrinkled my nose. It was a bit too close in colour to our uniform. 'No, what I want is something dramatic,' I sighed. 'Something elegant. I want to look like a real woman.'

Just then I spotted the most beautiful woman I'd ever set eyes on. She was being fitted for a dress and a lady with a mouthful of pins was bent double at the lady's feet, measuring her up. She stood as still as a statue, composed and glacially aloof. She looked like a movie star – Greta Garbo or Jean Harlow. Her tailored day suit had been discarded and she was obviously being fitted for something more glamorous for the evening.

If she noticed a sixteen-year-old scullery maid was staring at her, she didn't let on.

I gazed at her, trying to see what was different about her, then realized what it was. She had a suntan! Her smooth long limbs were kissed brown, which was more or less unheard of in them days, but this was an era when suntans were coming into fashion and to have one was a vital indicator of wealth. This woman obviously never had to work below stairs and away from sunlight.

She was being draped with a black metallic lamé, which shimmered under the light. The dressmaker positioned it this way and that, until finally the fabric hung and draped in sinuous folds over her tall slim body. The dress was entirely backless, revealing a tantalizing glimpse of the curve of her spine. The material skimmed her figure and the cowl neck at the front showed off her elegant décolletage. She looked like a goddess.

'I want to look like her,' I whispered in awe.

Flo gulped. 'I'll try me best, Mollie,' she said. 'But I ain't a miracle-worker.'

In the end we plumped for something a little less expensive than the fine material that the grand lady was being draped in. It was a nice black silky-satin material that cost four-and-a-half pence a yard. There was even a bit left over for some green material to line the dress.

As the cashier took my money and carefully wrapped my package in brown paper, Flo linked arms with me. 'See,' she grinned. 'You're feeling better already. Next stop, tea.'

As we strode arm in arm down Kensington High Street

in the direction of Hyde Park, I was just dazzled once again by the sights and sounds. London in 1933 was the most exciting place on earth. Big department stores were all the rage and everyone went to stores like Harrods, Woollands, Harvey Nichols, Selfridges and C&A to shop and Claridge's and the Ritz to socialize and dine. I suppose they do now, but back then you wouldn't get tourists traipsing round in jeans and backpacks. Everyone was impeccably dressed. Even the servants like Flo and myself, not to mention the countless office girls who flocked to London in their ever-increasing time off, looked put together and presentable in suits or dresses.

During the fifty years up to 1930, working hours had steadily reduced, meaning that most people had more spare time and 'leisure time' was becoming recognized as a concept. This was particularly true in London where increasing regulation of workplaces, including offices and factories, meant that working hours were limited. It wasn't unusual to see office girls doing just what Flo and I were doing now, window-shopping – and trying to spot society girls – in their time off.

Society girls like the Mitford sisters were the celebrities of their time, before soap stars, pop stars and – that very bottom of the rung – reality 'stars' were words we even knew. Spotting a Mitford sister or a member of royalty was the equivalent of spotting Victoria Beckham leave a London store and jump into the back of a blacked-out Range Rover. Knightsbridge and Mayfair were where the wealthy elite flocked to during the season and wherever the gentry went, the servants would follow.

Nowhere else was considered quite as 'with it' as

Harrods, though. Opened originally in 1849, it was famous for its motto *Omnia Omnibus Ubique*, 'All Things for All People, Everywhere'. Harrods could get you anything at all, from the rarest Chinese tea to a lion, if you so wanted. In 1917 they even sold an alligator, bought as a present for Noël Coward. But in 1933, the cost of most of the items on sale put them far beyond the reach of scullery maid Mollie and kitchen maid Flo, so we carried on walking in the direction of Hyde Park.

After her years of working in London, Flo knew her way about and nipped in and out of the crowds with me in hot pursuit, clutching my brown paper package. She pointed out landmarks as we walked.

'That's the Hyde Park Hotel, Number 66 Knights-bridge,' she said knowingly, pointing at a beautiful marbled entrance hall of an imposing red-brick hotel. 'Famous for its style and glamorous parties, it is. It used to have its official entrance on the other side opening out on to the park, but the queen banned it. Only royals are allowed to use the park entrance, everybody else has to use this side in Knightsbridge.'

I nodded. I doubted we'd ever get to walk through either entrance. The huge walnut doors swung open and shut as society folk streamed in and out, revealing a tanta-lizing glimpse of a plush marble hall and frescoed ceiling. Stairs of white marble flanked with balustrades led to the upper ground floor. Not since I'd first seen the V&A three years before had I felt so small and dazzled by such an important building. Some buildings have the effect of making you feel like a tiny mouse and all I could do was gaze in awe at its splendour.

'All the socialites go there for tea dances in the palm court,' Flo added.

'Palm court?' I said, puzzled.

'Yes, they have actual palm trees in the room.'

'Well I never,' I chuckled, shaking my head. 'Trees inside? It'd never happen in Norfolk.' I wondered what George would make of that and made a mental note to tell him when we got back to Woodhall.

We went on our way with me still laughing at the thought, when I saw something that wiped the smile clean off my face. As we bustled our way through Hyde Park towards Marble Arch we were assailed by a riot of noise and commotion. About fifteen men were stood on small crates of wood, hollering at the top of their lungs in front of a vast crowd of onlookers. Such noise you can't imagine. Everybody was competing with everyone else to see who could shout louder. A strange mood of menace and provocation hung in the air. It seemed hard to credit that it was just a stone's throw from the rarefied streets of Knightsbridge where society ladies danced amongst palm trees and sipped from china teacups.

'Whatever is this about?' I gasped to Flo, stopping to stare at these speakers, who were clearly oblivious to the jeers and shouts of hecklers as they ploughed on, spouting their views.

'Come on,' Flo said, her mouth tightening as she tugged at my sleeve. 'We'll get a tongue lashing if Mrs Jones finds out we've been here listening to these motley crowds. It's not a place we should hang about.' Her eyes grew wider. 'I'm serious, Mollie. Trouble breaks out and the police get called.' But I wasn't listening. This was just too much of a fun spectacle to pass.

'I am here to talk about our great empire,' yelled a small man with a puffed-up chest and a plum in his mouth. 'An empire that is crumbling beneath us as I stand here and speak. I take great pleasure in coming here to talk to you ignorant people.'

'Oh, sit down and shut up,' bellowed a man in the crowd. The speaker didn't even flinch.

'I am talking to you about our great empire,' he continued, holding his hands aloft for maximum impact, 'that in years gone by was great and yet is no longer our own.'

The crowd surged forward. 'Shut up, fascist!' one yelled. 'You don't speak for us.'

'Ladies and gentlemen,' he went on pompously, 'I take great pleasure in speaking to you ignorant people. We need to put Mosley in power.'

The crowd bristled.

'Go home,' shouted a lady with a voice like a foghorn. 'We don't want your sort here.'

The speaker turned on her and his upper-class accent slipped. 'Listen, lady, you're too young to remember the empire when it was great.'

'Do you take questions?' shouted another.

'No, I do not. I am here to warn against the future polluting of our coun–'

'Well you better take one from me, cos I object to this.'

Suddenly, as one, the crowd started to slow handclap him and sing, '*Get down, get down, get down.*'

A gentleman next to us looked at my stunned face and

smiled. 'Quite something, isn't it?' he said. 'You know, people have been speaking here since the mid-nineteenth century. This plot of land is the most famous in London.' With that, he gestured with his hand over the swathe of land from the pavement of Marble Arch to beyond some trees. 'Speakers' Corner,' he announced, leaning back and thrusting his hands into his pockets. 'Starts at the site of the old Tyburn gallows to the Reform Tree. People have been coming here to speak, meet, preach, canvas, convert and argue over politics and religion for years. Started with the Chartists holding mass protests about the suppression of rights of ordinary working people.' He snorted. 'Police tried to stop it, of course, but in 1872 Parliament granted the Park Authorities the right to permit public meetings. Milestone in the development of our democratic institutions, wouldn't you say?'

This man seemed so knowledgeable I simply stood and nodded my head.

'All the greats have been here,' he went on. 'Lord Soper, George Orwell, William Morris, Karl Marx.'

And now Mollie Browne.

He gestured to a man nearby. 'Spiritualist and religious nutters mainly, but the fascists are making their mark here now as you can see. Quite deplorable, most of them, but you have to respect the freedom of speech, wouldn't you say? It's what makes the British great.'

I nodded. 'Oh, absolutely.'

Suddenly another speaker started up next to us with such force I jumped out of my skin.

'Ladies and gentlemen,' he boomed in a thick cockney

accent. 'I ain't come here to be larfed at, spat at, aimed at, charfed at or any other old at for that matter. There are two sides to life. Spiritual and material. We've gotta get back to the natural side of life we was created for. We've got to accept Christ as our own personal saviour and obtain pardon, peace, patience and prosperity, for none but Christ can satisfy.'

'What about your old woman?' heckled a ribald onlooker. 'I 'ear she can satisfy all right.' A wave of raucous laughter broke out as the speaker was pelted with clods of earth and mud.

'Come on, Mollie,' hissed Flo nervously, dragging me away. 'It's turning nasty. Let's get out of here.'

But as we walked away in the direction of Marble Arch, the jeers of the men still ringing in my ears, I knew I'd be back. Something about this area, so thick with history, and the passion with which these men spoke, stirred something inside me. I was treading on the very ground where criminals had been taken by horse and cart to be hanged at the gallows in front of crowds of bloodthirsty onlookers. Today, in 1933, it seemed the public still wanted to watch blood spilt and enjoy a good old-fashioned spectacle. Unlike slightly more timid Flo, I loved this theatre of noise and commotion.

But what I loved most about London was its diversity. Not two minutes after watching a man get pelted with clods of earth while the fidelity of his wife was questioned, we found ourselves in an altogether more genteel place.

Having tea at Lyons Corner House in Marble Arch was

a dazzling experience. Flo led me past the art deco gold entrance and, once inside, all was serene, calm and restrained chatter as ladies and gentlemen took afternoon tea on tables laid with starched white tablecloths.

A waitress known as a 'nippie' in a black uniform, starched apron and a frilly hat with a black velvet ribbon in it, led us to a table for two. I smiled warmly and thanked her as she held back our chair. I knew what it was like to wait on others in a uniform so I wanted her to know I appreciated her efforts.

Well, what a tea we had: scones that could rival Mrs Jones's for lightness, lashings of cream and little silver dishes oozing with strawberry jam. As Flo and I tucked in and relished our surroundings, men in tuxedos played in an orchestra at the back of the vast room.

'Nice to be serenaded while we have our tea, isn't it, Flo?' I giggled, sipping my tea with one finger cocked out like I'd seen Mr Orchard do.

'I'll say,' she sighed. 'I feel like the other half. Talking of which, we best wolf this down.'

It seemed such a shame to leave this warm haven with people waiting on us for a change, but if we were even a minute late Mrs Jones would square us up. Running outside, we laughed together as we jumped on to the back of a hop-on, hop-off red bus and clambered up to the top deck.

'What a lovely afternoon,' I beamed, clutching my fabric to my bosom. 'Dresses and cake. Aren't we blessed, Flo?'

'We certainly are, Mollie,' she agreed. 'What more is there to life?'

'Boys?' I suggested.

We were still laughing when, all of a sudden, a strange thing happened. The bus was travelling down Park Lane when a man leapt to his feet and jabbed at the window excitedly. '145 Piccadilly,' he said. 'That must be the Duke and Duchess of York's children.'

All heads on the bus swivelled left. Situated as we were on the top deck, we could all see over the high brick wall that separated the gardens of a Piccadilly town house from Park Lane. There, enjoying the spring sunshine, were two little girls with their nanny. One was about seven years old and sat playing happily with a younger girl of about two. The two-year-old toddled about on unsteady legs as her elder sister, the seven-year-old, smiled and encouraged her.

A buzz ran round the whole top deck and, as the bus stopped in traffic, we all stared in silence. Little did we know it back then, but we were watching our future queen playing with her little sister, Princess Margaret.

This was some three years before the abdication crisis. Princess Elizabeth Alexandra Mary York was to become, after the abdication of her uncle and subsequent crowning of her father, Bertie, our future Queen Elizabeth II. But back then she was just a young girl innocently playing in the spring sunshine with her little sister, unaware that a whole busful of people were watching her and equally unaware of the plans that fate had in store for her.

They looked so sweet in their little dresses and I stared, quite spellbound, at their pretty peaches-and-cream complexions framed by soft fair curls. Their nanny, Clara Knight, known as Alla, who was later described as an ever-present benign dictator, kept a watchful eye on them.

It's a wonder Elizabeth seemed so normal, closeted away in her ivory tower. The rest of the world was quite obsessed with her. Chocolates, china sets and children's hospital wards, even a territory in Antarctica, were named after her; the people of Newfoundland had her image on their postage stamps; songs were written in her honour and Madame Tussauds displayed a wax model of her astride a pony. Yet there she was, a flesh and blood little girl, enjoying a normal childhood, seemingly oblivious to the attention.

Just as abruptly as it had stopped, the bus pulled off again and we left our future queen behind.

'Well I never,' said Flo.

I've never forgotten that moment and it seems frozen into my memory. Today the queen is eighty-six and I think she's a marvellous woman with all that she does, but I still prefer to think of her as she was back then, a happy, care-free little girl.

We was full of it, but when we got back to Cadogan Square there was a visitor in the kitchen. Mrs Jones's niece, who worked in service nearby, had dropped in and together she and Mrs Jones babbled away in Welsh. Flo and I didn't have a clue what they were talking about. As we got on with chopping vegetables for dinner, every so often they would throw us a look, jabber something in Welsh and then burst into laughter.

'Whatever are they talking about?' hissed Flo.

'Us most probably,' I whispered back.

Who knew, who cared, I'd had an absolute gem of an afternoon and I wasn't about to let them two take the shine off it. I'd clean forgotten my heartache over George and had enjoyed a simply amazing time.

Just then, Mr Orchard swept into the kitchen and turned to Flo and me with an icy stare. 'Mr Stocks requires your presence in the drawing room immediately.'

We stared at each other, alarmed. Oh no. Had he found out about us hanging around at Speakers' Corner? Or, worse, about us sneaking out to the village dance?

'Follow me,' Mr Orchard spat, turning so abruptly that the coat-tails of his jacket flicked out behind him. As we climbed the stairs that led to the good part of the house my stomach did little flip-flops. I didn't have a good feeling about this.

We were never summoned upstairs. Ever . . .

TIPS FROM A 1930S KITCHEN

•••

Christmas Pudding

Nothing tasted as good as the Christmas pudding Mrs Jones cooked. She adapted it from Mrs Beeton's recipe. Never fool yourself into thinking that a shop-bought one can ever taste as good as this. This makes enough for two puddings so you can keep one for next year. You don't need to freeze it. Why is everyone so obsessed with freezing? We coped perfectly well without a freezer. Just store it somewhere nice and cool and dry.

8 oz (225 g) beef suet
4 oz (110 g) mixed peel
1 lemon
8 oz (225 g) sugar
8 oz (225 g) raisins
Half a grated nutmeg
½ oz (10 g) mixed spice
8 oz (225 g) breadcrumbs
8 oz (225 g) sultanas
4 oz (110 g) currants
2 oz (50 g) desiccated coconut
4 oz (110 g) shredded almonds
Pinch of salt
Cup of milk stout (or Guinness if you can't get milk stout)
4 eggs
2 large glasses of brandy (one for the pudding, one for drinking while cooking)

Shred the suet. Finely shred the mixed peel. Peel and chop the lemon rind. Put all the dry ingredients in a basin and mix well. Add the milk stout, stir in the eggs one at a time, and add the brandy and the strained juice of the lemon. Mix and work through thoroughly until everything is blended well then spoon into a well-buttered pudding basin. Boil or steam for at least five hours before serving with brandy butter and brandy sauce.

Household Tip

In my day we polished pans with a mixture of vinegar, silver sand and lemon juice, but sprinkling a dirty pan with washing powder and soaking in boiling water before rinsing thoroughly does the job. If you want them to come up sparkling new, though, invest in some silver sand and mix with vinegar and lemon juice. It really does work.

7

Passion With the Footman

There is a charm about the forbidden that makes it
unspeakably desirable.
Mark Twain

All too soon we had left behind the servants' quarters and
had ascended into the smart hallway of Cadogan Square.
Like a couple of rabbits caught in headlights, we gazed
around at our new, opulent surroundings.

'Wait here,' ordered Mr Orchard as he left the hallway
and disappeared off into the drawing room.

Flo and I were soon joined by Irene, the housemaid,
who looked every bit as bewildered as us. 'What's this
about?' she whispered, tugging nervously at her apron.

I shook my head and was surprised to feel my heart
pounding in my chest. 'Darned if I know,' I replied.

The door to the drawing room swung open.

*Please, God, don't have found out about sneaking out to the
dance . . . please. I'll never do anything wrong as long as I live, I
promise.*

'Mr Stocks has requested your company in the drawing

room,' said Mr Orchard. 'He thought you might like to witness his niece before she is presented as a debutante to his Royal Highness at court.'

Flo, Irene and myself stared at him, utterly baffled. Mr Orchard, meanwhile, looked as if he had just handed us the Crown Jewels on a silver butler's tray.

'Yes, of course, Mr Orchard,' said Flo, recovering herself first. 'That would indeed be an honour.'

We all glanced nervously at each other before shuffling after him into the drawing room. Mr Stocks sat in the corner of the room in a leather armchair, looking on as a proud father might do, and there, in the middle of the room, was a vision in white.

A pretty young woman with dark hair stood demurely on the Turkish rug. She was dressed head to toe in a long white silky dress and long white satin gloves covered her slender arms. A single diamond glinted from her neck, which was as long and creamy white as a swan's. The chiffon train of her dress fell in soft folds around her feet. Her head was held so straight and high it was as if there was an invisible string pulling her up to the ceiling and on her face was a look so inscrutable it was impossible to guess at how she was feeling.

What a strange and bizarre situation. What on earth this girl must have felt, being gawped at by a scullery maid, kitchen maid and housemaid, was anyone's guess, but she was obviously adept at keeping her feelings under wraps. She can't have been much older than us, but standing there with our uniforms and aprons and bitten-down, slightly grubby nails, we must have looked like paupers next to a princess.

'This is my niece,' said Mr Stocks finally, breaking the awkward silence. 'She is about to be presented at court before starting the season. She looks quite lovely, wouldn't you agree?'

'Oh yes,' we all gushed as one. 'Pretty as a picture, sir. Most gracious.'

The girl bestowed us with a flicker of a smile.

We all stared at each other. We were only a couple of yards apart, but we were from totally opposite ends of the social spectrum. She was off to curtsey to King George V at Buckingham Palace, before attending the prestigious Queen Charlotte Ball. I was about to go back downstairs to peel a mountain of spuds. And yet I knew the gesture wasn't meant as a malevolent one by Mr Stocks. It wouldn't even have crossed his mind for a minute that it would look like he was rubbing our noses in it. In his mind he obviously thought he was being most considerate by allowing us young girls the 'treat' of seeing his niece.

We didn't really realize it then, but we were witnessing a most curious tradition and one that has long since died out. Now, of course, we look back on these traditions with a mixture of curiosity and amusement, but in those days a blue-blooded gal's 'coming-of-age season' meant everything.

Presentation of debutantes at court was an elaborate social ceremony that originated in the 1780s when King George III decided that the prettiest and most well-bred girls from the court circle should be presented to Queen Charlotte so that they could find an appropriate partner for marriage. The most prestigious and important party of the season remained the Queen Charlotte Ball throughout the 1930s.

Mr Stocks's niece would have been driven by Mr Thornton from Cadogan Square to Buckingham Palace, where she would have waited with other young girls on rows of chairs in an antechamber at the palace. One by one they would have been called to present themselves. She would have entered the royal chamber and have curtseyed first to King George V and then to the queen before being ushered out of the room. The court ritual denoted their entry on to the marriage market. The ensuing 'season' was a series of exclusive parties and events attended by debutantes where potential suitors could observe them. The season ran throughout the summer and its events included cocktail parties, dances, lunches and weekends at country estates. This system meant that the upper classes could preserve their hold over money and influence by only sharing their wealth and power with the 'right people'. Marriages of couples who met at these events were seen to have royal approval as the king had indirectly introduced them.

All the debutantes would be dressed in white to signify their virginity, which was an essential requirement for marriage.

It was important for Mr Stocks's niece to get every aspect of the tradition right. The curtseys had to be low and sweeping and no doubt her mother would have employed dance teachers to train her in the run-up to the season.

The rigid traditions around aristocratic marriage together with the loss of a generation of aristocratic sons in the First World War meant that there was a very small pool of eligible young men from suitable families for upper-class young women to marry. As it was inconceivable for an upper-class family to marry their daughters to less prestigious families, they often married men much older than themselves or remained unmarried.

The tradition finally died out in 1958 after Prince Philip moaned that it was 'bloody daft' and Princess Margaret apparently complained that 'every tart in London' was getting in.

I'm quite sure that Mr Stocks saw his niece as a cut above that, mind you. And so it was that she found herself getting ready to be paraded – sorry, presented – in the hope of securing a suitable husband.

'You may go back to your duties now,' nodded Mr Stocks.

'Thank you, sir, ma'am,' we said, backing out of the room. We stumbled a little less graciously from the drawing room and down the back staircase in stunned silence. But no sooner had the green baize door swung shut behind us than Flo and I burst out into nervous giggles.

'Well, that was strange,' I laughed. 'Whatever must she have felt like being gawped at by us? Thought she was the bee's knees, didn't she? Thin as a paper doll though, weren't she?'

Flo was a little more charitable. 'Yes, but she was ever so dignified,' she said softly.

'I s'pose,' I laughed. 'She's welcome to her balls though. Imagine, all those boring dinner parties and formal evenings. I think I'd die of boredom.'

Flo grinned as we arrived back in the kitchen. 'I guess it is a lot of effort to go to, to bag a husband.'

'Exactly,' I cackled. 'What a palaver, and like as not it'll be some wrinkly old rich man.' I shuddered. 'Imagine having to sleep with an old man night after night.'

Alan crept up behind me and sneaked his arms round me.

'You wouldn't have that problem with me, Mollie,' he said, squeezing me tight. 'Only firm young flesh here, I promise.'

'Oh, get away with you,' I scowled, pushing him off. 'Don't you ever get tired?'

'Not when it comes to you I don't,' he leered.

But later, as the debutante was being presented at court and I washed up dirty plates in the scullery, I thought seriously about the strange day I'd had, seeing the little princesses playing in their ivory tower under the watchful eye of their nanny and the debutante upstairs about to be presented like a piece of meat. It was a strange old world.

Did I envy the upper classes their lifestyle and privilege? The answer had to be *no*. I had a freedom that that girl could never enjoy. OK, I didn't have her money, but at least I'd never be pushed into a loveless marriage with a rich older man. I could go where I liked and see who I liked. I'd rather scrub floors than be trussed up like a dog's dinner and scrutinized at court any day. All that pomp and etiquette, it was a load of old cobblers. When the posh broadsheet papers came down the stairs after they'd finished with them upstairs, Flo and I would pore over them, laughing at the silly names and who'd married who.

Well, maybe more me than Flo.

'Mr Pompington Pomp Smythe is delighted to announce the marriage of his daughter Violet Pompington Pomp Smythe to Hugo Fussington Fwah Fwah,' I'd pretend to read, affecting a posh voice and sticking my nose in the air. I'd make sure never to do it in front of Mrs Jones, Mabel or Mr Orchard, mind you. They'd have had a blue fit to hear me speaking like that. I was proud of my Norfolk accent. It had character and I wasn't about to speak with a plum in my mouth to feel important. *Silly name, silly titles, silly traditions.*

'No, Mollie,' I said to myself as I plunged my hands into the dirty water and began to scrub. 'You're doing all right as you are.'

Tucked up in bed later, Flo turned to me as she wearily pulled the covers over herself and snuggled down.

'I'll make you a lovely dress out of that material we got today,' she whispered. 'You'll look just as gorgeous as Mr Stocks's niece by the time I've finished with you. You'll see.'

I smiled at my friend and found myself marvelling yet again at how wonderful she was. Good as gold, right to the core.

'You're a real friend,' I whispered back. 'They broke the mould when they made you.'

As the following weeks turned to months and Flo and I spent every spare second exploring London, I often found my thoughts drifting back to the debutante: where she was and whether she found a suitable husband at the myriad balls and parties she would be attending. I couldn't ask Mr Stocks. It was one thing him inviting us to his part of the house, but we would never have dreamt of presuming the gesture could go both ways and we could just 'pop' up and ask how her presentation went. Mr Orchard would have shot us on the spot.

Besides, we were all having too much fun to worry

Here's Flo again. She always had a smile on her face, no matter how hard we worked or how tired we got.

about his niece's marriage prospects. London was such a thriving, bustling place and Flo and I could simply never wait to change out of our uniforms and explore. Every spare second was spent eagerly anticipating the two hours after lunch service or our half-days off.

Sometimes when I had a different half-day to Flo I'd go back to Chapter Street and visit Aunt Kate and Uncle Arthur. Other times I would wander round the V&A by myself, standing stock-still and breathless with wonder at all the marvellous objects there. But I always most looked forward to my time with Flo.

Every outing was a voyage of discovery as we pounded the streets of London looking for excitement, thrills and even another glimpse of royalty. We screamed at *King Kong* when it made its debut in the London cinemas, gazed in every big department store window, ate roasted chestnuts bought from street vendors and giggled our way from Chelsea to the West End in search of adventures and fun. We were inseparable. You'd think working, sleeping and socializing together in such close quarters would have driven us mad. Not Flo and I – if anything it just seemed to bond us closer and not a cross word was passed between us.

Every day I noticed a difference in Flo's cooking and confidence. Mrs Jones had now all but stopped scolding her and trusted Flo to make even the most complicated dishes. From crêpes to soufflés, she could do it all. She even knew a bit of French and Italian cooking and could whip up a Consommé Royale or Italienne. Not that she ever bragged about her talents. In the same way that she was such a good seamstress – she could sew anything – likewise there wasn't much she couldn't cook. 'Tidy hands', my mother would have said.

I suppose I knew in my heart of hearts it was coming,

but one evening after dinner service Flo pulled me to one side.

'I got some news today, Mollie,' she said. A frown line had creased between her lovely deep-blue eyes and somehow she couldn't quite meet my gaze.

'I'm not going to like this, am I, Flo?' I said. 'Go on, spit it out.'

'I'm leaving,' she said sadly. 'I went to an agency and they've found me a job as a kitchen maid. I'm ever so sorry, Mollie, really I am.'

'But you're already a kitchen maid, Flo,' I protested.

'I know,' she said. 'But this is for the Marquess of Salisbury at Hatfield House in Hertfordshire. He's the Leader of the House of Lords, you know. It really is a step up.'

I felt my bottom lip start to wobble. 'But who'll help me keep Alan in line?' I cried. 'And who will I have to keep me company with old Mrs Grump?'

'He has a London property for the season,' she said brightly. 'It's in Arlington Street, just off Piccadilly near the Ritz, so just round the corner really. We'll be able to see each other in our time off.'

Poor Flo looked so desolate telling me, I had to put her out of her misery.

'Oh, come here,' I said, throwing my arms round her. 'I'm so pleased for you I can't even imagine. A marquess, no less. I'll have to curtsey for you now.'

'Get away,' she laughed, swiping my head affectionately. But behind the laughs we both knew it was the end of an era and that life at Cadogan Square would never be the same again. I'd never be able to replicate the easy camaraderie and trust I shared with Flo Wadlow with anyone else.

The next day she handed her notice in to Mrs Jones, who scowled like a bulldog chewing a wasp.

'Young girls nowadays,' she tutted as she wrote out a reference for Flo. 'Never stick at anything for more than five minutes. Flighty you all are.'

'Boys, dresses and dancing is all that fills your silly little heads,' I whispered to Flo.

'I heard that, Mollie Browne. Get back to ya scullery and get on with them dishes,' she said.

But despite her obvious irritation I could see she was disappointed. Flo was a lovely, calm, capable and efficient person to have around – an asset to any kitchen – and I knew Mrs Jones would feel the loss of her kitchen maid.

'That marquess'll be lucky to have you cooking for him,' she added, somewhat more softly. 'You'll learn a lot there, I reckon.'

Mr Orchard was greatly impressed at Flo's advancement up the servants' social scale, snob that he was. 'Oh, yes, I should say,' he observed from over the top of Mr Stocks's copy of *The Times* from the day before. 'You'll be working for the fourth marquess no less, former ADC to King Edward VII and King George V and Lord Privy Seal 1924 to 1929. A far larger staff, needless to say, and I daresay you shall have to refer to the butler there as "sir".'

Looking at him now I could easily see how he fancied himself in such a position – not that he'd ever dream of leaving Mr Stocks, mind.

'Yes, I feel quite elevated myself,' said Flo, smiling shyly.

That is what people fail to recognize about domestic servants today. We weren't just a load of simpering half-wits beholden to our masters. We had choices, we could come and go as we pleased and try our hardest to climb the ladder and elevate ourselves. What other job open to the working classes in that time gave you those options?

The morning she left, it was all I could do not to throw myself in front of the area steps and bar her way. Instead, I hugged her warmly.

'Here,' she said, pulling a package from behind her back. 'This is for you.'

Unwrapping it, I gasped as something black and shiny slipped through my hands. 'Oh, Flo,' I marvelled. 'This is magnificent.'

She'd promised she'd make me a dress to rival Mr Stocks's niece and she hadn't let me down. The long tailored black satin dress was nipped in at the waist but had a soft elegant scoop neckline. A flash of dazzling green lining peeked out from the neck.

'I've never owned anything so beautiful in all me life,' I cried, holding it up against me.

'You'll look the cat's whiskers in that, Mollie,' she smiled.

In a flurry of tears and hugs she was gone, her feet pattering up the steps as she went on her way to her new life. But just before she left she ducked her head round the door. 'Learn to gut them partridge, Mollie,' she said with a cheeky grin.

There was no doubt that Flo leaving was a cause for great sadness in my life, but this particular cloud did have one silver lining.

'I'm making you kitchen maid, Mollie,' announced Mrs Jones. 'You're up to it, but you have to stop butting up against Mr Orchard and listen good to me, you hear me?

'Oh yes, absolutely, Mrs Jones,' I said, nodding furiously. 'You won't regret it.'

I could not believe my luck. Well, there was a thing. Little Mollie promoted to kitchen maid, and at the young age of sixteen! How proud my mother would be. I was to receive seven shillings a week, a pay rise of a whole two extra shillings, but best of all, no more scrubbing the steps or blackleading the range and I wouldn't even have to empty my own chamber pot back in Woodhall. Irene would have to do mine now.

That's when I knew I'd really made it!

To take my place I recommended a nice fourteen-year-old girl I knew from back in Downham, by the name of Phyllis. Phyllis was to join us when we travelled back to Woodhall to start the season there. Suddenly I realized with a jolt of happiness that she would have to pluck and gut the pheasants! Not only that, but I would never have to clean out the old coal fire ever again! It was all I could do not to punch the air.

'Nice one, Mollie,' I said to myself as I got stuck in to a load of washing-up.

'What you looking so pleased for?' said Alan, interrupting my thoughts as he popped his head round the scullery door.

'Oh, nothing,' I smiled, plunging my hands deep into the foaming water.

'Bet you're missing your partner in crime, eh?' he said. 'She'll leave a big hole in your life, won't she?'

I turned on him and spat angrily, 'OK, come on then, out with it, Alan, let's have it – the ribald comment, the double entendre . . .'

Alan looked blank.

'You're not even going to slap my bum? Boast about your manhood?'

He looked utterly crestfallen and hung his head, bruised and deflated. 'My heart alive, Mollie, whatever must you think of me? I was just trying to be nice.'

'R-right, well,' I spluttered. 'You've got a smart mouth on you, that's all I'm saying.'

'I just know how you'll miss her, that's all. You two were joined at the hip.'

Sighing, I suddenly felt very tired. It had been a long day and I was roasting hot. I pulled my hands out of the water and pushed back a curl off my head.

'Come here,' chuckled Alan softly. 'You've got a smudge of dirt here on your top lip. You look like that Hitler chap everyone's talking about.'

Taking his finger, he dipped it in the foaming water and slowly and softly traced his finger over my top lip. His dark eyes never lost contact with mine and suddenly I felt quite weak. Maybe it was the heat, the fact that I'd been on my feet for near on twelve hours, or maybe it was the closeness of his body next to mine in the gloom of the scullery, but my legs started to wobble. Clawing at the neck of my uniform, I gasped and felt myself start to slither down against the scullery wall.

Alan reached out and, cupping me round the back and with one hand under my knees, he scooped me up and carried me into the kitchen. Gently he placed me on a chair and fanned my face with his apron.

'Cup of sweet tea over here please, Mrs Jones,' he said. He turned to me. 'Breathe deeply,' he ordered.

As I sat gulping in air, he gently rubbed my back. 'That's the ticket, girl. You'll soon be right.'

Fortified with one of Mrs Jones's strong teas and a slice of her Genoese sponge, I started to feel like myself again.

'You had me worried there, Mollie,' smiled Alan, stroking my head tenderly. 'Look after yourself.'

I stared after him as he left the kitchen, puzzled. That man had more layers than an onion. Funny, yet dark. Strong, yet weak. Jealous, yet strangely light-hearted. He was a complicated one, all right, and yet somehow when the two of us were together, the air seemed electric, highly charged. My top lip still tingled from his touch.

Mrs Jones stared at Alan as he retreated from the kitchen, then back to me, as she stirred her tea.

'There's trouble brewing there, Mollie, I tells ya,' she said, shaking her head slowly. 'He's a sandwich short of a picnic, that one.'

Trouble, it seemed, was brewing all over, not just between kitchen maids and brooding footmen. At more or less the same time as I was being appointed kitchen maid, the German president Paul von Hindenburg had no choice but to appoint Hitler, the Nationalist Socialist leader, as chancellor. Hitler seized the opportunity to cement his growing power. Instead of holding general elections, Hitler and his cabinet passed a new law, which declared presidential powers would be passed to the new head of state, the Führer. This gave Hitler huge power and, most importantly, control of the military. He began to speak at mass meetings and political rallies. These meetings became an everyday part of German life under the Nazis.

Throughout this time, Hitler's opponents became increasingly marginalized and gradually stripped of powerful or influential positions.

I only knew all this because Mr Orchard would read snippets out from Mr Stocks's *Times* in the servants' hall.

'This man's trouble,' he said over lunch. 'Mark my words. Rumour has it there's a Nazi group set up in London already, a hundred members strong with new members joining up all the time. Says here the Home Office don't know what to do with them.'

'They should throw them clean out,' spat Mrs Jones. 'Send 'em packing off to Germany.' Mrs Jones, like my mother, still had strong memories of the first war and the small Welsh village she hailed from had lost a whole generation of menfolk like Norfolk had. 'We don't want their sort here,' she added.

'Surely, Mrs Jones, it's better to have them here so our security services can monitor them,' replied Mr Orchard. 'Keep your enemies close and all that.'

'Well,' she sniffed. 'They're rum sorts, the lot of them. I for one shall be pleased to get back to the peace and quiet of Woodhall.'

'There won't be a war, will there?' said Irene, wide-eyed.

'Of course not,' snapped Mabel. 'It will never come to that. Our government won't allow it.'

I didn't really understand at that point the full gravity of these changes or the growing threat that Hitler presented, just that it left an anxious atmosphere in the room.

Shortly before we returned to Woodhall, Mrs Jones gathered us all in the servants' hall and informed us that during two weeks in August Mr Stocks would be taking a holiday and our services would not be required. Best of all, we were to be paid for our new leisure time. It was like having a Christmas and birthday all rolled into one. The hall was alive with chatter as people discussed how they would spend their new time off.

Leisure time up until then had barely been recognized, but now, thanks to the legions of people who had started working in offices and factories and the regulation of workplaces, the concept of 'workers' rights' and time off had finally started to sink in. People all over the country were developing something they called a 'hobby'. Working-class men were starting to go fishing, keep caged birds and pigeons or go to gardening clubs and start up allotments. All over London, dog tracks, skating rings, sports grounds and cinemas were popping up. Television didn't become available until 1936 but by 1933 half of all homes had a wireless.

'Two weeks,' chattered Irene. 'Almost unimaginable, ain't it? I'm going home to see me mum and sister and take a trip to the seaside.'

'Oh, me too,' I said. 'I can't wait to see my family.'

Mabel smiled with a faraway look on her face. She, no doubt, would have a liaison with her mystery man behind the woodshed.

Mr Orchard, paranoid about his privacy, said nothing.

Suddenly, in and amongst the excited chatter, I realized one person was staying strangely quiet. 'What's wrong, Alan?' I said. 'Cat got your tongue?'

He sat at the table, staring at the linoleum floor, his hands cupped round his mug, a look of deep sorrow engrained on his face. He waited until the room had emptied, then he fixed his gaze on me.

'I've got nowhere to go, Mollie,' he said finally, in a voice barely above a whisper.

Suddenly I realized I didn't really know a thing about Alan. Where he came from, where his family were.

'What about your mum's?' I asked.

He stared at me and the look of hurt and devastation in his deep dark eyes took my breath away. 'My mother's dead, Mollie. She's been dead a few years now. Consumption got the better of her. I'm an orphan.'

I found myself speechless. Finally, recovering from the shock, I took his hand in mine.

'My aunt raised me, but she didn't have much money,' he went on. 'Soon as I turned fourteen she sent me out to work as a hallboy and I haven't seen her since. So, you see, I haven't really got a family – or anyone, for that matter,' he added sadly.

'Oh, Alan,' I sighed. 'I'm so sorry. I had no idea . . .' My voice trailed off to nothing.

'It's all right,' he said, his mouth suddenly tightening. 'I grew up fast; I had to, no choice, see? But I won't pretend it's been easy not having a mother, like. No one to tell you how clever you are, bring you tea in bed when you're poorly, give you cuddles when you get scared in the dark. I have a vague memory of a woman. Pretty as a flower she was, holding me hand, and then . . .' He shook himself quickly as if to shake off the ghosts of his past.

My heart went out to him. What a crying shame. Imagine having no mum. I thought of mine, bustling round a cosy kitchen, my father warming his feet by the fire as Mother filled the room with delicious baking smells. Take a mother out of the equation and what you got? A sad and lonely life, that's what.

Talk about a light-bulb moment. This explained so much. His brooding intensity, his need to be liked, loved. He'd had a childhood of unfathomable loneliness, unlike me.

Suddenly the words tumbled from my lips before I could stop myself.

'Come and spend some time with me and my family,' I said. 'No one should be alone when they don't have to be.'

His face changed in a heartbeat and he gripped my hand tight. 'Really? You mean that? Oh, Mollie, that'd be smashing.'

He leapt up and lifted me clean off my feet and swung me round the servants' hall. 'You're a diamond,' he said, laughing. 'We can go to dances, cycle, swim – think of the fun we'll have.'

'Steady on,' I giggled, trying to hold my mop cap in place. 'Mr Orchard will see.'

His eyes glittered and, as he put me down, he pulled me so close I could feel his warm breath on my face.

'You won't regret this, Mollie,' he whispered.

Something told me I was already in way over my head.

Everybody's spirits on the return to Norfolk were as high as kites. Summer was here, we were back to the beauty of the countryside and we all had time off to enjoy. But there was just one snag for me: George!

I hadn't seen him since we'd left for London three months previous and I knew our relationship was dead and buried. I'd tried kidding myself that I liked him because he was such a nice chap and all, but liking someone is hardly the basis for a future together. And now there was this . . . thing . . . with Alan. Ever since I'd told him we could spend time together, the vulnerable man I'd glimpsed that night in the servants' hall had vanished to be replaced with the old cocky Alan, all cheeky winks and wandering hands.

As Louis collected us from the station, looking as gorgeous as ever, he waved from the car window. 'Hello, my lovely,' he sang. 'Someone's been moping round like a dark old cloud since you left. I daresay you'll get a warm welcome home.'

I groaned. How was it possible to feel this wretched?

The beauty of the landscape was lost on me as we whizzed down the country lanes, Louis chattering away ten to the dozen. I felt sick to my very core. My life, what on earth would I say to that poor fella?

Sure enough, as we pulled up outside, who was waiting, clutching a bunch of flowers and wearing a smart jacket despite the sweltering heat, but dear sweet George.

'Mollie!' he cried, his rosy cheeks lighting up when he spotted me. 'I've missed you so much. I came to give you . . .' His voice trailed off as Alan strode up next to me and placed an arm round my shoulders.

'All right, George,' Alan winked, sniffing the air. 'Been spreading muck, have we?'

George's face fell and I noticed a little vein on his temple start to twitch. He looked from me to Alan. Then, without saying a word, he smiled sadly, handed me the flowers and walked off, looking utterly defeated.

I took no pride in breaking his heart, I really didn't. I could have swung for Alan, I could have. From that day on I never knew George to court again. The tiniest things can alter the course of our lives forever and I often wonder what sort of man he would have become if I hadn't turned him over. Holding hands at the pictures, a shared sticky bun and a kiss in the snow – some people treasure these memories and make no room in their heart for any more.

The young lad in the back row, far left, is loyal farmhand George Thornton, Louis's younger brother, aged about seventeen. I fear I broke that poor man's heart.

Back then I was a flighty girl, living for the moment, and I daresay I gave no more thought to his stolen glances at me or the sadness in his eyes when he spotted me and Alan giggling together.

There was no real start to my relationship with Alan, but like a territorial animal protecting his lands I suddenly found I was drawn into his protective clutches. Like a couple of hormonal young creatures, our courtship was passionate, intense – and deeply unpopular below stairs.

Alan would use any excuse to sneak up behind me in the game room or the scullery, run his fingers down my back, spin me round and plant a long, lingering, passionate kiss on my lips.

'Steady on,' I laughed, the first time he cornered me. 'You'll bruise my lips.'

Our eyes would lock over the servants' hall table and Alan would fix me with a look of longing and lust so intense I'm surprised the table didn't burst into flames. The air between us crackled.

At first we managed to keep it secret, meeting in our half-days off or after lunch service. We'd hide behind a haystack for a quick fumble or run through the shady woods and rest against an ancient oak. Summertime at Woodhall was beyond beautiful and there was no shortage of places to meet for secret assignations. A balmy haze spread over the orchards and the fragrant hedgerows made a perfect spot to hide behind and while away a couple of hours.

The intoxicating scent of wild flowers seemed to have a powerful effect on Alan. 'Oh, Mollie,' he moaned one afternoon, ripping off my cap and running his fingers through my red hair. 'I want you so much. I knew you'd be mine one day.'

'Well, you'll wait then,' I said, slapping his hands away. 'If you really like me, that is.'

I liked him, I really did, and he was ever so good-looking. His dark eyes shone like conkers and his hair was so black it was almost purple in places. I daresay he could have had the pick of any of the girls at the village dance, but the fact that he had chosen me made me feel special. Whenever he tried to take things a step too far, or pushed things, I reminded myself of his unfortunate start in life. He'd had no one to love him growing up or to teach him boundaries.

Living and working together in such close proximity, it was almost impossible to keep a secret and soon the cat was out of the bag.

'I know you're seeing Alan,' muttered Mrs Jones, soon after we arrived at Woodhall. She was kneading dough to make a tart and I could see her knuckles turn white as she angrily turned the dough over, slapping it down and kneading it between her podgy fingers. 'I warned you courtship below stairs was forbidden, didn't I? The very day you started I told you! The boss won't like it, see, nor will Mr Orchard. Doesn't pay to date the staff.'

Biting my tongue, I said nothing, just carried on beating eggs in a large bowl.

'You know,' she said angrily, 'sometimes you don't know it all.'

What did she know about young love? She wouldn't know passion if it came up and slapped her between the eyes.

'Just cool it off, Mollie,' she said, turning to me with her hands on her beefy hips. 'I mean it.'

I stared miserably at my pudding bowl and said nothing. Who was she to say who I could and couldn't date? It was utterly infuriating. Just why should she and Mr

Orchard have the power to rule our lives? It was all right for Mr Stocks's niece upstairs. She was off being presented at court, with no end of parties and events for her to meet a suitable man. But what about me? How was I ever supposed to meet a man? When I spent ninety hours a week below stairs it was little wonder I ended up being attracted to someone I worked with!

To escape the heat from my private life I immersed myself in the heat of the kitchen. Cooking provides a wonderful escape to lose yourself in. Under Mrs Jones's expert tutelage, I was learning so much. I may only have been sixteen but already I could finally pluck, gut, draw, bone and truss a bird, fillet a fish with my eyes shut and make soufflés as light as air. I was forever making sauces, from béchamel to Béarnaise, caper to cardinal, bread to bordelaise, hollandaise to horseradish. Mrs Jones was a firm believer in sauce – the cooking of, not receiving, I hasten to add.

In 1933 sauces were all the rage. Nothing was served on a gentleman's dinner plate without some sort of hot accompaniment. Until the end of the eighteenth century, cooking was a neglected art in England. A Frenchman of that age once described us as a 'nation with one sauce'. Well, not when I was learning to cook. Mrs Jones was often wont to quote Alexis Soyer, who said in *Mrs Beeton's Book of Household Management*: 'Sauces are to cookery what grammar is to a language.'

She would hover over me whenever I made any sauce. 'It's all in the lightness of hand, Mollie,' she would say, planting a wooden spoon in my hand. 'I never ever want to catch you making a sauce with anything other than a wooden spoon.'

Hollandaise was the worst. I had to make a basic white sauce, put it on the heat and then add stock and egg yolks bit by bit and whisk by the side of the fire until it thickened. Woe betide you let it boil.

'It's ruined!' she'd shriek. 'Chuck it out and start again. Never boil a sauce, dolly daydream. Keep your mind off Alan and back on this hollandaise. A good sauce chef is about genius, Mollie, yer hear? I can only teach you so much, the rest is instinct. You have to feel it deep in here,' she said, thumping her plump hand against her left breast.

I could take or leave it, mind. It seemed no end of trouble to go to. The hours I spent grating horseradish for horseradish sauce, it's a wonder I have any knuckles at all left today!

The meat was what I loved cooking the most. When you grow up poor with not much meat, to be able to then cook and eat it nearly every day is wonderful. Most of what we cooked came from the surrounding farms or what Mr Stocks had shot, so it was all what you might call local and we knew its provenance all right. In fact, we knew to the last square inch where everything that landed on our plates came from. Everything we ate was either grown in the soil of Norfolk, grazed off the soil of Norfolk or swam in the seas off Norfolk – none of this meat from Argentina or fruit from Africa. It makes no sense to me that. Why buy food that's been flown from thousands of miles away when we have the most delicious produce right here on our doorstep? Daft, ain't it!

Back then we didn't just move with the seasons, we ate with them too. I learnt to make the most wonderful meat dishes, dishes you just don't see that often on menus nowadays. Game in aspic jelly, pheasant croquettes, loin of lamb, rabbit quenelles, partridge pie, stuffed quail, sweetbreads in aspic border, jugged hare with port, rabbit pudding and roasted saddle of mutton were all favourites. There was no end of techniques to learn and all the accompaniments, from stews to sauces, were of course made from scratch. I loved the smell of it all roasting and sizzling over the range.

Mrs Jones's eyes would light up when the gardeners brought the fruit and vegetables in straight from Mr Stocks's large kitchen garden. Garden makes it sound small, doesn't it? But it wasn't. The plot of land was out the back of the estate and was like stumbling across a secret, magical world. You followed a little lavender-lined path to a magnificent black wrought-iron gate with Mr Stocks's initials, MS, interwoven in capitals in the ironwork. Once inside the walled garden, beds of the most incredible-looking vegetables spread out in immaculate rows and were lovingly tended to daily by a team of gardeners. Rows and rows of trees groaning with fruit lined the ancient walls of the garden. There was even another greenhouse at the far end to grow more exotic fruit like pineapples.

Mr Stocks loved his fruit and vegetables and only those dug out of the ground or picked that morning were allowed to be served on his dinner plate.

The head gardener was responsible for picking the fruit and vegetables that Mrs Jones told him she needed for that day's menus. It was then delivered to her in big wicker baskets and placed on the kitchen table for her inspection. Fat asparagus, earthy new potatoes, all dug up just moments before and still covered in earth – they were as fresh as they come. She would brush off the dirt and insects as she inspected each item individually.

'The vegetables that grow in the ground you cook in the pot with the lid on and you start them in cold water. Vegetables that grow on top of the land you put in boiling water and you don't put the lid on,' she said.

It wasn't just cooking techniques, either. By watching and observing Mrs Jones closely I was able to see how she planned a week's worth of menus, what leftovers could be turned into something equally mouth-watering the next day and just how much or little to order to keep supplies topped up without being frivolous – a dirty word in the kitchens of Woodhall!

She saved her best smiles for my uncle Albert, the delivery man from Harcourts the butcher. Goodness knows whether she was getting kickbacks from the butcher for choosing him as the meat supplier to Woodhall, but Albert always got a coffee, a slice of cake and a rare smile when he delivered our meat order. It went both ways, mind. We would sell him what game Mr Stocks couldn't eat and in return we'd get the pick of the best beef, lamb, cutlets and sausages.

Soon after we arrived at Woodhall, the new scullery maid, Phyllis, started. Our trembling new recruit was just the same age I was when I started, fourteen, and had absolutely no idea what she'd let herself in for. She got the same regimental rundown from Mrs Jones that I'd got and my heart went out to her. She was a timid little thing and looked like she might burst into tears at any minute or blow away in the wind when Mrs Jones hauled her up about something.

As she scrubbed the floors and tackled the dirty dishes on her first morning I gave her a conspiratorial wink.

'It does get easier,' I smiled, making her a cup of coffee when we paused for elevensies. 'And don't mind Cook. She might seem like an ogre, but she's not so bad underneath it all.'

At the end of her first week she looked quite exhausted, poor girl, and she made the dreadful mistake of dropping one of the best gravy jugs.

'Whatever is wrong with you, girl?' screeched Mrs Jones as pieces of shattered porcelain skidded over the wooden floor. 'That happens again and I'll have to dock it out your wages. Watch what you're doing or you won't last long here. Just follow what Mollie does, all right?'

Poor Phyllis. I found her later in our bedroom, sobbing her eyes out.

'How do you do it?' she said. 'I can't do a thing right and it's such hard work. I'm dead on my feet.' Her hands were stained dark black from raking down the coal fire. 'I can't seem to get this coal dust off my clumsy old hands neither and there's nowhere to wash them,' she sobbed in despair.

I smiled gently, went downstairs and filled up a jug with warm water. Taking her hands in mine, I started to sponge off the worst of it.

'You'll get there, I promise,' I said. 'Don't mind that old dragon downstairs. She mostly blows hot air, not fire.'

Phyllis started to laugh.

'That's better,' I said. 'You're ever so pretty when you smile. Tell you what, I've got my mother's gramophone downstairs in the servants' hall. I'll teach you all the latest dance moves if you like. Someone very special taught me . . .'

'Oh, would you?' she beamed, all thoughts of the smashed gravy jug vanished. 'I'd love to be like you one day, Mollie,' she sighed.

'Whatever for?' I laughed.

'Well, you have pretty clothes,' she said, gesturing to the rail where Flo's black dress hung, '*and* a handsome foot-man boyfriend.'

I frowned. Seemed my relationship with Alan was a lit-tle more out in the open than I'd realized.

Finally August and the much-anticipated holidays came round.

Mr Stocks was only going to shoot grouse on one of his friend's grand estates up in Scotland, but you'd think he were going to Outer Mongolia the way Mr Orchard fussed. As his valet, he was responsible for packing his trunk and making sure everything was just so.

'A gentleman cannot turn up unprepared,' he said snootily. 'Irene, can you press Mr Stocks's linen handker-chiefs ready for his journey? I need his velvet house slippers and the cashmere bath slippers too.'

After that, he busied himself packing Mr Stocks's tweed suits, his shooting jackets, dinner suits and bow ties for the evenings and mid-grey flannel suit to travel in. His best cigars were taken down from the shelf near the range and delicately packed away in an engraved silver cigar case.

All I needed for the short journey back to Mother's was my bike and an old canvas bag with a few summer clothes thrown in.

It was arranged that Alan would stay behind in the servants' quarters, but would cycle up every day and spend time with my family and me. I was ever so nervous of how my family would take him. He could be a bit mouthy, after all. On the bike ride there I did what I usually do when I'm nervous – talk.

'I don't know why Mr Stocks only goes to Scotland on his holiday,' I said as we cycled. 'I hear it just rains all the time up there. If I had his money I should go somewhere hot and exotic.' I'd read all about Spain in a copy of Mrs Jones's *Home Companion* magazine once. 'I should love to go to Spain,' I sighed. 'The warmth of the sun on your skin all year round, bull fights, oranges as big as yer head. They even have them palm trees like they have in the fancy hotels. One of these days I'm going to go to Spain and seek out my fortune.'

I barely noticed that Alan had stopped cycling and was glaring after me.

'Whatever's wrong with you?' I laughed, turning round.

'I forbid it!' he fumed, throwing his bike down on the ground. 'When we're married I'll not have you go to Spain. You shall stay here and raise our babies, of course.' He pressed his face right up against mine and his dark eyes narrowed.

I stood rooted to the spot, stunned. By his reaction you'd have thought I'd said I was off to work in a bordello!

'Spain,' he scowled. 'Whoever heard of such a thing?'

A great sense of injustice settled in my heart and I felt the red mist descend. 'How dare you?' I screamed. 'Who are you to tell me what I can and can't dream? I have enough people telling me what to do at work without you trying to lord it over me. I warned you before, Alan. You don't own me.'

He moved as quick as a flash. Picking my bike up, he threw it into a ditch and exploded in fury. Before I even had a chance to speak, he marched up to me and gripped me so hard by my arms that I gasped. His eyes bulged in fury and flecks of spittle flew from his mouth as he shouted. His fists were bunched into tight balls round my wrists and twitched with rage.

'Get off me now!' I yelled. I fought against him with savage fury, but he had my arms locked down against my sides.

'You're flighty, Mollie Browne, and I won't have it,' he roared. 'I tell you, I won't have it.'

Just as quickly as the rage exploded, it disappeared. He released my arms, sank back against a grass verge with his head in his hands and started to sob.

It was like witnessing two men.

'I'm sorry, Mollie,' he wept. 'I don't mean to get cross with you. It's just that I love you so. You do know how to get to me.'

Hesitantly I sat down next to him and, even though my mind was spinning, I put my arm round him. He grabbed me and hugged me so tight I could barely breathe.

Where had this come from? I was only talking about oranges and now this!

'I just need security, what with my past and all. You will give me that, won't you, Mollie? You understand?'

I nodded miserably.

'Good,' he smiled. 'You'll marry me one day.'

I wasn't sure if it was a question or a statement so I said nothing.

The silence was loaded. I just got a hankie out of my pocket and dried his eyes. Finally he got to his feet, sighed and pulled my bike out of the ditch. Gently, he helped me on to it and then picked up my bag.

'I'll take this,' he said softly.

As we cycled to my mother's in silence, fear and doubt clawed at my heart. Alan was complicated – too complicated for my liking. You never knew what you were going to get with him. How could someone laugh and joke one minute, then be screaming blue murder the next? I thought longingly of George. He may have been a simple soul, but at least I knew where I was with him.

I didn't want to get married any more than I had wanted to work alongside that stuffy seamstress. Why did people always insist on owning you or putting you in your place? I was just sixteen, I wanted to travel the world, not get knocked up and locked up in Norfolk.

He'd recovered himself by the time we got to my mother's and was charm itself to her. She'd baked, of course, and my father and brother were sat round with their best clothes on. Mother had gone all out to make our cottage look as lovely as possible and all its inhabitants look respectable, and I loved her for it.

'You have a lovely home here, Mrs Browne,' Alan schmoozed, helping himself to a scone.

'Mollie tells me you're a footman,' she said with a friendly smile. 'How you finding that?'

'Fine,' he said. 'I'll make butler one day. Got to be able to keep Mollie when we're married, haven't I?' He reached over and squeezed my hand before cramming the well-buttered scone into his mouth.

Mother said nothing, but I could see the surprise register on her face. Alan would never have noticed it – just a flicker of an eyebrow and then it was gone. She and Father said nothing and were perfectly polite, but I could tell by the subtle nuances on their faces that they weren't taken with him. Apart from anything else, my father was a traditionalist. It wasn't done to talk about marriage like that over the table and he expected any suitor of his daughter to officially ask him for my hand in marriage.

Alan seemed oblivious to their subtle disapproval, mind you. That and the shotgun by the fireplace.

It was an awkward tea and I noticed with shock that my father had become more frail and tired, even in the three months that I'd been gone in London. His face was drawn and his eyes seemed lost in the grey pallor of his face. His chest rattled and halfway through tea he'd had to go outside, he were coughing that much. We sat in silence, all of us eating our scones and nervously drinking our tea as he coughed his guts up out there. The coughs seemed to come in great waves that exploded in his chest. The awful noise turned my heart over.

'Gassed in Ypres,' explained my mother to Alan apologetically.

By the time he staggered back in, he looked as if he could keel over at any moment. Waving my mother away as she jumped to her feet, he sank back into his chair, clutching his chest.

The rest of the tea passed with no more drama, but I felt quite exhausted by the end. When I mentioned Father's health to Mother as we washed up together later, she looked just as weary.

'Oh, let it be, Mollie, won't you? He's fine, just his chest playing him up. Nothing to worry about.'

'You're all right – for money, I mean?' I said. 'Cos I can give you some of my wages.'

Her face softened. 'When did you get so grown up?' she said fondly. 'Bless you, Mollie, but please don't worry about us. Your granny never sees us short. Besides,' she said, flicking her eyes in the direction of Alan, who was sat beside the fire with his boots resting up against the fireguard, 'you have your own worries now.'

Alan glanced over at us, obviously trying to listen to what we were saying, but somehow I couldn't seem to muster even a smile. For inside my stomach churned. Where was Flo when you needed her? I had made a dreadful, dreadful mistake. However would I get myself out of this one?

What's the saying? When the cat's away, the mice will play!

In Mr Stocks's absence, the youngsters of the house and grounds – myself, Alan, George, John the hallboy, Irene the housemaid and Phyllis the new scullery maid – had got wind of a dance that was happening in Downham. Somehow I'd managed to sweet-talk Louis into driving us all there in the Daimler and now excitement was running at fever pitch.

We all met outside Woodhall.

'The boss must never find out about this,' said Louis as he turned the key on the Daimler and it purred into life. 'He'll have my guts for garters.'

'Oh, stop worrying,' snapped Alan. 'Who'll tell him? Mr Orchard's back in London and Mrs Jones is out visiting. No one will ever know. Besides, he's back in a couple of days. We have to make the most of it.'

'Come on then,' sighed Louis. 'Jump in.'

I was wearing the gorgeous black dress Flo had made me and as I slid on to the plush leather seats of the Daimler, didn't I feel the bee's knees!

'Wait till people see us pull up outside in this,' I grinned.

'You look lovely, Mollie,' said George admiringly. 'Just like a society girl.'

Alan glared and put a hand on my knee.

This dance was bigger than the dusty old village halls we usually went to. The dance at Downham, which I had longed to go to since I was thirteen, was in the town hall and was thronged with young people.

When we pushed our way inside, the whole room was doing the Palais Glide, all moving in time to the steps. It looked like a riot.

'My favourite,' I squealed. 'Who's coming to dance?'

'You know I hate dancing,' grumbled Alan.

'I'll dance with you,' said Louis. 'Shall we?' He grinned, holding out an arm.

'Charmed, I'm sure,' I giggled, taking his hand. 'You lead the way.'

Dances nowadays aren't like dancing back then. With the exception of Alan, most people loved to dance – lived for it, in fact. With no television for entertainment, whiling away an evening at a dance hall was all the rage. Dressing up and going out to dance was the only entertainment we had, apart from the cinema. Everyone pushed the boat out and tried to look as smart as possible and everyone knew the steps. Well, you had to if you wanted to keep up.

We may not have looked as glamorous as our American cousins, who led the way with their big luxury dance halls and jazz bands, but we could sure swing it with the best of them. With no constant flow of booze for people to get bombed out of their heads on, people didn't get so drunk they couldn't dance. It may have been becoming more acceptable for women to drink in clubs in London, but here in Norfolk it was tea or fruit juice all the way.

Louis was just as light on his feet as he was at that first dance we went to and, wrapped up in his arms, I felt safe and warm. Somehow he managed to keep up a patter of chat while he danced and before long he had me in fits of giggles.

Dancing with handsome Louis in my black satin dress, I felt like a Hollywood movie star.

Why couldn't Alan make me laugh like this?

One dance turned to another, then another. All the while I was aware of a growing cloud of dark disapproval from the sideline. Every time I whizzed past him I just caught a glimpse of his face, frozen in anger. Well, who needed him anyway? Old stick-in-the-mud. I could dance if I wanted to. He wouldn't stop my fun. Besides, it was all harmless. Louis was promised to another. We were only dancing.

Louis and I were just foxtrotting our way round past the tea urn when a large hand clamped down on Louis's shoulder.

'I think that's enough now, don't you?' said Alan, his voice pitched dangerously low and calm.

Louis, unfortunately, couldn't see the warning signs and batted his hand away. 'Lighten up, Alan, we're only dancing. You should learn yourself and then you could keep Mollie company.'

Big mistake.

I could see the switch flick behind Alan's eyes and the vein in his temple twitched angrily.

'I said, take your hands off her NOW!' he boomed.

People around us stopped dancing and stared. I felt all eyes swivel and turn to us. Louis looked stunned.

'Alan,' I said nervously. 'You're making a scene.'

'You're making a fool of me,' he thundered. 'I won't stand for it.'

I felt humiliation burn inside and I just wanted the ground to swallow me up. Why did he have to ruin everything?

'Come on,' he spat, gripping my hand and leading me outside. 'Show's over, folks.'

As I was hustled to the exit, I could just make out Phyllis's and Irene's worried faces before the door slammed shut behind us. And then we were stood outside in the cold dark air. Angry tears of humiliation pricked my eyes. I'd looked forward to this night for ages. I'd felt like a princess in my dress in the back of the Daimler and now I felt like a silly fool.

'Why, Alan?' I cried. 'We were only dancing. Why do you have to ruin everything?'

Rage flashed over his face and then he was off. Thundering abuse and shouting with his face just inches from mine, his fingers jabbing at the neckline of my black dress, he spewed forth venom.

I stopped listening. There was nothing worth listening to anyway. I just watched his mouth flap open and shut. Funny how that face that had looked so handsome just a few months before, looked so ugly now. He didn't hit me that night, but I knew he wanted to and suddenly in a rare moment of clarity I knew just what Alan would become if I married him. I knew the life mapped out for me would have been one of misery and pain.

My mother had raised me to have respect for myself and others. I had to get away from him.

Back at Woodhall, with Mr Stocks home from his holiday and normal service resumed, you could have cut the atmosphere in the kitchen with a knife. Tension hung like steam in the air. It wasn't long before Mr Orchard pulled me to one side, his thin lips pursed in disapproval.

'It's come to my attention that you are courting Alan,' he said, looking down his nose. 'Despite Mrs Jones's express desire for you not to become involved with your fellow members of staff. You leave me no choice but to swap your half-days so you no longer have time off together. You must call a halt to this now.'

He'd obviously given the same speech to Alan, who was walking around the place in a foul mood.

'They can't keep us apart,' he whispered in a quiet

moment. 'What doesn't kill us will only make us stronger, Mollie. Needs be I'll get a job elsewhere and we can still be together.'

What did I feel? Mainly relief that I had an excuse not to spend time with him. I'd got myself into a hole and now I had to get myself out of it.

After lunch service that day I stepped outside and gratefully gulped in the fresh air. A low mist hung eerily over the woods and the sound of muffled gunshots rang out from a nearby shoot. I could make out Alan's face from the servants' door, staring out into the gloom.

Shivering, I pulled my coat tight round me, got on my bike and pedalled like the wind back to my mother's. She took one look at my face and folded me into her arms.

When she'd finished hugging me, she went to put the kettle on.

'Oh, Mollie,' she sighed. 'I knew he was no good. You have to give him up.'

'I can't, Mum,' I said, shaking my head. 'He'll square me up, I know he will. You don't know what he's like.'

'I do know what he's like,' she said. 'He's been coming in here in his time off, you know. I think he's trying to butter me up so as he can get closer to me.'

'Creep,' I spat.

'Look, love,' she said. 'He's not worth a breath of your anger. He's had a hard life and it's made him complicated. I feel for him, I honestly do, but I don't want him dating my daughter.' Her face fell. 'It would finish your father off if you married him.'

That settled it. I had to end it with my footman once and for all.

'I'm scared, Mum,' I admitted. For all my bravado and cheek, when it came down to it I was just a sixteen-year-old girl who needed her mother.

'Send him over here,' she sighed. 'I'll do it for you.'

Events were racing to a head as, in my absence, Alan had become locked in a showdown with Mr Orchard over his time off. As soon as I let myself back into the kitchen, one look at Mrs Jones's face told me all was not well. She stood with her back to the range, staring at Mr Orchard and Alan as they stood face to face, glaring at each other.

'It's not fair,' said Alan. 'We should be allowed time off together when we want.' He turned to me. 'Tell them, Mollie,' he said. 'Tell them we only want to be together.'

My blood raced. 'I – I –' I stuttered, nervously playing with the hem of my apron. I was paralysed with terror.

'It's all right, lass,' said Mrs Jones softly, saving me. 'I think, Alan, what Mr Orchard is trying to say is that you need to calm down and think about what's best for the household.'

'What about what's best for me and Mollie?' he said, thumping his fist down on the table.

You could have heard a pin drop as Mr Orchard's face hardened.

'I'll leave if you don't let us have more time together,' Alan raged. 'I mean it, so help me God, I'll go.'

The silence seemed to stretch on forever.

'Then go,' said Mr Orchard finally. 'I'll write you a reference.' With that, he turned on his heel and stalked from the kitchen.

Alan looked from me to Mrs Jones helplessly, before ripping off his green apron and throwing it on the table.

He glared at us with such terrifying force, I looked away and stared at the floor. A second later the back door slammed shut so hard the whole kitchen seemed to rattle.

He was gone.

I sighed heavily and slumped into a chair. I was surprised to find my hands were actually trembling.

'Right, show's over,' said Mrs Jones briskly to everyone. 'Can we restore this kitchen to the purpose for which it was originally built? Cooking!'

As everyone quickly went about their business, Mrs Jones came up behind me and, without saying a word, placed her hands on my shoulder and squeezed gently.

'Just take a minute, Mollie,' she said, when my breathing calmed down.

Alan went from there to my mother's and it was then she broke the news to him gently that I didn't wish to marry him or, in fact, see him again. Where he went and what happened to him I don't know and in many ways I still feel very sorry for him, despite his jealous rages. Being an orphan had shaped him in ways that had obviously driven him to the brink of madness. I just hope he found the security and love he so obviously craved.

The whole sorry episode taught me a lot as well – firstly, that when it came to men I had a thing or two to learn and, secondly, a girl really can't be without her mother!

You might think after all that drama I would have longed for a quieter life. Well, if you think that, then you obviously don't know me very well, dear reader, for what happened next back in London, well – how does that old saying go? Out of the frying pan and into the fire . . .

TIPS FROM A 1930S KITCHEN

•••

Trifle

If we were lucky at a dance, we might even get a bit of trifle. I love this recipe and have been using it for years. Or if trifle's not your thing, try making the brandy snaps, perfect for afternoon tea.

Line a glass dish with sponge cakes and soak with sherry. Add mixed tinned fruit (fruit cocktail is best) and chopped walnuts.

Cover with custard and, when cold, cover with whipped cream. Pipe cream rosettes on top and decorate with fruit and glacé cherries. Keep in fridge till required.

Brandy Snaps

2 oz (50 g) sugar
3 oz (75 g) butter
3 oz (75 g) syrup
2 oz (50 g) plain flour
1 teaspoon ground ginger
Large splash of brandy (omit for children's parties)
For rolling: wooden spoon with a well-greased handle

Melt sugar, butter and syrup, then allow to cool.

Add flour and ginger, mix well. Add brandy. Put small teaspoonfuls on to a greased baking sheet, leaving space for each snap to spread to about 4 inches (10 cm). Bake in a moderate oven until golden brown.

Allow to cool for a moment, lift each one with a palette knife and quickly roll over the spoon handle. Slide off when hardened. To serve, pipe the tubes full of whipped cream and decorate with a glacé cherry. If the biscuits cool too much before they have been rolled into tubes, pop them back into the oven for a moment to soften, then try again.

Household Tip

To refurbish linoleum, melt some beeswax and mix with a little turpentine. Use like a polish on the linoleum. It comes up like new.

8

Scandal Below Stairs

The secret of reaping the greatest fruitfulness
and the greatest enjoyment from life is to live
dangerously!
Friedrich Nietzsche

The date was April 1934. The location, the Royal Albert
Hall in London. Half a mile from Cadogan Square a
speech was about to take place that would put one of Mr
Orchard's monologues about the gentry into the shade.

Just before eight p.m. the spotlights dramatically swung
to the main entrance and illuminated a thin man with a
well-kept black moustache and a thick head of black hair.
Walking with a pronounced limp, he paced across the hall,
chest out and handsome head flung back. The limp did
nothing to slow his progress and he took his place behind
the lectern. In front of the assembled audience he oozed
an aura of power and confidence.

Behind him hung a giant black banner emblazoned
with the silver Italian fasces symbol. Copies of the *Daily
Mail* adorned the edges of the balconies. The audience,

mostly dressed in black shirts, leapt to their feet, anxious to capture every word uttered by their idol.

Although slight in stature, the speaker drew himself up, closed his eyes and prepared to talk. You could have heard a pin drop.

'Hold high the head of Britain,' he boomed. 'Lift strong the voice of the Empire. Let us to Europe and the World proclaim that the heart of this great people is undaunted and invincible.' His voice grew as his chest swelled. 'This flag still challenges the winds of destiny. This flame still burns.'

As his fist slammed down on the lectern the audience roared their approval. Encouraged by their obvious praise and devotion, and an unshakable conviction that he was born to rule, he went on. 'This glory shall not die. The soul of Empire is alive, and Britain again dares to be great.'

By the time he had finished, the crowd was in raptures. 'Hurrah for the Blackshirts,' they cried. 'Hail Mosley!'

He had spoken for an hour and thirty-five minutes without any notes or hesitations. It was quite a performance.

Today the Albert Hall is the venue for pop concerts and the Proms. Back in 1934, fascist leaders were packing it to the rafters.

Such was the fiery force of his oration and the confidence in his beliefs, fascist MP Oswald Mosley held his supporters in the palm of his hand. Fresh from his tour of Italy where he'd studied Mussolini's new movement, Mosley had returned to London determined to unite the existing fascist movements.

Just two years previously, in 1932, he had formed the British Union of Fascists. At their first meeting in London, thirty-two members put on black shirts and the Blackshirt movement began.

As well as the Albert Hall, he took to London's Hyde Park to preach about his new party. His popularity grew. As a charismatic speaker and able politician, Mosley spoke about ideals such as patriotism, order and discipline and social justice which many people found appealing. He argued that Great Britain needed to become a more advanced civilization and proposed that the Blackshirts would be a new, improved British people capable of achieving this. Many people were attracted by his speeches and were not aware of the dark side of the fascist ideology.

I was one of them!

Well, actually, back in them days I didn't really give two hoots for the politics, being a flighty seventeen-year-old and all. I just liked the look of some of the handsome Blackshirts.

Most people were taken in that spring when we returned to London for the season. The *Daily Mail* had just published an open letter of support for them entitled 'Hurrah for the Blackshirts' and now, in 1934, their meetings and rallies were attracting thousands. In just two years the BUF had swelled in numbers with a membership approaching 40,000. The Blackshirts came from all walks of life and the membership included both men and women of all ages. Those most closely linked to Mosley were well-educated, often with a military background and from well-off and well-connected families. I'll never forget the first time I clapped eyes on our Blackshirts, Henry and Percival.

Phyllis and I had our customary two-hour break after lunch and I was giving her the same tour of London that Flo had shown me. I'd bounced back after my disastrous encounters with Alan and George and my confidence was fully restored. I was pleased as punch to be back in London. My ego hadn't been too badly bruised and, with all the arrogance of youth, I couldn't wait to see what men were out there to have a flirt with.

Now Phyllis was the new girl, all wide-eyed at the sights and sounds of London.

'Come on, Phyllis,' I'd blustered bossily, secretly chuffed that I knew my way round and she didn't. 'We'd best rush. Best tour you'll get, this. They've opened up a new Woolworths on the King's Road. Let's go and have a look.'

Strutting down the road like I owned it, I suddenly heard a whistle.

'I say there, you, the red-headed girl,' said a rich and deep sexy voice. 'Where you off to in such a hurry?'

Whirling round, I was delighted to find myself face to face with a tall, handsome man dressed entirely in black. He looked like the Milk Tray man with muscles.

'Come back here and have a chat with us,' he smiled. 'The name's Henry and I simply insist you don't pass me by without telling me your name.'

'Mollie,' I giggled. 'Why you all dressed in black then? You'll bake out here.'

He thrust a pamphlet at me emblazoned with the headline *Join the BUF*. But I wasn't really looking at the pamphlet. I was too busy checking out what was beneath the shirt. He had muscles on his muscles. He was tall, well over six foot, and built like a barn with a mass of blond hair that he'd slicked back off his face and a strong jawline. He oozed youth and strength.

'We're Blackshirts. We're here to protect our leader, Oswald Mosley. This here is our headquarters, otherwise known as the Black House,' he went on, gesturing to a large building next to an army barracks.

'You must be very strong then if you're hired to protect someone,' I flirted.

He raised his eyebrows and a slow smile spread over his face. 'Perhaps you'll get to find out. What time does a ravishing girl like you get off work then? I can meet you outside your office if you like. Bet a girl like you knows the best places to go in London.'

'Ooh, we don't work in an office,' piped up Phyllis. 'We work in Cadogan Square. I'm a scullery maid and Mollie here's a kitchen maid.'

'A kitchen maid, eh?' he drawled slowly, looking me up and down. 'Well, kitchen maid Mollie, reckon you can come and meet me up at Hyde Park tomorrow? Our boss is making a speech and we'll be there to protect him from attack from some of these mindless left-wing opponents. You might learn a thing or two.'

'There's nothing you can teach me,' I winked, with more bravado than I felt.

'Is that so, Mollie?' he said, grinning. 'Ten bob says you come.'

I could tell by his arrogant smile he already knew I'd come, but I wasn't about to let him know that. I simply smiled and walked away.

'See you around then,' he called after me.

'Not if I see you first,' I shot back.

Phyllis was full of it. 'Oh, you're ever so daring, Mollie. Did you see that lad he was standing with? I liked him. Yours is pretty good-looking too.'

Feeling very smug at the handsome couple of lads we'd landed a date with, instinct told me to keep quiet about this one and, just before we got back to Cadogan Square, I pulled Phyllis to one side.

'Best keep this one under our hats,' I whispered. 'Mrs Jones and Mr Orchard have funny ideas about things sometimes.'

The next morning Phyllis and I were bubbling over and I could scarcely keep my mind on the hollandaise sauce I was making.

'I'm so relieved that Alan's not here any more,' said Mrs Jones, deftly gutting a fish next to me. 'He was more trouble than he was worth, that one. Caused no end of bother. I knew you'd see sense, Mollie,' she went on. 'I'll make a kitchen maid of you yet. Just got to keep your mind on cooking and not boys.'

I nodded and smiled, but I wasn't really listening. I was too busy dreaming of my blond-haired Blackshirt. I didn't really know what a Blackshirt was, nor – if I'm honest – what a fascist was. Even if I'd had the time to read Mr Stocks's leftover copy of *The Times*, by the time it made its way down to the servants' hall Mr Orchard had taken it to read in the housekeeper's sitting room. So you see, with no access to newspapers or a wireless to listen to, I knew nothing of world events or the politics of the day.

That may seem barely credible to you, but the kitchen of a big upper-class house was like a bubble. The outside world and current affairs simply never permeated the intense order and day-to-day routine that we lived our lives by. There was some comfort in these ever-present routines, but it also meant we were living in a time warp. We toiled away underground and, metaphorically speaking, in the dark. As long as Mr Stocks's meals went up like clockwork, the pans were sparkling, the steps gleaming, the servants' bell always answered, what did it matter that dark forces were brewing on the rarefied streets outside? We would no more discuss politics while working than Mr Orchard would forget to faithfully sound his gong at half past seven each night.

As soon as the last dish was scrubbed and placed on the rack, Phyllis and I tore upstairs like a whirlwind. She started getting changed into an old cotton dress.

'You can't wear that!' I gasped. 'You've got to make a bit of an effort. This is London, not the country.' With that, I changed into a new polka-dot fitted dress that I'd just bought from Marks & Spencer for half a crown.

'There,' I said as Phyllis zipped me up at the back. 'You've got to look the business.' I smoothed down the dress and noted with satisfaction that it showcased my curves superbly. I was seventeen now and had come on a long way since that shy fourteen-year-old who hated being naked in front of Flo. I'm not saying I knew what to do, but having a couple of boyfriends had given me confidence in my looks and my body. I even put on a pair of short white gloves like I'd seen Flo do.

Soon we were heading for the area steps.

'Don't forget to be back by half past four, girls,' shouted Mrs Jones as she gratefully sank into the small armchair in her sitting room. 'We have to have tea ready.'

'Don't worry, we will,' I sang, slamming the door behind us.

Out on the streets, the bright spring sunshine bouncing off the gleaming white mansion houses of Cadogan Square was blinding. Coming out of the kitchen basement and up the stairs always reminded me of how a mole must feel when it pushes its way, blinking and dazzled, above ground.

Billy, the Harrods errand boy I'd flirted with back when I'd first arrived at Cadogan Square, cycled past and I wiggled my hips as I strutted along the road.

'Oi, Mollie, you look lovely,' he called, whistling appreciatively. 'Coming to see me, are ya?'

I shook my head. 'Not today, Billy, sorry,' I grinned. *I had bigger fish to fry now.*

We were meeting Henry and Percival at Hyde Park, just behind Speakers' Corner. If I'd thought the park was busy and raucous that first time I'd seen it, it wasn't a patch on what it was like now. It was sheer bedlam. Knowing that Mosley was here to make one of his speeches at this rally, his most loyal supporters were out in force – as were vast crowds of anti-fascist demonstrators. They crashed and clashed together, their voices growing louder and louder as they competed with each other for supremacy and the last word. Overhead, a police gyrocopter circled, the first time the Met Police had ever used one to keep an eye on a large meeting, apparently. The noise sounded like the buzzing of a thousand bees growing closer and closer. There must have been hundreds of people there, standing around, waiting for Mosley's arrival. The air was thick with menace, tension and the threat of violence. All it took was one man to push another and you knew a riot would break out. A line of policemen stood elbow to elbow, poised and ready should violence erupt. They had their hands crossed behind their backs as their eyes darted this way and that, looking for signs of trouble in the crowd. I thought back to dear old PC Risebrough in Norfolk and his campaign to trap a scheming gang of strawberry-thieving kids. Something told me he'd be a bit out of his depth here.

'I don't like the look of this,' trembled Phyllis. 'I wasn't expecting this.'

'Don't worry,' I grinned. 'We've got our own personal bodyguards, remember.'

Just then I spotted Henry and Percival. Their striking blond good looks and tall black-clad shoulders towered over the assembled crowd. Henry leant back against a tree, a confident, arrogant smile playing on his handsome face. When he spotted us he looked even smugger.

'I knew you couldn't keep away, Mollie,' he drawled. 'A girl like you likes danger, doesn't she?'

Totally oblivious to the foul looks that were thrown our way, Phyllis and I stood next to our respective Blackshirts and proceeded to giggle and flirt outrageously, throwing our heads back with exaggerated laughter at their jokes. Henry didn't seem much interested in me or my life, just more concerned with telling me about his military background and posh degree. He was a bit up himself, but I reasoned when you looked as good as he did you were entitled to be a bit arrogant.

Just then, a frisson of excitement ran through the crowd and I noticed Henry's shoulders tense as he leapt upright, his back suddenly becoming ram-rod straight.

'Mosley's here,' he muttered to Percival. 'Look lively.'

I whirled round to see a tall man with a bristly moustache march confidently through the crowd, flanked either side by more Blackshirts. He may have had a slight limp, but that did nothing to detract from his own obvious sense of self-regard. As he drew close I felt a strange chill wrap itself round my spine.

His eyes were as dark and cold as a shark's and he had cheekbones you could have cut glass on. As he swept past he threw a chilly look in our direction. Henry stiffened and threw his arm up in a one-handed salute.

'Hail, Mosley!' he barked. His manner was one of utter deference.

It was a brief moment, but I knew in an instant that Henry was the sort of man who would never see me as an equal. He was completely in thrall to this strange man.

'Why does he walk like that?' I whispered to Henry once he'd passed.

'Wounded in a plane crash during the war and returned to the trenches before his leg was completely healed,' he replied proudly. 'Became infected and he had to have two inches removed.'

He and the other assembled Blackshirts gathered around Mosley as he took to his stage. Phyllis and I followed, eager to get close to the action.

'Wonder what he'll say?' I muttered to Phyllis.

Henry silenced me with a single icy glare. 'Sssh,' he said. 'He's about to speak.'

Mosley drew himself up straight, raised a single hand aloft and, with that, an enormous roar echoed round Hyde Park.

'Attention,' hollered a man to his right, but despite the high pitch of his voice it was drowned out in the general hubbub.

Oblivious to the noise, Mosley launched into his speech.

'In the lives of great nations comes the moment of decision, the moment of destiny. And again and again in the great hours of its fate, this nation has swept aside convention, has swept aside the little men of talk and of delay, and has decided to follow men and movements that march forward to action. Let those who dare follow us in this hour. And I say, in the ranks of our Blackshirt legions march the mighty ghosts of England's past with their strong arms around us and their voices echoing down the ages saying "Onwards!"'

Another great roar went round the park and the gyro-copter seemed to circle lower. I glanced across to look at Henry's face. His handsome features were bathed in adoration as he gazed at his idol and nodded his head in agreement. At that moment I don't think it would have mattered if I'd ripped off my polka-dot dress and done a naked lap round the park. I doubt he'd even have noticed, so intently was he listening to his master's speech.

'We must be worthy in our mission,' went on Mosley. 'Because a Blackshirt is a revolutionary dedicated to the service of our country. We must have the power to endure, we have the qualities of a true Britain, and we carry with us the destiny of Britain. I would like to be the companion of every one of you, every man and woman . . .'

'We don't want you as a companion!' hollered a man.

'Hear, hear!' shouted more men.

Ignoring them, he carried on, his voice growing louder. 'Our faith is greater than your faith,' he shouted to the hecklers.

You could almost see their chests rise in furious indignation. A chant started up, slow and steady at first then gradually growing louder . . .

'*Out fascists out, out fascists out, out fascists out!*'

'The government is surrendering to Jewish corruption,' Mosley shouted, his nostrils flaring in rage. 'But we shall never surrender, we shall triumph over the forces of corruption because in us the flame to light the country and later light the world shines strong.'

'What's he on about?' hissed Phyllis, nudging me in the ribs. 'What flame?'

I shrugged my shoulders; I didn't have a clue what he meant. 'He's just spouting a load of old claptrap, far as I can tell,' I whispered, making sure Henry didn't hear me.

Mosley was coming to the climax of his speech. A vein was twitching in his temple, just like I'd seen on Alan when he got worked up about something, and his fists were swinging about like jackhammers.

'To all the world a message: England lives and marches on.' With that, he punched his fist into the air, his moustache twitching in jubilation. The Blackshirts roared their approval.

'Get rid of the rats!' shouted an angry heckler. Then he picked up a clod of earth and hurled it at Mosley. The crowd had been tensed and poised like a coiled spring, waiting for someone to strike the first blow. Some things in life are inevitable. As I watched the clod of earth sail through the air in a perfect arc, I knew that single action would be enough to spark all-out chaos.

It missed, but Mosley jerked his head round in surprise.

Seconds later the crowd was a seething mass of elbows and arms. A scrummage of limbs flailed about on the ground as men fought with their fists. Caps were dislodged and grunts filled the air as the crowd erupted. The police blew their whistles and jumped into action, but you could see they had their work cut out restoring peace to this crowd.

'Got to go, see you soon, Mollie,' shouted Henry as he and Percival rolled up their sleeves and disappeared into the tangle of flying fists.

Poor Phyllis. Her eyes grew as wide as saucers.

'Come on,' I laughed. 'Let's get out of here.' Grabbing her hand, I elbowed people out of the way and we ran for dear life. By the time we reached the far end of the park my blood was racing with sheer exhilaration.

'Blimey,' I gasped, leaning against a tree to catch my breath. 'That was exciting. Don't think my heart's ever pumped as fast.'

We were still on a high as we descended the area steps, flushed with the drama of the afternoon.

'Did you see Mosley's face?' I chuckled as we burst into the kitchen.

Mr Orchard was just picking up Mr Stocks's tea tray to

take upstairs but at the mere mention of Mosley's name his head snapped round.

'You're late,' he barked. 'And what's this about Mosley?'

I went to kick Phyllis, but it was too late.

'We saw him up at Hyde Park,' she burst out, all innocent excitement. 'What a palaver. You should have seen it.'

My heart sank as I saw Mr Orchard's eyes turn to me, then narrow.

'And what, might I ask, were you doing up there?'

For the love of God, Phyllis, don't say.

'Oh, we were meeting some Blackshirts up there,' she giggled. 'Right handsome they were too.'

Too late.

Mrs Jones whirled round and dropped her whisk and Mr Orchard's face was frozen in shock. When he recovered himself, he glared at me.

'Mollie, might I have a word with you in the housekeeper's sitting room?' he said.

I had never seen him so angry in all the years I'd been working there. Words were bandied around like bullets. *Totally unacceptable . . . shame . . . I forbid you . . . if the boss finds out . . .* On and on he railed, growing angrier by the second. I'd had enough. As before, when Mother tried to get me to work in that tiny shop or Mrs Jones banned me from the dance or Alan used his aggressive tactics to try and control me, at the sound of Mr Orchard lecturing me about who I could and couldn't see, something inside me just shut down.

I may have been a seventeen-year-old kitchen maid, but I knew my own mind. I'd had it, simply had it, with people trying to control my life.

I was saved from further scolding by the servants' bell tinkling in the hall. Mr Orchard shot to his feet.

'I must tend to Mr Stocks now, but do I make myself perfectly clear, Mollie?' he asked.

Mr Orchard, the snooty butler who kept a watchful eye on me and my shenanigans. He was always giving me a telling-off but, looking back, I probably deserved it!

'Perfectly,' I said, meeting his gaze. On the outside I was calm, but inside I was churned up. *Of all the pompous . . . Why was I always the butt of his sour temper?*

Word quickly got round the kitchen of mine and Phyllis's afternoon activities. For the rest of the day Mrs Jones and Mabel clucked and shook their heads like a couple of hormonal hens.

'Don't you be leading that Phyllis astray,' said Mabel. 'She's a nice young girl. Those Blackshirts are nothing but trouble.'

I bit my tongue. Listen to the old crone on her high horse. I knew she'd been having her fun behind the wood-shed, not that she'd ever admit as much. How dare she sit in judgement on me!

Mrs Jones, who seemed convinced that most men were the root of all evil, was hopping mad.

'And I thought you seeing Alan was bad enough,' she raged, shaking her head. 'Don't you be going getting your-selves in trouble, especially not with them.'

Phyllis and I kept our heads down and got on with our jobs, but in our bedroom, after service that night, I was still seething.

'They're not telling me how to run my life,' I muttered to Phyllis. 'I'm going back there tomorrow, just see if I don't.'

'But Mr Orchard said —'

'I don't care what he says,' I raged. 'I've had it with people trying to control me.'

That night I fell asleep with the roar of the crowd and the policeman's whistle ringing in my ears. The powerful events of the day were to shape all our lives in ways I could not have foreseen or even imagined, but trouble was brewing out there in the streets, back alleys and royal parks of London. To me, though, it was all one big thrill, a tantalizing taste of the unknown and a brush with the dark side.

I knew Henry was trouble, of course I did. But what's more attractive to a young girl than a bit of danger . . . *a bad boy*?

The next day after lunch I went alone back to Speakers' Corner. This time the sight that greeted me was even more bizarre than the day before. There was handsome Henry, still in his uniform, but hopping about beside him was someone truly astonishing.

I'd never seen a black man before, much less a semi-naked one.

A tall and striking man wearing voluminous purple pantaloons, embroidered African-coloured waistcoat, bare arms and bare feet, cut a striking figure against the sea of Blackshirts. His flamboyant outfit was topped with an elaborate headdress of red, white and blue ostrich feathers that seemed to reach high into the sky.

He was letting Henry have it from both barrels and his feathers quivered as he jumped from foot to foot in excitement. His enormous feet were totally bare as he leapt around doing a sort of strange tribal dance, while simultaneously wielding an umbrella.

It was like watching Mary Poppins on drugs.

'Each item and every colour I wear symbolizes the brotherhood of man,' he boomed. 'Red, white and blue stands for the British Empire, which comprises Jews, Muslims and Blacks.'

I was absolutely flabbergasted by this strange character, not to mention his bizarre rantings, and stood rooted to the spot. Henry, meanwhile, didn't seem even remotely fazed by the sight of a six-foot-tall black man in purple pantaloons and ostrich feathers spouting off in his face.

London in 1934 was indeed a truly strange place.

'Get away, you old crackpot!' Henry yelled, dismissing him with a flick of his hand.

'Crackpot am I?' the man yelled back. 'Well, hear this. You know why the Germans hate the Jews, why you hate the Jews?'

Henry and the assembled Blackshirts rolled their eyes.

'Because they are too much like you,' he went on.

'You're crazy,' spat one of the Blackshirts and then – somewhat viciously – 'Get that boot polish off your face.'

'It's true,' he persisted, swinging his umbrella about and ignoring their racist remarks. 'Contrary to the shallow idea that racism is rooted in otherness, one can truly only hate someone who is like oneself and whom one therefore understands.'

This last speech was too much for them and they pushed him away. I didn't know it back then, but I was watching the most famous black man in the country. Racing tipster Prince Monolulu was a familiar sight, not just at Speakers' Corner, but also on racecourses around the country. The British at that time were fascinated by the exotic and had taken this colourful character to their hearts. He appeared on racecourses between the wars in his eccentric outfits where he drew huge crowds. The Prince sold tips in envelopes and engaged in endless banter with people around him, his most famous call being 'I gotta horse!'

No newsreel of the Derby was complete without a film of him shouting his catchphrase. He embroidered fantastical stories about being descended from a remote royal tribe from Abyssinia and claimed to have been a model in Germany, an opera singer in Moscow and a fortune teller in Rome. In actual fact his real name was Peter McKay and he was from the West Indies.

Prince Monolulu met a rather sad end on Valentine's Day, 1965. He was being treated in Middlesex Hospital when a friend visited him with a gift of a box of Black Magic chocolates and offered him a strawberry cream, which he accepted and promptly choked to death on. Choked to death on a strawberry cream? You couldn't make it up, could you? Poor fella. Back then I certainly enjoyed watching him giving the Blackshirts some flack.

Henry spotted me and waved me over. 'Hello, my ravishing redhead,' he said with a smile. 'Wondered whether we'd see you again after all that trouble yesterday.'

'Who *was* that?' I asked, staring after the man as his headdress disappeared off amongst the hecklers.

'Oh, him,' Henry said nonchalantly. 'Just some silly old fool.'

He slung a powerful arm possessively round my shoulder and fear nagged in my chest. I had come up here alone, no one knew where I was and if they had known they would probably have imploded with anger. What if he tried something? Thank God we were in broad daylight in London with no hedges to lean up against or haystacks to hide behind. There's no telling what a man like Henry could get up to there!

Suddenly I felt way out of my depth. Over-possessive

footmen were one thing, but bullyboy fascists were in a league of their own. If Mr Orchard or Mrs Jones knew I was here I would be sent home in utter disgrace.

Suddenly a vision of my dad's face swam into my mind. Exhausted, his poor lungs shrivelled from mustard gas, he had sacrificed his health and his life to fight the Germans in the war. How would he feel if he knew his daughter was cavorting with a fascist follower? And not just a follower but a Blackshirt, paid to enforce his master's beliefs? I had a feeling he wouldn't be right happy about it.

I stood feeling intimidated, wishing the ground under Speakers' Corner would swallow me up, as Henry and his fellow Blackshirts discussed their boss's next speech and spouted some truly terrible opinions.

Something told me that on this occasion I might just have crossed the line. Using an excuse to get away, I fled back to Cadogan Square, my heart pounding around like a bouncing tennis ball in my chest.

For the rest of the day I put my head down and worked hard, the heat from the kitchen providing the perfect place to escape my troubled mind. Phyllis kept trying to catch my eye, but I ignored her and went about my business. Suddenly I missed Flo desperately. She would have known just the right thing to do or say.

The next day was a lovely hot summer's day and as I had a half-day I knew the perfect antidote. I'd always loved swimming back in Norfolk as a child and every time I'd passed the Serpentine in Hyde Park I'd looked longingly at the cool strip of sparkling water and thought how much I'd love to bathe in it.

The famous stretch of water, created in 1730, was a magnet for pleasure-seekers and pleasure boats filled with people regularly chugged up and down its long snake-like waters. Four years ago, in 1930, a rectangular area had been opened up specifically for swimmers. Everyone was chatting about Lansbury's Lido, in fact it was the talk of the town, because for the first time it had permitted mixed bathing. Imagine! Men and women in next to nothing, all swimming in the same waters!

Mr Orchard had virtually spat out his morning coffee when he'd read news of it in Mr Stocks's *Times*, back when it had first opened.

'I don't believe it! Mixed bathing in the Serpentine,' he'd gasped. 'Whatever next?' He was just as incensed when, two years later, they removed the railings that separated a paid-for area from the hoi polloi. In many ways the removal of those railings was a significant milestone. In marked the start of the breakdown of boundaries between the classes, the gradual erosion of upstairs/downstairs. Little wonder then that it put the wind up our butler and all that he held dear. If he'd had his way there would have been railings all round Cadogan Square and Knightsbridge, marking out the boundaries between the gentry and the commoners. Back then, I couldn't think why people were so obsessed with boundaries. To my mind they were just there to be pushed anyway. As for the Serpentine's new mixed-sex pool, honestly, I couldn't see what all the fuss was about. The way he talked about it, you'd think it was some hotbed of raunchy impropriety, not just a swimming lake. But he wasn't alone in his contempt for it.

While I was hurriedly stuffing my one-piece bathing suit and a towel into a bag, an anonymous police super-intendant was airing his considerable disquiet about the pools and the conduct of its bathers. In a memo drafted at Scotland Yard in the summer of 1934, the disgruntled superintendant wrote:

Women of doubtful character are displaying themselves in flimsy bathing dresses. Vulgar men and boys are drawn to the area and some female bathers have complained of their costumes being ripped off by an over-excited male populace.

The practice of many bathers on sunny days of rolling the costume down to the waist can only be overcome by considerable activity on the part of the constable on duty, in patrolling the area and directing such bathers to wear the costume correctly. This direction is very often received with bad grace and sometimes with opposition.

The Yard put much of the misbehaviour down to the removal of the railings, which had had Mr Orchard's knickers in a twist. The aggrieved superintendant went on:

Hundreds of bathers, including men of an undesirable type, are evading the charge by undressing in the free swimming area, packing their clothes into an attaché case and walking to the paying zone. Subsequent over-crowding has the effect of keeping away many decent-minded women who strongly resent the vulgar gaze of men and boys.

Well, I wasn't about to roll down my one-piece and go topless, but I wasn't averse to witnessing a bit of scandal neither, so off I trotted in the direction of Hyde Park.

Unfortunately, English weather being what it is, by the time I'd made it to the park the clear blue skies overhead had been replaced by ominous-looking dark and angry clouds.

'Storm clouds seem to follow me, all right,' I noted to myself with a wry grin.

At Lansbury's Lido there wasn't so much as a sniff of a fella in sight, vulgar or otherwise. What's more, it was freezing cold. Wind was whipping over the water, sending ripples along the Serpentine, and leaves spiralled down from the trees and skimmed over the water's choppy surface.

Popping into a changing hut, I shrugged off my dress and changed into my white one-piece. Teeth chattering, I poked one naked toe out of the hut. A blast of Arctic wind whistled up my bare leg.

'Brrr,' I shivered. Then I gave myself a good telling-off. 'Come on, Mollie Browne. You're as tough as old boots. You're from Norfolk, for goodness' sake.'

Maybe it was the Viking ancestry in me, but I wasn't about to be put off by a trifling bit of wind. If I could climb three floors down the side of a house, I could brave a bit of cold water.

I strode out in the direction of the swimming area. With every step I took, my legs seemed to turn a more curious shade of blue. Most people had hotfooted it inside into the warmth, but one solitary man stood watching me, amusement and shock twinkling in his eyes. I thought back to the time I'd hurled myself into the Denver sluice as a child. Suddenly, a mad, impetuous urge took hold of me. You could take the girl out of Norfolk, but you couldn't take Norfolk out of the girl.

Here goes nothing.

'Geronimo!' I hollered in a loud battle cry and raced towards the diving board. Soaring through the London skies, I felt brave, invincible, free . . .

Then I landed in the water with an almighty splash.

'Cor blimey,' I gasped, spluttering as I bobbed to the surface. The cold was like icy needles pricking me all over and my breath came in frantic shrieks. Floundering about, I doggy-paddled to the side and pulled myself up, gasping for air. I landed with a slap on the cold concrete floor.

'Bravo . . . Bravo,' came a loud, booming voice.

I looked up to see the man I'd spotted earlier standing over me.

'A very brave, if somewhat foolish, display,' he said, smiling down.

The man was dressed in a warm-looking suit and hat. Suddenly, looking at my bare legs and arms, I felt very underdressed.

The man was fiddling with a camera hanging round his neck.

'W-what you got that for?' I shivered.

'I'm a photographer,' he said. 'Tell you what, why not pose for a picture over there on the diving board?'

Images of Mr Orchard's disapproving face popped into my mind.

'I oughtn't to,' I said.

'Go on,' oozed the man. 'It'll be fun.'

Never let it be said that Mollie Browne didn't know how to have fun. 'All right then,' I said, grinning. 'Just one.'

Strutting my way over to the diving board, I perched on the edge. Sucking in my tummy and sticking out my chest, I smiled as brightly as I could – no mean feat when your teeth are chattering furiously.

Quick as a flash, the man picked up his camera. *Pop . . . pop . . . pop* went the flashbulb.

'Thanks awfully,' he said and, packing up his stuff, he made to leave.

'Just a minute!' I yelled after him. 'Where are you from?'

'Me?' he said, a wicked smile spreading over his face. 'Only the Sunday newspapers. Congratulations, you're tomorrow's news.'

Oh crumbs.

By the time I'd made it back to Cadogan Square I'd convinced myself there was no way on earth anyone would see it. Besides which, what did it matter? Where was the harm? I hadn't been cavorting with some vulgar young man, just hanging about on a diving board.

The next morning, one look at Mr Orchard's face told me that a) he had seen it, and b) it did matter. Very much. His face had gone a funny shade of purple and, without saying a word, he lifted one arm and pointed in the direction of the housekeeper's sitting room.

I slunk in and sat down heavily on a chair.

Why did I keep getting into trouble? Why?

'I presume you have seen this . . . this scandal rag?' he spluttered, throwing a copy of the *News of the World* down with a thud on to Mrs Jones's wooden desk, which she used to write up the day's menu. 'You should do, seeing as you appear to have a somewhat prominent position in it.'

The paper fell open and my heart sank. There I was in all my semi-naked splendour, perched on the edge of the diving board. My tummy was sucked in, my chest pushed brazenly out and a cheeky smile was plastered across my face. Over the top of the picture screamed a headline: SHIVERING ON THE BRINK.

I looked up at Mr Orchard's livid red face and quivering nostrils.

'It's me,' I said lamely.

'Yes, Mollie, it is you,' he thundered. 'Apparently shivering on the brink.' He said the last words as if he were reading 'kitchen maid caught in sordid romp'.

'I'm sorry,' I blustered. 'I was only having a swim. I didn't know there would be a photographer there.'

'Why, Mollie,' sighed Mr Orchard heavily, removing his half-moon spectacles and rubbing his eyes, 'do you insist on repeatedly bringing shame and disgrace on this household?'

'I'm sorry,' I said again.

'Mr Stocks is an elderly gentleman and if he finds out about this I wouldn't be at all surprised if he doesn't give you your marching orders. Imagine, a kitchen maid in his employment appearing in – in –' He could hardly bring himself to say the words and when he did he spat them out with venom – 'the *News of the World*. First the Black-shirts and now . . .' He flicked the paper away and sniffed in disdain. 'Now this unsavoury business. Can't you ever stay out of trouble?'

It was a good question and, under the circumstances, a

fair one. Given my behaviour, shivering on the brink seemed to sum up my current position in Cadogan Square rather neatly. I suppose to you today reading this, appearing in your swimming costume in the *News of the World* wouldn't seem like much, but back in 1934 in Cadogan Square it was absolutely scandalous behaviour, at least in the butler's eyes. No matter that society girls were obviously getting up to far worse – rumour had it that Diana Mitford was having an affair with Oswald Mosley and he himself had cheated on his wife, Lady Cynthia Curzon, with her younger sister *and* their step-mother.

As always, it was one rule for upstairs and another entirely for downstairs. I was supposed to be seen and not heard, work hard and keep my private life as scrupulously private as Mr Orchard obviously did. I never knew where he went after hours, what he got up to, and I never would. You weren't supposed to conduct yourself or flaunt yourself publicly, full stop. Much less in a newspaper.

The *News of the World* was a scandal rag even back then. At a tuppence per issue, my father always took it on Sundays. In fact, it was aimed at the newly literate working classes, something the gentry obviously didn't approve of. Apparently, Frederick Greenwood, editor of the *Pall Mall Gazette*, was in his club one day when he met Lord Riddell, the then owner of the *News of the World*, and in the course of conversation Riddell said to him, 'You know, I own a paper.'

'Oh, do you?' said Greenwood. 'What is it?'

'It's called the *News of the World* – I'll send you a copy,' replied Riddell and in due course did so. Next time they met, Riddell said, 'Well, Greenwood, what do you think of my paper?'

'I looked at it,' replied Greenwood, 'and then I put it in the waste-paper basket. And then I thought, "If I leave it there the cook may read it" – so I burnt it.'

It quickly established itself as a purveyor of titillation, shock and criminal news. Much of the material came from coverage of vice prosecutions, including alleged brothels, streetwalkers and 'immoral' women. That photographer had obviously been hanging about, hoping to catch a bit of the so-called lewd behaviour that had got the Met police all fired up, when he'd chanced upon me.

The paper's motto was 'All human life is there'. And now too, it would seem, was Mollie Browne.

After that I crept about like a nervous kitten, under the ever-watchful eyes of Mrs Jones, Mr Orchard and Mabel. I wasn't daft. I knew they suspected I was up to no good at every turn and sneaking out to meet fascists on my half-days off. Mrs Jones used every excuse to keep me close to her and suddenly I found myself bogged down in some very time-consuming tasks like picking the tiny bones out of mackerel and grating enormous piles of horseradish. I toed the line, but underneath it all I was longing to get out and be free. London was just bursting with adventures to be had and I couldn't wait to get upstairs and experience it all.

By June of the 1934 season, shortly before we headed back to Norfolk, I found my mind wandering back to Henry. Would it hurt if I saw him again? He was ever so handsome, after all. Surely just one more time wouldn't matter? After all, we were returning to Norfolk soon.

I was pondering this one morning as I headed to the servants' hall with my cup of coffee for a well-earned rest at eleven o'clock. I found everyone in there poring over the newspapers.

'What is it?' I asked.

All eyes turned to me and I sensed trouble.

Oh no. Not another centrefold of me, please.

'What's wrong?' I ventured nervously. 'What you all reading?'

'Your boyfriend's been up to no good again, I daresay,' crowed Mabel, hardly able to conceal the glee in her voice.

'What boyfriend?' I asked.

Mr Orchard rustled the paper. 'I warned you against those Blackshirts, didn't I, Mollie?' he snapped. 'They're bad news.'

'What have they done?' trembled Phyllis, instantly fearing the worst.

'Last night the British Union of Fascists held an indoor rally at Olympia in London which drew a crowd of twelve thousand,' said Mr Orchard, reading straight from the paper. 'Some five hundred anti-fascists managed to infiltrate the hall. When they began heckling, they were attacked by one thousand black-shirted stewards. Several of the protestors, illuminated by bright spotlights, were beaten up by the Blackshirts.'

An uneasy silence fell over the servants' hall as Mr Orchard looked up at me, glared, and then carried on reading.

'In ugly scenes, Blackshirts began stumbling and leaping over chairs to get at the source of the noise. There was a wild scrummage, women screamed, black-shirted arms rose and fell and blows were dealt. The arena was soon full of hooting and whistling, and chairs, boots and shoes were flying in the air. Mosley interrupted his speaking for these violent outbursts and then calmly continued once each heckler was subdued.'

He threw the paper down on the table and looked at me with a self-satisfied smile. 'See, I told you so. Mosley is an imitation Hitler and his Blackshirts nothing but a band of violent bullyboys.' His voice was quivering with rage. 'He is simply begging for the opportunity to reduce England to a Nazi German province. Well, now everyone can see them for what they really are.'

He pushed the paper over the table towards me, and there it was: photo after photo of Blackshirts forcibly ejecting men and women. Not only that, but the antics of the Blackshirts at the Olympia rally had made the front pages of most newspapers that fateful day.

The rally was a turning point. A public outcry ensued, Lord Rothermere and his *Daily Mail* newspaper withdrew its support, they were banned by the BBC and membership of the BUF went into decline. It fell from 40,000 to 5,000 in the following year; people no longer wanted to be associated with the movement, as the violence at the heart of it became more apparent. The scenes were nothing like the famous Cable Street confrontation that was to happen two years later in 1936, where the BUF were prevented from marching through the East End by opposition demonstrators and requests from the police trying to keep the peace, but it was enough. Enough to highlight to me how much of a silly, naive young girl I'd been.

It had a profound effect on me. Shame and humility

washed over me that day in the servants' hall. I was, in many ways, a youngster playing at an adult's game. First Alan, now this. I always thought I knew best in matters of the heart. As much as I was loathe to admit it, perhaps I wasn't always right. I made a vow there and then. No more larking about, no more photos in the *News of the World*, no more unsuitable fellas.

I was never going to be truly respected here by my superiors. Not after this debacle. It was time to knuckle down. It was time I got a new job and proved my worth elsewhere. It was time to seek my fortune, somewhere hot, somewhere far away, where no one had even heard of Blackshirts and scandal rags. Somewhere like . . . *Spain*?

TIPS FROM A 1930S KITCHEN

...

Proper Fish and Chips

In my day, fish and chips were always wrapped in news-paper (sometimes even the *News of the World* – I often wonder if anyone had the pleasure of seeing me in my swimmies smiling back at them while they ate their cod and chips). We used to pay 3d for a portion of fish and chips. If you saved up your old newspapers and took them in with you when you bought your fish and chips they'd pay ha'penny for twelve papers so it was worth doing! Fish and chips served in newspaper always tasted better. It's such a shame the health and safety brigade got on to it and banned it. Course, at Cadogan Square, we could never have served up fish and chips to Mr Stocks wrapped in a paper. Mr Orchard would have had a blue fit! This is the way we did them and they tasted delicious.

Peel and slice potatoes into chips. Heat enough lard in a pan to cover chips and wait until lard is hot, put chips in pan and cook until soft. Take out of pan. Reheat fat until very hot and place chips back in for two minutes or until they're really crisp. Drain on kitchen paper. Save lard for next time.

Cut fish into required sizes and dry with kitchen paper. Flour well and dip into beaten egg. Cover well with white breadcrumbs and shake off surplus. Heat lard, put in fish and cook until golden brown, then drain and serve with anchovy sauce.

For the anchovy sauce, melt 2 oz (50 g) butter, add 2 level tablespoons flour and mix well over a low heat. Add milk until the sauce reaches required thickness. Add anchovy essence, salt and pepper, and simmer for one minute.

Household Tip

A cotton bud dipped in mouthwash is the perfect thing to clean those hard-to-reach places on ornaments, etc. – also good on computer keyboards and mobile phones, so I'm told.

9

Castles in Spain

To travel hopefully is a better thing than to arrive.
Robert Louis Stevenson

I'll never forget seeing Wallis Simpson coming out of a
hotel on Park Lane in London, in early 1935. I close my
eyes and I can still see her hard face and whippet-thin
body descending a staircase, with Edward scurrying after
her like a lapdog.

Some people just have 'It' – a sort of star quality that
makes people stop in their tracks and stare. Today, there
are no end of programmes devoted to finding people
with that extraordinary quality that makes them stand out,
just as there are many celebrity couples who fill column
inches. Well, back then we didn't have Posh and Becks,
Angelina and Brad or Beyoncé and Jay-Z. We had Wallis
and Edward, and the whole of the country was buzzing
about their scandalous relationship. Edward was causing
shockwaves with his obsession with this American divor-
cee and I must admit that I, like everyone else, was happy
to take my part in the vilification of Wallis Simpson.

It was a whole year since my own illicit flirtation with one of Oswald Mosley's Blackshirts had got me into trouble below stairs and since then I had kept my head down and worked hard. I suppose you could say I knew a fair bit about being involved in a relationship that was destined to fail and there is no doubt that the blossoming love between Wallis and Edward was just as looked down upon as my own with Henry the Blackshirt.

London – indeed, the whole country – disapproved of this twice-divorced, domineering American whose steely ambition glinted as brashly as the rocks on her fingers. How could he court a woman who had cheated on her husband and expect us to accept her? Preposterous. Folk from high society upstairs to kitchen maids downstairs and the working classes all frowned upon it. Looking back, the country's condemnation of their love affair was probably over the top, but in those innocent yet judgemental times their relationship seemed scandalous and out of step.

She was up to no good and we knew it. Servants' halls and drawing rooms the length and breadth of the country were alive with gossip about it. We didn't have the Internet back then and British newspapers didn't report on their relationship, yet somehow we all knew.

Never underestimate the ability of servants to spread gossip! I'd spent the last year hearing titbits about their blossoming relationship conducted at parties and on yachts in the Mediterranean and now here, in the early spring of 1935, I was actually seeing her in the flesh! The jostling crowd and the ripple of electric excitement that ran through it had been enough to alert me to the possibility of something scandalous. If there was so much as a whiff of something good going on, I wanted to be a part of it! I'd only popped out because Mrs Jones was running short on sugar – still, two minutes wouldn't hurt.

Pushing my way to the front of the crowd, I gasped when I realized who I was looking at. Happen I was right to barge my way through, after all.

'Is that who I think it is?' I breathlessly asked a young lady to my left, probably a secretary on her lunch break.

'Yes,' she whispered, hardly able to contain her excitement at the story she'd have to tell when she got back to the office. 'It's Edward and that new lady of his, Wallis. They've just got back from some holiday in Europe apparently.'

'Fancy,' I gasped.

The secretary turned to look at me and her eyes flashed angrily. 'Hard-faced bitch, ain't she? Look at 'er. Who does she fink she is?'

I stared at Wallis in her immaculately cut navy wool suit and the first thing that struck me was the determined set of her jaw. She had a reputation as a ruthless social climber with a voracious sexual appetite and, by the way she conducted herself, she clearly wasn't doing herself any favours.

She was as brassy as Mr Stocks's front-door knocker.

A policeman was holding back the crowds so she could walk down the steps and into a waiting motor car. Wallis stopped and glared frostily at us all in the crowd. Edward, still walking down the steps, received the same icy glare when he reached the car, and by the way she took his arm and hustled him in, you could tell who wore the trousers in that relationship. He, meanwhile, gave her a look of utter devotion and adoration. He looked like a lovesick puppy, silly sap.

An impressive emerald and diamond bracelet, probably a gift from Edward, glinted on her tiny bird-like wrist as she gripped the car door and lowered herself in. With one final malevolent stare, she disappeared into the back of the big flashy car and their chauffeur drove them off up London's Park Lane.

'Did. You. See. Her!' spat the secretary through pursed lips. 'Apparently she's juggling Edward *and* her husband.' A scowl settled on her face as she crossed her arms firmly across her chest. 'Floozy.'

'It won't last,' I said. 'She's up to all sorts and he's a playboy bachelor.'

The secretary looked left, then right, then lowered her voice and leaned in. 'Apparently she seduced him into bed with some saucy tips she picked up,' she said in a wicked whisper.

My eyes widened. 'Can you imagine?' I murmured, thoroughly enjoying this juicy bit of gossip. I'd only popped out to get a packet of sugar – this was an unexpected bonus!

'And,' she went on, 'she stays so skinny by having Earl Grey tea, grapefruit juice and nothing else. Imagine!'

I shook my head in wonder. 'Imagine,' I agreed.

I wouldn't get a day's work done below stairs if that was all I ate. In nearly four years of service there had barely been a day when I hadn't started with a plate of bacon and eggs and ended with a lovely roast dinner. I wasn't over-weight – Alan had told me I had a lovely figure – but I had decent curves all right. Judging by the size of Wallis, I doubted whether she'd ever let a plate of Mrs Jones's beef and Yorkshire pudding past those brittle lips. She went straight up and down, like a piece of paper. Still, I suppose when all you do all day is drape yourself over a yacht, you don't need that much sustenance. Wallis Simpson would no more scrub steps or rake down a coal fire than she would fly to the moon.

That was the problem with her and some of these other society folk. Their lives were too rarefied, too indulged. They didn't know what it was to live in the real world. Their days were just a whirlwind of yachts, parties and champagne. The life of bloomin' Riley! Ridiculous. The woman wouldn't know a decent day's work if it came up and hit her between the eyes. Imagine her cutting it a day below stairs under Mrs Jones's stern eye.

The secretary threw one final furious scowl in the direction of their car before stomping back off to work.

All my life I'd had to listen to endless lectures about the evils of shameful behaviour and, more recently, Mr Orchard's sniffy reproaches about bringing shame on the house with my conduct, yet some hussy like Wallis could flaunt it about all over Europe and do whatever she pleased. Double standards, if you asked me. Still, I sniffed as I marched back to Cadogan Square on foot, I was better than that old trollop!

As I walked, I pondered my situation. I had been in Cadogan Square for four years. Flo had long gone, seeking her fortune elsewhere; Alan had vanished in a furious blaze of anger; even Phyllis, the new girl, was well settled in and gaining in confidence daily. I, meanwhile, was stuck stock-still, every day rolling out the same with a kind of dull inevitability. From peeling spuds to laying out cook's table and making pastry, I could do it all with my eyes shut now.

I'd been just fourteen, a girl, when I started. Now I was nearly nineteen and still unmarried. Was I in danger of becoming an old relic like Mr Orchard and Mrs Jones, destined to spend my life as their whipping boy? On the other hand, could I leave my nice cushy number? I may have started work at six thirty a.m. and rarely finished until nine thirty or ten p.m., but in that respect I was no different to any other domestic servant and the work was all the same. Once you've scrubbed one lot of steps, you've scrubbed them all. I daresay some other member of the gentry would still demand a five-course dinner each and every night. But at least Mr Stocks was a gentleman. Two weeks' paid holiday a year was unheard of below stairs, as was getting two hours off after lunch every afternoon, not having to do the annual spring clean and getting a cash present instead of the usual old scratchy stockings at Christmas. Not to mention the delicious leftovers that made their way below stairs every day. I didn't know many kitchen maids in the 1930s who got paid holiday and got to eat sirloin steak every Sunday! Nor could I ignore the fact that, as an elderly gentleman, he wasn't downstairs pestering us young girls. I knew from overhearing local gossip at dances that some of the prettier young servants were forever being pestered to sleep with their young male bosses. It started with a patted bottom and a sly wink and ended God knows where! Tiptoeing along creaky corridors after hours as frisky male gentry ended up the wrong side of the baize door!

In Granny Esther's day, most of the local gentry saw it as a perk of their social position to bed the best-looking girls, like it was their feudal right to sleep with their kitchen maids. Can you ever imagine? Like Granny Esther, it would be the young girls who were left to deal with the consequences and God forbid you had an unwanted pregnancy. So in some respects I was very lucky. An elderly gentleman who cared for his staff and left us alone was definitely a plum position to have found myself in.

Then a terrifying image of me aged fifty flashed into my mind, red-faced and sour and still grating horseradish and making fairy cakes for Captain Eric at Cadogan Square. I shuddered at the very thought. No, I had to get out. I'd go as stale as month-old bread otherwise. There were domestic staff agencies everywhere. I would write to one and register my interest. Someone would take me on, surely? I may have been a handful, but I could graft all right, and there was little I didn't know about cooking now, thanks to Mrs Jones and Flo.

During the last year Mr Orchard and I had reached an uneasy truce. He'd never brought it up, but I sensed I'd never be forgiven for appearing in the *News of the World* in my swimming costume or for cavorting with fascist Blackshirts or for my relationship with the footman. I'd broken virtually every rule in the house. Thank God I'd never got myself in the family way. Mind you, I'd never be that daft!

My thoughts evaporated as I arrived back at Cadogan Square. I was bursting to pass on my news.

'Guess who I saw?' I crowed, dumping the bag of sugar

on the kitchen table. No one looked up from their duties. 'Only Wallis Simpson, coming out of a hotel,' I went on, undeterred.

Mrs Jones finally looked up and her red jowls wobbled in annoyance. 'Hussy,' she sniffed, returning her attentions to a large trout she was filleting.

'Fancy that, Mollie,' said Irene, the housemaid, when she heard. 'Was she as skinny in real life?'

'I should say,' I laughed. 'Like a paper doll.'

'Anyway, never mind that, I've got better news,' Irene replied.

'Better than seeing Wallis Simpson?' I scoffed.

'Yes,' she said. 'Boss has said we can have time off to watch the Silver Jubilee. Got to be better than clearing out your chamber pot, Mollie Browne,' she teased, patting me affectionately on the arm.

Now that *was* good news. Time off, any time off, was a good thing. My spine tingled in excitement. Not since I'd seen King George V travelling along the Lynn Road in Norfolk and Princess Elizabeth playing in her back garden in London had I felt so excited. The prospect of seeing our beloved royals was always something to look forward to and, unlike seeing Wallis, was cause for celebration, not derision.

As the big day of King George V's Silver Jubilee drew nearer, the feeling of anticipation and excitement was mounting. Not just below stairs at Number 24 Cadogan Square, but in homes all over Britain. I suppose, in many ways, it was a little like the wedding day of Prince William and Kate Middleton and, just as for their royal wedding, and indeed the queen's Diamond Jubilee, so too did plans reach fever pitch for the king's Silver Jubilee. There may be seventy-six years between these events, but the deep sense of national pride was just as strong, if not stronger, back then.

We adored our royalty. We felt nothing but pride for our king and were ready to celebrate the twenty-fifth anniversary of his coronation. He was popular, loved and respected by the masses for his common sense. Course, many now see him as an aloof and stern figure, making his stuttering son's life hell in the film *The King's Speech*, but King George V was very popular and held in high esteem, especially after his leadership during the First World War when he'd visited factories, front lines and hospitals. He had set an example of confidence, courage and sacrifice and a recent recovery from a serious illness only cemented that affection. He was devoted to his wife, Queen Mary, and to the empire.

Consequently, there was an enormous outpouring of patriotism. Street parties were planned all over the country and bunting and flags fluttered from every street lamp. Even the smart railings of Cadogan Square were ablaze with red, white and blue. Babies dressed in Union Jacks were pushed along in their Silver Cross coach prams and little children dressed in red, white and blue crêpe paper dresses ran giggling through the streets. Stamps and medals were issued and even new public parks opened in his honour.

By the time the day of the celebrations dawned, 6 May 1935, me, Irene and Phyllis were a giggling, over-excited mess.

'Here, girls,' said Irene, handing us all a flag on a stick. 'I've got us these to wave as the coach goes past.'

'Thanks, Irene,' I said. 'Wonder if I wave it high enough he might notice me and give a wave back.'

'Unlikely,' grumped Mrs Jones unkindly. 'He never noticed you when it was just you and him on the Lynn Road.'

I poked my tongue out as soon as her back was turned. Old grouch.

'You not coming, Mrs Jones?' piped up Phyllis.

She whirled round, hands on hips, all ready to play the martyr. 'How can I?' she blazed, glaring at us accusingly. 'I've a soup to finish, pastry to make, not to mention savouries and puddings for tonight and I've got an empty kitchen. Now you make sure you come straight back as soon as that coach has gone past, you hear me?'

'We will,' we all chorused.

But even Mrs Jones's surly mood did nothing to dull our spirits and we raced up the area steps and into a great tidal wave of human life, all making their way along the smart streets to Hyde Park.

For the first time the streets around Cadogan Square were heaving with gentry and their domestic servants all walking together, shoulder to shoulder, in one mass of happy humanity. It was the first time Cadogan Square had come anything close to resembling a community. Everyone was dressed up, everyone excited about the spectacle ahead.

Many life-altering things happened in 1935. The driving test became compulsory, Penguin Books published the first paperbacks in Britain, steel was produced in Corby,

Stanley Baldwin took over as prime minister and the Nobel Prize was given for the discovery of the neutron, but for those that can remember, King George V's Silver Jubilee stands out as the happiest of times. Up and down the country, every single road, more or less, held a street party with games, fancy dress, floats, bunting and afternoon tea, but here in London we were actually watching history unfold.

By the time we reached the roundabout at Hyde Park, the crowds were heaving and hundreds of people lined the streets. Little did I know, but my old chum Flo was watching it by the Ritz, not half a mile away.

'Here, girls,' I said. 'Follow me.'

With that, we pushed our way to the front of the railings. It was a tight squeeze. All around us the atmosphere was jubilant. People held up vast banners: 'King George, Queen Mary, long may they reign. God bless them.' Everyone was dressed in their Sunday best and had bright smiles plastered on their faces.

'There's an awful lot of people, ain't there?' trembled Phyllis, still not fully recovered from her experience at Speakers' Corner.

'Stick with me,' I grinned, squeezing her hand.

We knew the carriage would be coming soon, en route from Buckingham Palace to St Paul's Cathedral. Suddenly a huge round of applause and deafening cheers broke out. My skin prickled with goosebumps as the atmosphere in the crowd became electric.

'It's the king!' screamed Irene, waving her flag like mad. 'Long live the king!'

The crowd swept forward as one, a great tidal wave of love and respect washing over us. Then I saw them, perched upright in their magnificent carriage drawn by six horses. Queen Mary, dressed in a beautiful white coat with a fur stole, her diamonds glittering in the spring sunshine, looked our way as we hollered and cheered like crazy. She gave us a curt little nod.

'She hasn't changed much,' I chuckled to the girls.

Talk about pomp. Hundreds of guards on horseback trotted past, resplendent in their scarlet jackets.

'God save the king!' I yelled, along with hundreds of others.

There were no snidey comments, no sarcasm or envy. No front-page examination the next day of what they were wearing or how they behaved. Just total and utter deference. Every single person, man, woman and child, cheered and clapped with total enthusiasm.

Today the royals have to earn our respect; back then it was a given.

In response to the extraordinary adoration of the cheering crowds, the king later said: 'I cannot understand it, after all I am only a very ordinary sort of fellow.'

As soon as they had gone and the crowds started to disperse, Irene turned to us with a sigh. 'Oh well,' she said. 'Back to me chamber pots.'

We fell about laughing and, as I linked arms with my friends from below stairs, I didn't care that we didn't have a street party to go to and it was straight back to work. We'd seen the king and queen up close and it was a total and utter joy.

'Thanks for letting us watch the procession, Mrs Jones,' I said gratefully when we got back. 'Oh, you should have seen it, we was so close to the king and queen.'

'I'm sure you were,' she said. 'Now hop to it, them carrots won't peel themselves.'

Later, as we prepared Mr Stocks's evening meal, we were allowed, as it was a special occasion, to listen to the king's speech on the wireless:

'At the close of this memorable day I must speak to my people everywhere. How can I express what is in my heart as I passed this morning through cheering multitudes, to and from St Paul's Cathedral, how could I fail to be most deeply moved. Words cannot express my thoughts and feelings. I can only say to you, my very dear people, that the queen and I thank you from the very depths of our hearts for all the loyalty and, may I say, the love with which this day and always you have surrounded us.

'I dedicate myself anew to your service for the years that may still be given to me.

'I look back on the past with thankfulness to God. My people and I have come through great trials and difficulties together. They are not over. In the midst of this day's rejoicing I grieve to think of the numbers of my people who are still without work. We owe it to them and not least to those who are suffering from any form of disablement all the sympathy and help we can give.'

My mind flickered to my poor old father, shivering out in his hut, rasping for breath, and my mother still putting on her best face, and a sudden sorrow settled over my heart. What did the future hold for him, for my mother, in fact for all the thousands of people disabled by the war and fighting poverty and destitution? Goodness only knew . . .

I tuned back into the speech.

'Other anxieties may be in store but I am persuaded that with God's help they may all be overcome if we meet them with confidence, courage and unity. So I look forward to the future with faith and hope.'

It was a stirring speech and, as the national anthem struck up, we all went about our work with a renewed sense of hope for the future.

A year later our beloved king was dead.

1936 was the year of the three kings. With the sad passing of King George V came the accession and then abdication of his son, Edward VIII. I should have known that gusty spring morning, when I'd seen the couple in London and noted the look of utter love that shone in Edward's eyes, that he would always put love before duty. And so, as Edward was pressured to hand the throne and control of the empire over to his brother, there was change in my life too, albeit on a slightly smaller scale.

We were back in Woodhall in Norfolk in the summer of 1936, four months before Edward's famous abdication speech, when Mrs Jones turned to me out of the blue one morning and remarked: 'It's time for you to get a better job, Mollie. You've been here five years now.'

I stopped rolling out pastry and stared at her, flabbergasted. 'Well,' I admitted, 'I have been thinking about it.'

'You've learnt all you can learn here now,' she went on. 'You can easily get a job in a bigger house. Pains me to say it but you're not a bad little cook – when you keep your mind on the job and not on unsuitable boys, that is.'

I might have imagined it, but she was smiling, actually smiling at me, in a sort of encouraging way. Blimey. Wonders would never cease.

'Get yourself down to Collins Agency in King's Lynn on your next half-day off. I'll write you a reference. You'll be able to get something easy.'

'Thanks, Mrs Jones,' I mumbled. 'I'll do that.'

Me in the grounds of Woodhall, in a rare moment off duty, aged about eighteen.

Sure enough, on my next half-day, I dressed up smart and, clutching my reference, headed on the bus to King's Lynn.

A stern, bespectacled lady took one look at my reference, looked me up and down long and hard and then referred to a heavy leather-bound book on her desk.

'Well, we do have a position that you would be suitable for,' she said. 'Lord Islington needs a kitchen maid. He has houses in Hyde Park and a country estate in Bury St Edmonds, Rushbrook Hall.'

My heart sank a little. A lord was a step up, but I'd been a kitchen maid for years, ferrying between London and a country estate. It would just be more of the same. But I knew I had to be realistic. I was nineteen, nearly twenty. The next logical step up was cook, but I was way too young and inexperienced to make that position. So for now, it looked as if I was trapped as a kitchen maid.

'I'll book you an appointment to see Mrs Pickering, Lord Islington's secretary,' she said, slamming shut her leather-bound book, indicating that the interview was now over. 'Make sure you take your references.'

On my next half-day I took no end of buses and trains to get from Norfolk to Bury St Edmonds in Suffolk. An old bus lurched and bumped along a country road and by the time it spat me out at a stone gatehouse next to some imposing gates, I was hot, dusty and tired.

Trooping up a long drive to a large moated mansion set in acres of parkland, most people would have been impressed. But as I trudged over the moat, I muttered to myself: 'Why have the gentry always got to have such long bloomin' driveways?'

I was parched by the time the butler hustled me round the servants' entrance and into Mrs Pickering's office. She gave me a cursory inspection, looking me up and down through her half-moon glasses. Honestly. It made you feel as if you were livestock at an auction, not a kitchen maid being interviewed for a job.

'Well,' she said, after a thorough read of Mrs Jones's reference, 'you have the necessary experience. There could only be one possible problem.' She frowned. 'His Lordship has a castle in Spain which he intends to move to imminently, so the post requires someone who desires foreign travel.'

My head snapped up like you see in a cartoon. All traces of travel fatigue vanished. 'Spain?' I gasped. The sun came out and choirs of celestial angels blew trumpets on fluffy clouds. I could have shouted 'Hallelujah' and planted a kiss right on the end of this stern woman's nose.

'I'll take it,' I announced.

'The salary is ten shillings a week . . .'

'I'll take it,' I said again.

'You will have a half-day off once a week and every other Sunday and your duties include . . .'

I stopped listening. It didn't matter if I had to drag a sack of coal from London to Suffolk with my teeth, I was going to take it. Because it meant that finally, finally, my dreams would be realized. I would get to travel to Spain.

It's worth keeping in mind that I didn't really know much about Spain. Few did back in 1936, but in my eyes it was a hot, humid, exotic, fantastical place full of swarthy men and palm trees. Not since I'd climbed to the very top of the tallest tree in the village as a ten-year-old tomboy had the world seemed so big and so full of adventure and magic.

Now I was getting to live my dreams. I was going to live in Spain. No one in my family, in fact no one I knew, had ever travelled abroad. Alan, that possessive footman, had told me it was an impossibility. Well, I'd show him, I'd show them all! Mollie Browne was going to Spain to live in a real-life castle. Who knew what amazing adventures beckoned!

On the bus back to Woodhall, my heart was bursting

with rapturous joy. Back in the kitchen I raced over to Mrs Jones and planted a big wet kiss on her cheek.

'Get away with ya,' she scolded, wiping her cheek angrily. 'What's come over you, big daft dolly daydream?'

'I'm off to Spain, that's what!' I babbled excitedly. 'Me, in Spain, what about that?'

Mr Orchard looked up from a bottle of wine he was decanting. 'Has anyone warned the natives?' he said drily.

'You're just jealous,' I snapped back. Cheeky, yes, but he couldn't sack me now.

He raised one eyebrow a fraction. 'I wish you the very best of luck, Mollie. Something tells me you will need it. And, tell me, just who is the lucky man or woman who has the dubious honour of being your new employer?'

'Lord Islington,' I said proudly. I could tell even Mr Orchard was impressed.

'Aah, Lord Islington,' he said as if he took tea with him regularly. 'Lord Islington, otherwise known as First Baron Islington, educated at Harrow and Christ Church Oxford. Former Governor of New Zealand, Privy Counsellor and most recently Under-Secretary of State for the Colonies. Seventy years old now, I believe, but a most impressive gentleman.'

'You sound as if you've swallowed a copy of *The Times*,' I giggled.

'Less of your sauce, Mollie,' snapped Mrs Jones.

It was September 1936 when I took my leave of Wood-hall.

In a way I was sad to go, but life moves on. Besides, Phyllis was getting my job, so she was getting a leg-up too.

As I packed my small case and clambered down the back staircase for the last time, I found Irene and Phyllis waiting at the bottom, wearing solemn faces.

'Who's died then?' I laughed.

'This place won't be half as much fun without you,' sniffed Irene, getting a large hankie out of her apron pocket and blowing her nose loudly.

'Yeah,' agreed Phyllis. 'Who's going to get me into trouble now?'

In the servants' hall Mr Orchard offered me a stiff handshake, but Mrs Jones surprised me the most when she threw her arms round me and I found my face stuffed into her vast and fleshy bosom. It was like being folded into a giant pile of dough. When I was finally allowed up for air, her pudgy little face lit up with a rare smile that reached her eyes.

'I'll miss you,' she said, 'but I'll come and see you at your mother's for tea on your next half-day off.' And then, as if embarrassed by her unusual show of affection, 'Don't you be giving that cook any cheek, you hear me, and don't burn the béchamel sauce.' She pushed back a lock of red hair from my face and added softly, 'And stay out of trouble, Mollie Browne.'

Untangling myself from her floury embrace, I grinned.

'Trouble – me?' I said, all wide-eyed innocence. Then I virtually skipped out of the servants' door and on to my new life.

Just outside I found dear, sweet, loyal George waiting with a bunch of flowers. No matter that I'd broken his heart, this loyal farmhand wasn't going to let me go without saying goodbye.

'May I write, Mollie?' he asked, pressing the flowers into my hand.

'Course,' I said. 'Where's Louis then? He not come out to wish me good luck?'

At the mention of his handsome older brother, George looked crestfallen. 'He's visiting his lady friend,' he mumbled.

Feeling a little tactless, I smiled and stroked George's ruddy cheek. It reddened even more at my touch.

'No matter,' I said, kissing his warm cheek. 'You're here and that's what counts. You're a real pal.'

Then I hopped on my bike and cycled past the woods where I'd enjoyed many a secret tryst with Alan, past the woodshed where I'd overheard racy Mabel and her secret lover, and round to the front of the drive, where I disturbed a pheasant who shot into the air with an indignant croak.

'Watch out!' I chuckled. 'Or you'll end up in Mrs Jones's soup.'

I took one final backward glance at the grand old hall where I had spent the past five years in service. The sight of the imposing antlers either side of the large front door brought a smile to my face as I remembered me and Flo tiptoeing past them, scared witless, that night we'd sneaked out to the dance.

I had laughed, cried, scrubbed, plucked, filleted, diced, scoured, fried, roasted, betrayed and been betrayed, been bullied and bossed, learnt to dance, kiss and cook at this grand and magical old house, deep in the countryside.

All in all, Woodhall had been the very best of times.

I may have started as a nervous fourteen-year-old

scullery maid, but I was leaving a confident woman on the verge of a new life in Spain. Other people, like Granny Esther, may have knocked my profession down, told me I was nothing but a skivvy for the thankless upper classes, but I knew domestic service was opening up new worlds for me.

I turned and pedalled down the long gravel drive. With a warm, light breeze kissing my face and my red hair flying behind me, I had soon reached the end. I was just about to cycle round the corner, out of sight forever, when I heard Mrs Jones call after me, hands planted as ever on those beefy hips:

'And don't forget, Mollie Browne – never stir a sauce with anything other than a wooden spoon.'

I was due immediately at Lord Islington's London property near Hyde Park, but I managed to stop at Mother's for a quick cup of tea before I got the train. Granny Esther was there when I arrived.

'Don't know why you want to go all the way over to Spain,' she grumbled. 'Perfectly good jobs to be had here in Norfolk.'

I shook my head in despair, making sure to do it by her blind eye.

'Don't give me cheek, Mollie,' she snapped. 'What do you want to go abroad for anyway? It'll be filthy dirty and them natives have some strange ways about them. They eat funny food –' she paused for effect – 'with their hands.'

I snorted, which just seemed to irritate her more.

'Heathens,' she spat. 'They don't wash, you know. No hygiene about them.'

Granny seemed to have conveniently forgotten her

habit of pouring paraffin before serving up butter when she used to run her country shop.

All the same, I pondered her original question. Just why was I so desperate to go abroad? I couldn't put my finger on the exact reason. Most girls my age I knew were desperate to marry and start having babies. Not me. My mostly disastrous brushes with romance hadn't exactly left me panting for more. I just had this feeling, this strong primeval urge inside me to travel, to see something of the world. I knew that made me different to my contemporaries, but then I'd never felt the same as everyone else anyway.

Ever since I'd sat in that big old tree as a ten-year-old and mapped out my future, a future far away from Norfolk, my heart was always yearning for more. Now I'd conquered London and I was about to set sail for Spain. Nothing was quite so thrilling as the unknown.

I was blissfully unaware that the Spanish Civil War had just started and Franco's fascist troops had mobilized, or that there was widespread poverty, unrest and turbulence. I just wanted to gaze at this hot and dusty country, watch dark-skinned men wrestling bulls under the balmy Mediterranean skies. No more rainy Norfolk days, no more thick and stifling London fog, no more breaking the ice on your jug of water so you could take a wash or shivering in an attic under an old blanket. Just endless sunshine.

It was the lure of the strange and exotic that acted like a gravitational pull to me. Besides, I had to take the chance. Opportunities like this hardly ever came up for a girl like me. Foreign travel was something you never even considered if you were from a working-class background. The only person in my family who'd ever left Britain was my grandmother's sister Rose, who'd moved to Australia, and that had taken her three months by boat! Not like nowadays, where people think nothing of hopping on a plane.

I knew I'd be travelling by boat with the rest of the staff. Just the thought of setting sail from Portsmouth made me tingle with excitement.

When I finally reached Lord Islington's Hyde Park property, I was overawed by the size of it. But it's funny – looking back, I hardly remember anything about that house or the people that worked in it. Just that it was very, very large, with endless dark rooms cloaked in heavy velvet curtains that blocked out the light and no end of staff to cater for one seventy-year-old lord.

The place was in total chaos. Packing boxes were crammed into every available space in readiness for the move to Spain and Mrs Pickering walked from room to room with a clipboard, organizing everyone.

The cook was French, which was very exotic in my eyes, and was married to the butler. She was most impressed that I knew how to make a decent Consommé Royale.

'Zis is good zat an Engleesh girl knows zis,' she said, and not for the first time I found myself thanking good old Flo.

I'd not been there long when a familiar face poked round the door.

'Here, Mollie, this is grand, ain't it?' whispered a male voice.

'Ernie Bratton as I live and breathe,' I cried, throwing my arms round him. 'What you doing here?'

'Captain Eric's in town so we're staying up at Cadogan Square. Mr Stocks and the rest of the staff are all back at Woodhall, so it's just the two of us.'

Ernie Bratton was Captain Eric's valet and a nicer bloke you'd be hard-pressed to find. He was handsome all right, in his twenties with lovely thick curly dark hair and film-star looks. There was no chemistry between us, more's the pity, but he was a lovely chap and his ready smile always cheered me up.

'It's great to see you, Ernie, but you best not stay. You'll get me in trouble with my new boss.'

'S'right,' he said, thrusting something into my hand. 'I only came to give you these.'

'What is it?' I asked, baffled.

'Tickets to the Chelsea Arts Ball at the Albert Hall.'

'How on earth did you get these?' I gasped. Servants never went to dos like this. I didn't know how much the tickets cost, but I knew the cost of them put them out of the reach of girls like me.

'Captain Eric gave them to me. His lungs ain't so good at the moment so he doesn't feel well enough to go. He said I could invite who I wanted, so I thought who better to have a laugh with than you!'

'Well, what about that?' I gasped, hugging the precious tickets to my chest like they were made of solid gold. 'He's a gent and no mistake.'

Ever since I had listened to Uncle Arthur tell fantastical tales about the goings-on at the society balls he worked at,

I had longed to see one for myself. Village halls were one thing, but this was something else altogether!

What a glorious, glorious night that was. For that one night only, I wasn't a kitchen maid. I was almost one of them.

In the black satin dress that Flo had made me and with my red hair freshly washed and gleaming, I thought I was it. I didn't have a scrap of make-up on. Not that it mattered – I was so fresh-faced I could carry it off. I completed my look with a green velvet bolero jacket, and by the time I jumped off a red double-decker bus to meet Ernie outside, I had ants in my pants.

'Mollie,' he gasped, 'look at you! You scrub up well.'

'Ta,' I smiled. 'You don't look so bad yourself.'

Ernie was wearing a smart tuxedo, probably one of Captain Eric's, and as I linked my arm through his, I reckoned we looked quite the couple.

''Ere, Mollie,' he whispered in my ear as we walked up to the Albert Hall. 'They'll never know we're a kitchen maid and a valet!'

The Chelsea Arts Ball was one of the most important events in the London social calendar of the 1920s and 1930s. It was attended by up to 7,000 socialites, artists and other Londoners in extravagant costumes. We knew from reading Mr Stocks's newspaper that it always caused a stir and attracted a lot of media attention.

On the door, a private steward, hired to keep the undesirables out, checked our tickets. I could hardly believe it when we were ushered inside.

Once in, Ernie and I stared around open-mouthed in

wonder. It was a glimpse inside another world. The Albert Hall sparkled like a giant snow globe. Vast glitter balls hung from the ceiling and lights of all different colours glinted from every corner.

'I'll go and get you a lemonade,' said Ernie.

A bar serving cocktails and champagne was set up in the corner, but I didn't care for alcohol. I just wanted to dance.

'Can't believe we're here,' I whispered when Ernie returned with our drinks. 'It's so lavish, ain't it?'

I've heard tell that people dressed in extravagant fancy dress, but I don't recall seeing anyone like that, though the women were done up to the nines in backless or slinky evening gowns and all the men in the full fig.

'Come on then,' I said to Ernie. 'I haven't come here to hang around like a coat stand all night.'

'You're mad as a hatter,' he grinned. With that he set down his drink and held out his hand. 'Would madam care to dance?' he asked.

'Yes, she would,' I replied.

What a night! Dance? We didn't stop. I didn't care who I danced with – Ernie, any strange bloke, it didn't matter to me. I just wanted to be up there on the dance floor. I must have foxtrotted, waltzed and two-stepped my way round the Albert Hall until the soles of my shoes were nearly worn through. The band played 'Red Sails in the Sunset', 'Lullaby of Broadway', 'Chapel in the Moonlight' and 'The Way You Look Tonight', all marvellous songs of that era. As Ernie swung me across the dance floor I felt like Ginger Rogers being swept around the room by Fred Astaire in the film *Swing Time*.

By the time our eleven p.m. curfew drew near and Ernie told me it was time to go, I was on cloud nine. No matter that the ball would go on until three a.m. and we had to leave before the end. Or that the only thing that passed my lips was lemonade and not the champagne cocktails other people were quaffing. I didn't care. When I'd first visited London all those years ago as a knock-kneed twelve-year-old, I'd sworn that one day I'd attend a big fancy society ball, and now finally I had. And the cherry on the top of my dazzling night? When we got outside, rain was drumming on the pavement so Ernie paid for us to get a taxi home. A taxi! This might not sound much to you, but servants never got taxis, so this was a very big deal. In fact, it was the first time I'd ever been in one.

Alighting from the taxi outside Lord Islington's huge house opposite Hyde Park, I felt like Cinderella! I might not have had Wallis Simpson's life of luxury or the king and queen's wealth and privilege, but I was doing all right, just the same.

'Well, Mollie,' I murmured as I snuggled dreamily down under my eiderdown up in the attic of the huge house. 'You *did* make it to the ball.'

The next day I could scarcely wipe the smile off my face as I helped prepare the boss's breakfast. I would dine out on this night for years to come.

Spain and high-society balls! Life was definitely looking up!

It was only a matter of weeks before my fairytale life came crashing down around my ears.

I was just laying out Cook's table when Mrs Pickering

came into the kitchen and clapped her hands. Everyone stopped what they were doing and looked up expectantly.

'I have some news,' she said in a tone of voice that instantly struck dread into my heart. 'It is with great regret that I have to inform you that Lord Islington died here at home last night on the sixth of December 1936. It goes without saying that there will be no need to continue packing for Spain.'

My whisk fell on to the stone floor with a clatter. It may sound callous that my only thought was for myself, but my heart plunged into my boots. *No. No. No . . . he can't be dead.*

And just like that, my dreams of Spain and faraway adventures under a red-hot sun melted away to nothing.

TIPS FROM A 1930S KITCHEN

•••

Lemonade

Not being a terribly sophisticated girl, I drank lemonade when I went to the Chelsea Arts Ball. Truth be told, I preferred it to the taste of champagne. It's easy to make your own and when served chilled on a hot summer's day is absolutely delicious. It's no secret that every cook of my era used Mrs Beeton's recipes and the lemonade recipe in her *Book of Household Management* remains one of the best to this day.

Strain the juice of two lemons into a half pint (285 ml) of cold water and then sweeten to taste with 4 oz (110 g) of caster sugar. Next stir in a teaspoonful of bicarbonate soda, add plenty of ice and mint, and drink while cool. I sometimes adapt Mrs Beeton's recipe by adding a grating of fresh ginger, which adds a nice zing.

Household Tip

To get rid of greasy fingermarks and spills on polished wood, simply wipe with a cloth soaked in vinegar before polishing with wax.

10

A Cook at Last

I have always thought that there is no more fruitful
source of family discontent than a housewife's
badly-cooked dinners and untidy ways.
Mrs Beeton,
Mrs Beeton's Book of Household Management

Four days after Lord Islington's death, on 10 December
1936, Edward VIII abdicated. His reign had lasted 326
days. My own ill-fated job had lasted just a few months.

I thought of that innocent young girl I had witnessed
from the top deck of the bus playing in her back garden
in London. Now Elizabeth would be ten and all too aware
of the huge responsibilities facing her and her family as
they moved into Buckingham Palace and the harsh glare
of intense public scrutiny. But what about me? What new
role did I have in life now that I was officially out of a job?

Lord Islington's body was still warm when we all
trooped back to Rushbrook Hall to start the tedious task
of unpacking all the boxes once bound for Spain. A

month later my job finished and I was on a train back to Norfolk. As the train puffed its way across the fens, my dream of a new life in Spain grew more distant with every mile passed. And by the time I walked down the Lynn Road, a heavy January fog cloaking the fields in a grey drizzly gloom, it had vanished.

With each weary, rain-sodden step I took, fresh waves of humiliation and frustration washed over me. I had bragged to anyone who would listen about my grand job. What's more, I'd given up a perfectly good job to join that household. I couldn't just go back to Woodhall and ask for my old job back. Old snooty knickers would have a field day. Besides which, Phyllis had my job now.

What a daft fool I'd been to walk away from that position. Castles in Spain? I really had been painting castles in the sky if I thought I could ever actually live in one!

All along the way neighbours and friends popped their heads out of their doors to call out a cheery greeting.

'Ar ya reet, Mollie love?' cried my mother's friend when she spotted me. 'What you doing here then? I thought you was off to Spain.'

Mortified, I mumbled the whole sorry story about Lord Islington's untimely death. By the time I made it home I must have told that story a hundred times. Had I really boasted to that many people about my future?

Once inside, the door slammed and I collapsed on to a kitchen chair with an exaggerated groan. Mother, busy raking out the coal fire, looked up and raised her eyebrows.

'My life's over,' I sighed dramatically. 'Why did I tell all those people I was off to Spain? I'm going to be a laughing stock. There won't be a person in Downham who won't know of my misfortune by now.'

My head hit the wooden kitchen table with a thud.

'I know what they'll be saying,' I mumbled. 'That'll larn her, old big mouth Mollie with her fancy job.'

Mother simply smiled, wiped her hands on her apron and came and sat next to me. Gently lifting my head up from the table, she cupped my chin in her hands and gazed at me with her lovely soft hazel eyes.

'Chin up, love,' she soothed. 'You're a clever girl with some decent experience under your belt. You'll get a new job in no time. You'll see. How's about I see if I can't rustle up a bit of steak and kidney pudding for your supper tonight?'

Now that really is a sign of a wonderful mother. She'd probably been up cleaning and washing since the crack of dawn and, what's more, my father's health had deteriorated and he was currently having a spell in a sanatorium, but instead of telling me to pull my socks up, she simply offered me words of love, a hug and a big serving of steak and kidney pud. Thank God a mother's love is unconditional or else she'd have been well within her rights to boot me up the bottom.

For the next few days I moped about the place and even Mother's home-cooked suet and apple pudding drowned in double cream couldn't put so much as a flicker of a smile on my sorry face. My brother was irritating me, the relentless rain drumming on the window sills was boring into my skull and all my old school friends were either married with babies or working every hour God sent in apprenticeships.

I thought of Flo. How I longed to see her, but she was working for her marquess at Hatfield House, which was too far to bike.

As always, my mother, quiet force that she was, had the answer. Thanks to her Friday-morning market gossip she knew everyone and everything that went on round our way. I came in from fetching in the eggs from the garden one Friday morning to find one of Mother's friends, Elsie Jackson, and her husband, Tom, sitting warming their feet by the fire.

'Hello, Mollie.' Elsie smiled brightly when I walked in. 'Bumped into your mother at the market. Happen I heard of your misfortune. What a shame. Spain's supposed to be a lovely place, so they say.'

My heart sank. Did everyone have to know everyone's business round these parts?

'Tom here's a chauffeur up at Wallington Hall. They're looking for a cook. If you're looking, that is.'

I frowned. 'Cook? I'm not sure I'm up to that just yet, Elsie,' I said, putting the eggs down carefully on the table. 'Besides, I'm only twenty. I can't run a kitchen.'

'Course you can,' smiled Mother. 'I've seen your cooking. No one can make pastry like you and you're a grafter, all right.'

'Besides,' said Elsie, 'they're desperate. Their cook's ill.'

Mother was sitting forward in her chair now. 'Why not, Mollie?' she urged. 'Try it and if you don't like it, then leave.'

'That's settled then,' said Elsie. 'Tom here'll run you up there directly.'

Tom up until now had done what most men do in the

company of chattering women – he'd stopped listening and dozed off. At the mention of having to leave his comfy fireside seat, his head jerked up.

'What, now?' he spluttered. 'I was looking forward to one of them sausage rolls I can smell cooking.'

Elsie booted him swiftly and, sighing, he stood up. He knew when he was beat. The power of two strong Norfolk women when they've set their mind to something is almost impossible to overcome.

'Come on then, lass,' he sighed, reluctantly dragging himself away from the warmth of the flickering fireside. 'Let's see if we can't make a cook of you.'

On the way I had a think about it. A cook's job at a country estate was a big job all right, and virtually unheard of at my age, but what did I have to lose? I'd learnt a lot at Mrs Jones's side and cut my teeth on her apron strings, so to speak. And just like that, with all the exuberance of youth, I bounced back from my Spanish setback and set my sights on a bigger goal.

Wallington Hall was buried deep in the fens around the River Great Ouse and only four-and-a-half miles from my mother's. As we drove, ancient villages with strange names like St John's Fen End, Barton Bendish, Wormegay and Marshland St James whizzed past.

'Wallington's a shooting lodge set in six hundred acres of private grounds,' said Tom. 'Pheasants, duck, geese, woodcock, partridge, pigeon – you name it, they shoot it. It was a shooting lodge for the Earls of Warwick, but it's been in the Luddington family for years now. It was built in 1525, mentioned in the Domesday Book, so it was.'

'Nearly as old as you then, Tom,' I joked.

'Don't you be showing Mrs Luddington your saucy side,' he warned.

We fell into a comfortable silence as we drove through the estate's grounds. The patchwork of fields, woodland, copses and duck ponds was teeming with wildlife. Suddenly the car lurched off the road and started to bump its way through a field. 'Hang on tight,' said Tom as we ricocheted over mole hills. 'No road up to the Hall.'

Through the drizzly January gloom I got my first look at Wallington Hall.

'I'll be,' I gasped, quite spellbound.

Tom glanced sideways and chuckled when he saw my face. 'Quite something, ain't it?' he said.

Looming up out of the misty fields, the Hall rose into the grey skies like something from a Gothic fantasy. Some parts looked to be Tudor, some medieval and other parts eighteenth century. Least that's what Tom had told me. To my untrained eye it just looked big, impressive and dark. It was definitely a house with a story to tell. You got the feeling that there was things, inexplicable forces, watching you from behind the stepped gables and moulded battlements.

'It's haunted, so they say,' nodded Tom.

'Get away,' I laughed.

But he wasn't laughing back.

'No, really, Mollie,' he whispered. 'That there facade hides a grizzly Elizabethan tale of tragedy, betrayal, dark deeds and a slow and agonizing death. Rumour has it there's buried treasure in the parkland too.'

Gobsmacked, I was about to ask more when he brought

the car to an abrupt stop. 'Out you get then,' he said brightly. 'You get this job and you'll be the youngest cook in history, I reckon.'

I gulped. At the mention of slow and agonizing deaths my confidence suddenly seemed to vanish. By the time I knocked on the vast porch door it had all but deserted me.

The door swung open and a butler stared back at me.

This is beautiful Wallington Hall where I worked as a cook. The ancient shooting lodge, set in 600 acres of private grounds, is mentioned in the Domesday Book. It even had its own resident ghost.

'I'm here about the cook's job,' I said, trembling.
He surveyed me coolly.
'I have references,' I added.
'This way,' he said. 'I'll see if the lady of the house can see you now.'

I followed him through the servants' quarters to the servants' hall until eventually I was led through the baize door and on to 'their side of the house'.

I knew from my brief glimpses at Woodhall and Cadogan Square that the other half liked to live opulently, but this was something else. The fireplaces seemed as big as Mother's cottage. Rich and ornate tapestries hung from wood-panelled walls and hardly a spare inch of wall wasn't covered with the head of some poor deer, whose eyes followed me malevolently as I scurried after the butler. Mahogany cupboards groaned with sparkling crystal and family silver, no doubt heirlooms passed down through the generations.

Finally I was taken into the drawing room and told to wait. Not since watching *Frankenstein* at the cinema had I felt this unnerved. I half-expected a ghoul carrying his own head to walk into the room! A grandfather clock ticked ominously in the corner and some poor stuffed stag stared down at me from on high. Gripping my references tightly, I shifted uncomfortably in my chair.

'What are you looking at?' I muttered at the stag, half-wondering if I wouldn't end up in the same predicament myself.

The door swung open and in walked one of the prettiest and most flustered ladies I'd seen in a long while. She smiled warmly and I instantly relaxed.

'Good morning,' she said, holding out a slender pale hand. 'My name's Nell Luddington and you must be Mollie.'

She was as fragile as a fawn with kind brown eyes smiling out from under arched eyebrows. She can't have been that much older than me. I later found out she was just twenty-six, but her expensive silk blouse and tweed skirt, coupled with her impeccable manners, made her seem much older.

'My husband and I are in the most dreadful predicament,' she said, just as a young hallboy brought in a tray of tea. I saw myself getting checked out by the boy and knew my ears would be burning the minute he got back to his side of the house.

'Our cook is quite ill with pneumonia, poor lady,' went on Mrs Luddington. Pouring the tea, she wrinkled her perfect nose. 'We don't know when or if she'll return.'

I felt like saying, *More like she heard of the ghost and took her leave.* Instead, I just smiled politely.

'We are offering a wage of one pound a week. Will you come and see how you get on, just in the short term? We're frightfully in need. I'm not really sure I know how we're surviving. The butler, bless him, is trying his best, but Mr Luddington is missing his puddings.'

I hesitated.

'We don't go in for a lot of fancy cooking,' she added, pressing a teacup into my hand.

'Well . . .' I began.

The cup of tea was swiftly followed by a ginger snap.

Her brown eyes took on a slight air of desperation. I'll admit it, there was a small part of me enjoying this. Who'd have thought it? Little old Mollie being offered a cook's job at just twenty.

'We've recently bought a fridge,' she said with a last roll of the dice.

A fridge! Well, that settled it. Nowhere I had worked

had ever had the luxury of a fridge. In fact, no one I knew had one. Wait until I told Mother about this.

'I'll take it, Mrs Luddington,' I said, standing up.

'Oh, I am so pleased,' she said with a smile. 'You can start tomorrow, can't you?'

I was about to take my leave when she placed a delicate hand on my arm. 'Just one thing,' she said. 'You don't mind ghosts, do you?'

I gulped and shook my head. Then, with my head still spinning from the speed of my appointment, I stumbled outside to find Tom Jackson leaning over a fence stroking a horse.

'Meet the new cook of Wallington Hall,' I said.

'Well done, Mollie lass,' he grinned. 'I knew you'd do it.'

When I reported for duty the next day, Mrs Luddington welcomed me warmly and gave me a tour of the house and kitchens.

Under a bright winter sun and clear, frosty skies the house took on an altogether different appearance. It really was magnificent. The Hall was surrounded by woodland, fields and lakes for as far as the eye could see. Beautiful thoroughbred horses grazed in the paddocks that surrounded the house. Beyond them, a low mist hung over the lakes and woods.

I honestly think the grounds were the most beautiful I'd ever clapped eyes on. How lucky this woman was to own all this land at just twenty-six.

'If you want to meet my husband you'll usually find him out there, shooting,' she said, gesturing towards the misty woods and arching one perfectly groomed eyebrow.

'Those woods resound to the sound of gunfire,' she said. 'We run a commercial shoot, so you'll find yourself catering for a vast number of shooting parties. That doesn't intimidate you, does it?' she asked.

'Oh no, Mrs Luddington,' I reassured her. 'I'm used to that.'

I knew through local gossip that they charged for shooting parties, unlike Mr Stocks, who just used to open up his land to his friends. Rumour had it she was the niece of an earl and from a very well-to-do family. No doubt that meant she was from old family money, but probably not terribly well off, hence the reason they needed to get an income from the shoot. Her husband, my new boss, was one Major James Hilton Little Luddington (a right mouthful, but fortunately I only had to call him 'sir') and Wallington Hall had been in his family for generations. Mrs Luddington certainly looked like she had the breeding to match his all right, as she turned on her heel and I scurried after her slender, silk-stocking-clad ankles.

'Follow me and I'll show you round the Hall,' she called out.

As she swept down hallway after hallway, rattling off conversation like gunfire, I struggled to keep up with her. My eye was turned, you see, by the beautiful paintings and artefacts adorning the walls and sideboards. Large oil paintings of stern-looking men with bushy moustaches astride magnificent hunting horses stared down at me. This was better than the V&A. Imagine living surrounded by all this splendour.

My eyes were drawn to a magnificent painting of one of her husband's ancestors as I bustled after her. I didn't notice that she had stopped and I smacked clean into her.

'Sorry,' I blustered. 'Just gawping at all your beautiful things.'

'You are up to the cook's job?' she said, narrowing her brown eyes. 'You are awfully young, after all.'

Come on, Mollie. Get it together.

'Of course I am, Mrs Luddington,' I said in my most businesslike tone. 'You can count on me.'

'Good,' she said briskly, drawing herself up. 'Now, as well as the shoots you will have to cater for myself, my daughter Sarah, who's five, Ted, who's three, and our new baby, Johnnie.'

Baby? This didn't look like a woman who'd just given birth. She was whippet thin. Then again, this was the gentry. She had legions of staff and no end of time to recuperate. I doubted she'd have got out of bed for at least two weeks. Makes me laugh. I was back doing the housework the day after my first child was born. No such fate for Mrs Luddington.

'Besides us, you will need to cater for our nanny, Connie, our under nanny, two housemaids, the butler, the footman and a kitchen boy, who is there to help you, of course. Tom, our chauffeur, and his wife live in one of our cottages on the estate, as do the groundsmen, gamekeeper and gardeners, so you shan't need to worry about them.'

I gulped and smiled as brightly as I could. That was an awful lot of cooking by anyone's standards.

'You'll find me here in the day nursery most of the time,' she said, gesturing to the door behind her. 'Of course, I will meet you each morning in my office to go through the day's menus at ten thirty prompt.'

I idly wondered what the nanny and under nanny were like. I knew domestic staff could be a bit sniffy about nannies, as if, because they lived on 'their side' of the house, they somehow thought themselves above their station. Well, I didn't give two hoots for all that nonsense. I'd take them as I found them, as I did everyone.

As we marched back down the corridor I suddenly felt the temperature plunge and I shivered.

'Did you notice that?' Mrs Luddington asked, pausing and placing one delicate hand on a thick wooden door.

'Yes,' I said. 'Why's it so much colder here than anywhere else? I feel like a cold chill's just run down my back.'

'Aah,' said Mrs Luddington, a little smile playing on her face. 'I see I'm going to have to explain all about our resident ghost, who unfortunately resides in the bedroom right below yours.'

'A ghost?' I quaked.

'Do you believe in ghosts, Mollie?' she went on, her brown eyes boring right into mine. Suddenly I found myself shifting uncomfortably. 'I'm rather afraid that most of the servants do tend to believe in ours.'

'I . . . well, yes, that is to say no . . . maybe?' I stuttered.

Unfazed by my obvious nerves, she went on: 'In the mid-1500s a lady by the name of Elizabeth Coningsby inherited Wallington and then married a rather unpleasant-sounding man by the name of Sir Francis Gawdy.

'Sir Francis was an infamous judge who sat on the commission which tried Mary, Queen of Scots, at Fotheringhay in 1586 and was a member of the court which condemned

Sir Walter Raleigh in 1603. I rather fear Elizabeth was a perpetual affliction to Sir Francis, who by a trick of the law managed to possess himself of his wife's estate.

'He also destroyed a whole village to make way for all our beautiful parkland and converted the local church to his dog kennel. You can imagine this made him somewhat unpopular with the locals, so much so that after his death he was refused burial and was eventually flung without ceremony into the churchyard nearby and covered in a heap of stones. Before his death he was rumoured to have buried his fortune somewhere in the grounds.'

'Buried treasure?' I gasped, wide-eyed, suddenly remembering what Tom had told me. 'And what about his wife?' I asked.

'She met a tragic end in this room,' Mrs Luddington sighed. With that, she pushed open the heavy door to reveal a small, chilly bedroom.

My heart leapt into my throat. 'Urgh,' I gasped, startled. There was just such a hideous presence. Such a deep, festering feeling of misery that seemed to rise up from the floorboards in waves.

'After a local uprising she locked herself in here to escape, but once the rioters dispersed she found herself too weak to unbolt the door. Her own staff deserted her to join the rioters.

'She perished miserably from hunger and thirst right there on the floor. Apparently her ghost has been sighted wandering in this part of the house – a small, grey and spiteful figure in Elizabethan dress.'

I stood rooted to the spot in silence. 'What a truly horrible story,' I gasped eventually. 'Poor woman! Despised by her husband and then left to rot and starve to death in her own home. No wonder she can't move on, poor wretched soul.'

'Yes, it is rather a sorry tale, isn't it?' agreed Mrs Luddington. 'Could have leapt from the pages of a historical novel. Except, of course, it all actually happened right here.'

Suddenly I felt quite depressed.

'Still,' smiled Mrs Luddington brightly, 'I'm sure you'll be much happier here than poor old Elizabeth Coningsby.'

I hoped so!

That night, as I drifted off to sleep with a blanket over my head, the fact that for the first time ever I had my own bedroom was totally lost on me. I was sleeping slap bang over a scorned ghost. The wind rushing through the branches outside sounded eerily like the soft moaning of a dying woman. And if I listened really hard, over the soft hooting of an owl that drifted through the night sky, could I make out the faint sound of scratching? *A desperate woman clawing at the locked wooden door below?*

'Get away, Mollie,' I scolded myself. 'You're daft as a brush. It's just mice.'

This was a strange old place with its haunted bedrooms and buried treasure in the grounds! I'd never been anywhere quite like this before.

I eventually drifted off, with disturbing images of rioters and headless horses galloping through my dreams. The next morning I was exhausted, but the sound of a small tap at the door woke me up.

'Half past six,' called out a boy's voice, followed by retreating footsteps.

I opened the door to find someone had left a cup of tea for me, just as I always had for Mrs Jones.

'I could get used to this,' I grinned blearily, picking up the steaming mug of tea.

After my tea and a bracing wash with freezing cold water from a jug, I felt much better, almost ready to take on the day, scorned ghosts and all. Carefully, I took my new uniform out from the wardrobe and held it up like it was made of butterfly wings. Talk about proud! Mrs Luddington and I had come to an agreement that instead of buying me a new cook's uniform I could use my cousin Kathleen's old nursing uniform. I had three pure cotton knee-length dresses, two in brown, one in mauve, and all with pristine starched white aprons.

Aunt Kate had given them to me when her daughter, my cousin, had dropped out of a nursing apprenticeship at Guy's because she'd been unable to cope with the workload. She might have been too soft and let them go to waste, but I wasn't about to. Mrs Luddington and I both agreed that with a little alteration they'd make perfect cook's uniforms. I think she'd been secretly a bit pleased at not having to fork out for a new one.

By the time I'd dressed myself in a brown one and smoothed down my white apron, I felt the bee's knees. I was determined to do my best. I was cook now, after all. *Queen of the kitchen at last!*

Walking down the narrow back stairs, I found myself whistling despite the ungodly hour. Mrs Beeton wrote (and I do agree with this): 'It is a thousand times tested truth that without early rising and punctuality good work is almost impossible. A cook who loses an hour in the morning is likely to be toiling all day to overtake tasks that would otherwise have been easy.' She was right as always. Cooks have to steal a march on the day and that always meant rising before the rest of the household stirred.

If you're wondering why I was so cheerful, despite living over a ghost and the prospect of a mountain of work, it was because, quite simply, I was the boss now. No one can understand it, unless you have been a skivvy that is, that enormous feeling of pride that comes with rising up through the ranks and knowing you are no longer a dogsbody. Here the lady of the house spoke more than just two words to me. Thanks to my rise from kitchen maid to cook, I actually mattered here. No more scrubbing, plucking or being talked down to for me.

Walking into the kitchen, I looked around and smiled. It was big and dominated by the usual vast scrubbed oak table; copper pans hung from the stone walls and a beautiful cream and black Aga dominated one wall. And, joy of joys, we had a fridge, an actual fridge. No more packing great chunks of ice in a lead-lined box and nearly freezing your fingers off just to reach the milk. When I tell you that even as late as the 1940s only 25 per cent of homes had fridges, you will see what a rarity ours was in 1937. The price of such luxuries simply put it beyond the means of most families, so food was kept cold on a marble slab at the back of the larder, in iceboxes or outdoors.

A housemaid was on her hands and knees scrubbing at the wood floor with a bar of carbolic soap, but when she spotted me she jumped to her feet.

'Can I get you another cup of tea?' she asked nervously. 'Er . . . what shall we call you?'

I laughed. 'Well, Mollie, of course.'

The kitchen boy, who could only have been about fifteen, shot out of nowhere and presented a cup of tea to me.

'Already done it,' he snapped at the young girl. 'Here you go, Mollie.'

I could definitely get used to this. They were actually talking to me and looking at me with respect. I smiled back warmly. I wasn't going to have any of that snootiness that I had experienced. As long as they pulled their weight I would talk to them like they were my equals. What was the point of being horrid or sarcastic to them? I'd had enough of that treatment to know it wasn't nice to be on the receiving end of a telling-off.

I'd like to be able to tell you what that nervous girl's name was and the butler, footman and other staff of the house for that matter, but I can't. The memory of them is expunged from my brain because, quite simply, there was too much else going on in there at that time. Because from that moment on, and for the next two years, I worked harder than I have ever worked in my life. During the day my routine was like a more intense version of a soldier in the army. Every minute and second was accounted for and it's a wonder my poor old brain didn't burst.

A typical day went something like this:

6.30 a.m.   Wake when kitchen boy knocks and leaves tea.

8.00 a.m.   Cook staff breakfasts.

8.30 a.m.   Cook breakfast for children and nannies in the nursery.

9.00 a.m.	Get Mr and Mrs Luddington's and visitors' breakfast ready.
9.30 a.m.	Clear down breakfast and plan and write up day's menus.
10.30 a.m.	Meet with Mrs Luddington and go through menus.
11.00 a.m.	Start cooking lunches so children and their nannies can eat at 1.00 p.m. in the day nursery and the Luddingtons at 1.30 p.m.
2.00 p.m.	Staff lunch.
2.30 p.m.	Clear down after lunch.
3.30 p.m.	Start making afternoon tea for Luddingtons and nursery teas. Prep for evening meal.
5.00 p.m.	Start cooking evening meal to be served to the Luddingtons at 8.00 p.m.
8.00 p.m.	Evening meals must be ready for butler to take to dining room.
8.30 p.m.	Staff evening meal.
9.00 p.m.	Have pudding ready for butler to take through and cheese, biscuits and coffee ready.
9.30 p.m.	Clear down evening meal and then off duty. Play cards, order food, plan more meals or read. (Sometimes I'd get to go to a dance and I could leave earlier on those occasions. Doors to Wallington Hall were always locked at 10.30 p.m. sharp so you had to be back for then.)

It was a hectic schedule and there was no time for dawdling. I was always to be found scurrying around the kitchen, flushed as red as a tomato, pencil behind my ear, a half-drunk cup of tea going cold on the kitchen table as I struggled to keep my eye on the ball.

But back to my first day.

I started on the staff breakfasts – easy, I could do those with my eyes shut. I rustled up eggs, bacon, kedgeree, sausage, toast, mushrooms and black pudding for nine people including the two nannies, followed by breakfast for the 'other side' of the house – more cooked breakfast for Mr and Mrs Luddington and boiled eggs and soldiers for the children.

Then I sat down and drew up the menus for the rest of the day. Checking the larders, I noticed we were running worryingly low on food supplies and some of the meat didn't look all that bright neither. I made a mental note to swap supplies from their current butcher to Harcourts, where my uncle worked. Well, you've got to do right by your family, haven't you?

I drew up a tasty-sounding lunch menu of mushroom soup, followed by roasted venison with all the trimmings. What was it Mrs Luddington had said her husband had, a sweet tooth? I put down a trifle, fruit salad and apple crumble for pudding. He had to fancy one of those. No man could resist Mollie's trifle. Then we'd have cheese and biscuits.

Dinner was more of the same except a bit fancier. I'd make some of those nice savouries that Mr Stocks had when he was entertaining, a consommé, a lovely bit of sea bass and roasted pheasant, and perhaps my mother's special recipe for steamed suet pudding with apples and cream.

How could they resist?

I duly presented my menu to Mrs Luddington at our ten thirty a.m. meeting in her office.

'This sounds lovely, Mollie,' she said with a smile.

This was easy.

I stood up, beaming, and was just about to leave when she called me back.

'In two days' time my husband has a shooting party coming down from London for the rest of the week. There will be ten in all to cater for, as well as the beaters and the groundsmen, and meals for the household, of course.'

I paled.

'Is that OK?' she asked, tapping her notebook impatiently.

'Course, Mrs Luddington,' I said. 'As you wish.'

I walked back through the baize door, my legs shaking, and saw the hallboy and kitchen maid look up nervously at me. Suddenly for the first time I realized perhaps why Mrs Jones had always been flustered and grumpy. This was an awful lot of responsibility, especially for one so young. I had nearly twenty-five people to cook breakfast, lunch and dinner for day after day for a week. I couldn't afford to get it wrong either. No wonder she could be a little sour at times!

'Right,' I bellowed. 'We've got a lot to do this week. Mr Luddington has a shooting party coming. Let's get to it.'

From that moment on I barely drew breath. At just twenty I was in a position of huge responsibility, but I didn't worry as much about it as I would if I were, say, forty. I daresay if you were looking nowadays to talk to a cook in service in a big house in the 1930s, you wouldn't find any alive as most of them were in their forties and fifties. There's probably only Flo and me left who can recall this age. We both made cook's position in our twenties, which was rare.

I do feel, though, that youth served me well back then. I just got on with it. I channelled my fizzing energy into conjuring up feasts three times a day, seven days a week. By the end of that first week, mind you, I was beat. Parts of my body throbbed that I hadn't known existed. I had mashed, scrambled, stirred, basted, sliced and diced, all the while keeping my eye on five different bubbling pans and my mind focused on what needed doing next.

On the first day of the shoot I'd sent out twenty portions of hare soup, piping hot Irish stew, apple pie and bread and butter pudding for dessert followed by cheese and biscuits, baked potatoes and salt beef sandwiches for the beaters and groundsmen, shepherd's pie for the children, then for dinner twenty servings of consommé, lemon sole, roast beef and all the trimmings, followed by trifle, spotted dick and savouries. All totally home-made and all made from scratch without the use of any kind of electronic equipment. I'm not saying this to brag. I just want people to know how different cooking was back then compared to now. We didn't have blenders, microwaves, steamers, electric kettles, electric whisks or food processors. Nothing could be made at the touch of a button. Everything was whisked, stirred, grated, chopped, beaten and blended by hand. By me! I grafted, and I mean properly grafted, to cook feasts and all from scratch. I do think the food tasted better for it too.

Fortunately all the plates came back clean, no one choked on a stray bone and Mrs Luddington even sent the butler down to tell me how well the food was received.

At the end of the shooting party I was just about to haul myself up the back staircase to bed when I realized that I hadn't even made a start on ordering food for the next month! Woe betide we ran out. There were no supermarkets nearby we could just nip to, to top up supplies. Everything had to be individually ordered from local stores and bread and meat from local bakers and butchers. Fortunately the Luddingtons got all their creamy milk in fresh from a local farm they owned and vegetables came from the magnificent kitchen garden that backed on to the house. I stayed up until nearly midnight making sure I knew exactly what supplies we had in and just what we needed. I remembered how Mrs Jones knew to within an ounce how much sugar, butter and flour she had and seemed to instinctively know when to get more supplies and by how much to keep her going.

My brain was so fuddled I got in a dreadful muddle trying to make sense of it.

The next day I had a half-day off. After lunch it was all I could do to drag my weary body back to my mother's, but even then I didn't rest. I took my order book so I could run over my supplies and make sure I had it just so. Once there, I let myself in, rested my head on the kitchen table and within seconds felt myself drifting off.

'Knock knock,' came a cheery Welsh voice from the back door.

'Mrs Jones!' I gasped. 'What brings you here?'

'Half-day off, Mollie. Thought I'd come and see how

you're getting on.' Now she was no longer my boss she was certainly a lot more pleasant to me.

'You haven't changed a scrap,' I smiled.

'Fancy you have, Mollie,' she smiled back. 'When you started at Woodhall you couldn't cook water and now look at you. So, how you finding it?'

'It's pretty hard keeping on top of it all,' I confessed. 'I don't know how you've done it for so many years.'

She chuckled and patted my arm. 'Think you can cope?'

'I reckon,' I said, rubbing my eyes. 'I'll say this though. It's a lot easier having a boss than being a boss.'

Mrs Jones's rotund body shook like a jelly as she heaved with laughter. 'I won't say I told you so, but don't worry. You were trained by the best. Now come on, lass, move over and let's talk over your provisions and check you've got all you need so as you don't run short.'

The softening of Mrs Jones was a godsend and I picked her brain on many an occasion after that. She and I even became friends, regularly meeting at my mother's for afternoon tea on our half-days off or going to see films like *Gone With the Wind* at the Regal in Downham. For all the lip I gave her, and all my antics, I like to think she was as fond of me as you would be a cheeky niece.

That night, back at Wallington Hall, when my head finally hit the pillow, it wasn't ghosts and buried treasure chasing through my dreams but sinking soufflés and burnt saucepans dancing before my eyes.

By the end of that first month I felt more like a conductor in an orchestra than a cook in a big house. I lived and breathed food. Every plate had to be turned out to perfection and my brain was razor sharp. I regularly found myself stirring consommé with one hand and basting meat with the other. And before each service I would lay all my utensils out like a surgeon does before he operates.

Mistakes just couldn't happen. They're not easy to rectify when you haven't got a microwave or blender or any other labour-saving device to hand. The only time I did make a mistake was when my meringues didn't rise. Cooking food in an Aga where you can't control the temperature is very tricky, but I always managed somehow to bluff it. Pavlova often became Eton Mess, crushed up and served with strawberries and cream, to disguise a saggy meringue. I got away with it, mind, as at the end of the month Mrs Luddington called me into her office.

'I'm frightfully pleased with your progress, Mollie. You're a very good cook for such a young woman.'

'I was trained by the best,' I grinned.

'Would you please stay on?' she urged. 'I don't think our cook is ever going to be well enough to return.'

The offer of a permanent job was beyond my wildest dreams. Once I got used to the workload, I actually began to really enjoy it. I even began to get a bit experimental, cooking such delicacies as beef Wellington. Mother bought me my own copy of *Mrs Beeton's Book of Household Management* and in time it became so well thumbed it actually fell apart.

It was all utterly marvellous. I was my own boss. As long as I got all the meals out ready for the butler to take through, three times a day, then the evenings were my own. I earned a pound a week (a fortune for a twenty-year-old in 1937), ran a kitchen that looked out over

321

glorious parkland and I even had a fridge. Better yet, Mrs Luddington was a really lovely woman and didn't affect any airs and graces. I didn't see much of her husband, but she actually took time to treat me like a human being. I like to think it's because I always took time to get things right and go the extra mile that she was so sweet to me.

Here I am, a fresh-faced cook, aged about twenty-two.

After my first Christmas there she even came 'below stairs' and handed me a beautifully wrapped gift of a silk scarf and buttery soft brown leather gloves. 'Just a little something to show our appreciation, Mollie,' she'd smiled.

'We'd hate to think you were unhappy and wanted to leave.'

I was nearly at a loss for words when I unwrapped the beautiful presents and couldn't wait to get them home to show Mother. I even stopped and got Father a bottle of whisky out of my wages.

'I am so proud of you, Mollie,' Mother said.

Sadly things weren't looking quite so rosy for my father. His 'bad spells', as my mother called them, were becoming more and more frequent. His face wore a permanently haggard and drawn look and you got the feeling he was hiding the worst of it. The explosive coughing fits he had were now so frequent, all you could do was rub his back and get the cloths ready for when the blood bubbled out of his mouth.

'This is for you, Dad,' I said proudly, handing him the bottle of whisky I'd bought. 'Cost me nine and sixpence out my wages. Thought it would do your lungs good.'

Sadly, if you've been gassed by the Germans it takes more than a wee dram of whisky to make you feel normal again.

'Bless you, Mollie,' he croaked, stroking my hair and shaking his head. 'My little Mollie all grown up and a cook for a grand family. What about that?'

'Yeah,' I laughed. 'Bet old PC Risebrough would have a blue fit if he knew.'

Despite my success in the kitchen, I was still no closer to finding the love that eluded me. Where were the husband and kiddies to call my own?

True, there were no fascist bodyguards or explosive

footmen here, but there wasn't much in the way of men full stop, unless you counted the odd weather-beaten farmer.

Not that I didn't get my share of offers, mind you . . .

I'll never forget the grand high-society wedding we hosted at Wallington Hall and all the saucy scenarios it threw up. That was an eye-opener all right on the comings and goings of the other half.

Major James's sister, Anna, was to be married, and the Luddingtons had agreed to host the wedding at Wallington Hall. Mrs Luddington broke the news to me over our morning meeting.

'We will of course be getting in caterers, as even you can't cater for that many, Mollie,' she said. 'But we'd be honoured if you could make the wedding cake.'

'Oh, I'd be delighted,' I gushed, secretly thinking that I'd never actually made a wedding cake before. That was a real measure of my confidence back then. I'd never attempted a wedding cake, but I reasoned it couldn't be that hard. Like anything in cooking, planning is key. I realized if I made it a fruitcake I could make the actual cake weeks in advance, then ice it nearer the time.

As I busied myself baking, Wallington became a hive of activity. The wedding seemed to breathe new life into the estate. The butler and housemaids were working non-stop as a stream of family silver came below stairs to be cleaned. A huge marquee went up in the parkland outside, teams of gardeners tended to the grounds and countless bottles of champagne were placed in the scullery to keep cool. The Hall hummed with nervous anticipation and the smell of fresh roses and carbolic soap wafted down its wood-panelled corridors.

By the time a steady stream of Daimlers and Rolls-Royces bumped over the fields on a sunny summer morning, the old Hall was in a state of near nervous exhaustion. Many of the Luddingtons' close friends were staying in the Hall for a few days over the period of the wedding festivities and a lot had arrived the day before. Most of them were society folk and the servants' hall had been alive with gossip about them.

''Ere, there's a famous society lady staying in one of the guest bedrooms,' said the young housemaid one morning. 'Verity's her name. Ever so pretty she is. You should see her clothes, so delicate and fine. She's got the most beautiful skin, too.'

I had heard of her and seen her in the society pages of the newspapers too.

Soon after, I had my own brush with the other half. I was just finishing off the icing on the top tier of the wedding cake and had stood back to admire it when the door to the kitchen swung open.

'Well, that really is a thing of beauty,' drawled a deep voice.

I twirled round to find myself staring at a man named Johnnie. Johnnie was one of Mr Luddington's friends. He often came down from London to stay at weekends. I'd also seen him at Wallington before on shooting parties and I reckoned he fancied himself. By the way his eyes roamed over my body, I could see that wasn't all he fancied. He was also clutching a half-drunk champagne bottle in one hand and his dog's bowl in the other.

'I say, Mollie,' he said, weaving his way across the

kitchen. 'You don't mind if I call you Mollie, do you? I just need to fill up my dog's bowl with water.'

'No, sir, that's fine,' I said nervously.

'Don't call me sir.' His red face came within inches of mine. The smell of booze on his breath made my eyes sting. 'Just call me Johnnie, why don't you?' he said softly and winked at me. 'I do so love this glorious red hair of yours, Mollie.' With that, he set down his champagne bottle and dog's bowl on the kitchen table and took a lock of my hair in his fingers.

Suddenly I became aware of his other hand, snaking round behind until it came to rest on my bottom.

'Do you know what room I'm staying in, Mollie?' he leered, giving my bum a hearty squeeze.

Johnnie may have been stinking rich, but to me he was just stinking.

'Get yer hands off me!' I said loudly, pushing him away. 'You'll get me the sack, you will.' I laughed it off so as not to create a situation but as Johnnie retreated from the kitchen, I was bristling.

Daft toff, who did he think I was?

He may have been handsome, rich and still only in his twenties, but I wouldn't have dared risk a dalliance with Johnnie. I'd have been given my marching orders if Mrs Luddington ever found out.

Thankfully, the rest of the wedding passed without incident. The bride looked glorious, the sun shone, and when the butler and the footman took my three-tier cake outside and placed it on a table dressed with white roses, I felt proud as punch.

The sound of upper-class voices, the clinking of champagne glasses and a swing band rang out over the fields until night sneaked in over the estate. As we were cleaning up the kitchen at the end of the evening, the butler came in carrying an ice bucket containing a few bottles of champagne.

'Compliments of Mrs Luddington,' he said, popping a cork and pouring all the staff a glass of champagne.

'She was ever so impressed with the cake, Mollie,' he smiled, handing me a glass. 'To a job well done,' he added, raising his champagne flute aloft.

'A job well done,' we all agreed. I raised the glass to my lips and took a sip. Spluttering, I set the glass down. 'Blimey,' I giggled. 'The bubbles just went right up my nose.'

You might find this hard to believe, but I had never touched so much as a drop of alcohol before, much less fancy French champagne. Women, at least not respectful women, just didn't.

It was curious how, after just a few sips, a warmth snaked down my chest and I found my voice growing a little louder. 'S'good stuff this,' I slurred, taking another healthy swig from the glass.

Within half an hour I was roaring drunk.

'Tresshure . . .' I slurred, gesturing wildly with my hands. 'Buried tresshure . . . s'out there in s'dark.'

The butler looked baffled as I weaved my way to the back door of the servants' quarters.

'Off to find tresshure,' I said, making a lunge for the handle and missing.

Eventually I staggered out into the dark of the night and was seized with a sudden desire to cycle home to

Mother's. It was pitch black out there in the fields as I swerved like a maniac to avoid the bushes that seemed to loom up out of nowhere. I had no lights and still managed to cycle nearly five miles home, drunk as a lord. I don't remember much of anything after that. How I got home unscathed is nothing short of a miracle.

When I awoke in the morning it was to the realization that I hadn't stumbled across Sir Francis's hidden hoard of treasure, but I did have an absolutely cracking hangover.

Mother chuckled when she saw me in my old bed.

'Looks like someone had a good time last night,' she said. 'Whatever do you look like?'

Groaning, I lifted my head off the pillow and peeled my eyes open. My eyeballs throbbed and my mouth was as dry as a sun-baked ditch.

'Why do people drink when it leaves you feeling this wretched?' I whispered. 'I'm sick as a dog.'

'Shouldn't you be back at Wallington making breakfasts?' said Mother.

Hells bells, I was late!

Getting on my bike, I pedalled like the wind, all the while seized with the urge to stop and vomit into a hedgerow. Never in all my life have I felt as sick as I did that morning after the wedding. Why people drink is utterly beyond me. I have never touched so much as a drop of champagne since.

That morning, I turned out nearly fifty rounds of kippers, growing greener by the second. My stomach was churning when the housemaid rushed in, brimming over with excitement. She was obviously oblivious to my pain as she screeched at the top of her voice, 'You'll never guess whose socks I found at the bottom of Miss Verity's bed!'

I stared blankly.

'You know,' she urged. 'That society lady.'

'Whose?' asked the kitchen boy, eager for any snippet of gossip.

'Only Mr Johnnie's,' she giggled. 'I know they're his as they've got a sort of grey lining.'

The staff were full of it.

'Never!' gasped another housemaid. 'Dirty old scoundrel.'

Silly old Johnnie. You really couldn't keep anything hidden from the servants! Whether Mrs Luddington ever found out about randy Johnnie and her friend Miss Verity I don't know, but I daresay he wasn't the only one who couldn't keep it zipped up. Nevertheless, the wedding was a resounding success for Wallington Hall and the Luddington family and I was very proud to have played my part in it.

'We're all going out on Mr Luddington's boat for the day,' Mrs Luddington announced one morning, not long after the wedding. I knew Mr Luddington had a boat he liked to take out on the Norfolk coast, and he'd often return at dusk with some big old fish he'd slap down on the kitchen table for me to gut, fillet and serve up for dinner. Now it seemed the whole family was going to enjoy some time out. 'Why don't you take the day off?' Mrs Luddington continued with a smile. 'You deserve it.'

'Thank you, Mrs Luddington,' I replied. 'Very generous.'

Finding myself in the rare position of having nothing to do, I strolled across the parkland to find Tom the chauffeur leaning over a fence and stroking the mane of one of Mr Luddington's magnificent horses. Joining him, I stroked the horse's velvety neck. Taking fright, he flared his nostrils, tossed his mane back and took off over the fields.

'Thoroughbred,' explained Tom. 'He's a booty all right, but a flighty one, make no mistake. Won't let anyone ride him. Everyone's tried, even Mr Luddington, but no one can stay on him for long,' he chuckled. 'They all end up face down in the dirt.'

Uh-oh. There was that feeling! The same feeling I always got when there was a challenge or dare being issued. The words were out of my mouth before I had a chance to stop myself.

'Happen I can,' I boasted. 'I'm brilliant with horses. I know all about them. I spent my childhood riding them.'

'You?' spluttered Tom. 'Don't talk daft, Mollie. You're just a slip of a girl. You'll never stay on him.'

The human condition really is a funny thing, isn't it? The strange processes that go round the old grey matter. As soon as someone tells me I can't or shouldn't or won't do something, it quickly becomes nothing short of irresistible.

'Just watch me,' I said, climbing the fence and swinging my leg over. 'I'm not afraid of anything or anyone, including this horse.'

'This should be fun,' Tom laughed, following me into the field.

Tiptoeing up to the creature, I placed one hand gently on his quivering nose. 'Steady boy,' I soothed, stroking his trembling neck.

Tom was right. He really was a beauty. His chiselled neck and gleaming mane glistened with drops of rain and his high withers moved with the grace of a dancer. No matter that I'd only ever ridden a carthorse before. After dealing with a creature as frisky as Alan, my temperamental footman, I could cope with this beast!

'Give us a leg-up,' I whispered to Tom, who was hovering behind me.

Gently holding on to the horse's neck with my left hand and throwing my right arm over his back, I put my left foot into Tom's cupped hands and propelled my body up and over, on to the thoroughbred's magnificent back.

I'd made it. I was on!

Gulping, I realized the ground looked quite far away from up here. I stroked the horse's mane and straight away he started to nervously dance about, skittering from side to side.

'Hold on, Mollie,' said Tom. 'He's got that look about him. I think he's going to –'

Suddenly the horse reared up on his hindquarters and, with an outraged snort, took off at full speed.

'– bolt!' cried Tom.

His words were lost on the wind as we careered across the field. The bushes and trees became a blur of green as we thundered along.

'Whoa, boy,' I whimpered, clinging on to his mane for dear life. 'Slow down.'

My heart was in my mouth. We were heading straight towards the edge of the field and the ditch! Oh crumbs. This was going to end badly.

Suddenly I had the strangest sensation of flying.

Everything went into slow motion as the ditch rushed up to meet me. Funny the things that pop into your mind when you know you're about to make a total fool of yourself. I only hoped Mrs Luddington was well on her way to the coast and wasn't around to see her cook hurtling through the air.

I landed face down in the mud with an almighty splat.

'Urghhh,' I groaned as every last bit of breath left my body. And there I stayed for a full minute, my body in shock, as I registered the fact that I was face down in a watery ditch filled with frogspawn and cow dung.

It stank down there!

When I finally peeled my face out of the mud, winded and gasping for breath, I saw Tom standing over me. Tears of laughter were streaming down his ruddy cheeks as he slapped his thigh. 'I thought you said you'd ridden afore, girl?' he hooted.

'Yeah, but only carthorses,' I confessed, picking a bit of congealed frogspawn from my hair. Tom was bent double and clinging to a fence post for support, his whole body shaking with laughter.

'It's not that funny,' I muttered crossly. 'Now help me out of this ditch.'

'I'm sorry, Mollie,' he said, wiping his eyes with an old handkerchief and holding out his hand. 'But your face when he took orf with ya. Funniest thing I've seen all year. Anything injured?'

'Only my pride,' I groaned.

With that, he helped me to my feet and shook his head. 'Just as well you can cook better than you can ride a horse, lass, or we'd all be in trouble.'

Fortunately Mrs Luddington never found out about my encounter with the ditch and it was shortly after this that she gave me a lovely surprise at one of our usual morning meetings.

I found her delicately pulling something from a large white cardboard box. From beneath folds of soft white tissue paper she lifted the most exquisite dress I'd ever seen.

'Oh my,' I breathed. The black dress had a lacy bodice and a full skirt. Layers and layers of soft net sprang out from the tiny waist, and beneath the net I glimpsed a daring flash of scarlet silk.

'What a beautiful dress, Mrs Luddington,' I said. 'Where will you wear that?'

'It's yours,' she said kindly.

'W-what?' I stuttered.

'And this,' she said, reaching into the box and pulling out a soft wool fawn-coloured, tailored suit.

I was utterly gobsmacked. The couture dress and the suit must have cost her hundreds of pounds, and she was giving them to me like they were old buttons.

'I haven't worn them for ages and they're just sitting gathering dust. I rather thought you might like them, Mollie. We're about the same size.'

'Like them?' I gasped. 'I'd love them!'

Never had I owned such beautiful clothes and after dinner service that evening I locked myself away in my bedroom and tried them on. They fitted beautifully. The dress had been made to perfection by a French seamstress. Hours of work must have gone into the bodice and sewing on the layers and layers of fine net. Twirling round in front of the mirror, I laughed as the underskirts lifted up to reveal its dazzling flash of crimson.

This wasn't a dress. It was a masterpiece.

Mrs Luddington was an absolute gem to give something so beautiful away. That goes some way to showing what a lovely lady she was. Most ladies of that era gave their cast-offs to their lady's maid or to a head housekeeper. The fact that she'd given the clothes to me made me feel so special.

Best of all, it wasn't long before I got to show the dress off.

In January 1938 there was a dance at Marham Aerodrome and nothing on earth would have kept me away. The RAF were stationed there and rumour had it there were some good-looking chaps amongst their number. The perfect place to give my new black dress an outing! No matter that it was six miles away or that I'd have to bike there. I was going and, what's more, I was going in *that* dress.

Goodness only knows what I looked like speeding down the country lanes on an old bike in a fancy black dress. The black net and scarlet underskirt billowed in the breeze and with my hair streaming behind me I felt I might take off at any moment. Partridge and all manner of birds burst out of the hedgerows as a more exotic bird sped past them.

Clambering off my bike at the aerodrome, I became aware of someone watching me.

'I simply must have the first dance with you,' announced a well-spoken man.

I looked up to find myself gazing directly into the most

piercing blue eyes I'd ever seen. The owner of the blue eyes stared at me, amused, as I smoothed down the netting on my dress and pushed my windswept hair back into place.

'We'll just see about that,' I shot back as I walked into the hall. I gave him my customary cheek, but inside I already knew I would dance with him because with that one look I'd realized my life was about to change.

It's funny. Sometimes you just know. And from the moment I clapped eyes on Timothy Moran, a corporal in the RAF, I knew he was the one for me. Perhaps it was the flash of my scarlet underskirt as I clambered off my bike that hooked him in, but he seemed as taken with me as I was with him.

No matter that he couldn't dance for toffee and trod all over my feet, he was everything I could want in a man – funny, clever, well spoken without being pompous and handsome to boot. The fact that he was in the RAF had a certain appeal. Who knows if I'd have fallen for him as much if he'd been a farmer, say, but having a fella in the RAF, well, there's a certain glamour and prestige attached to that. As he talked of all the places he was likely to be posted to – Cyprus and the Far East, to name but two – my eyes lit up.

My handsome young corporal had been well educated at a Jesuit public school in Lincolnshire.

'My mother had high hopes I'd join the priesthood,' he confessed halfway through our third dance.

'I'm glad you didn't,' I replied cheekily.

By the fourth dance I'd learnt that his mother had just died and he was desperate to marry and start a family.

By the sixth dance I knew I'd be his wife and the mother of his children.

Timothy was well over six foot tall and his broad shoulders seemed to fill the whole hall. Sighing, I rested my head against his chest and allowed him to waltz me around the aerodrome. Nowhere felt more comfortable or safe. Being with Timothy Moran was like taking a long slow sip of ice-cool water. I could have stared into those startling blue eyes of his all night.

At midnight I happened to glance at the clock and I froze.

'The time!' I gasped. 'I've got to get back to Wallington. I've got to be up at the crack of dawn!'

'I'll see you home,' he smiled.

Together we cycled home in the dark, my heart racing as we sped round every bend. He planted a soft little kiss on my cheek, promised to come and see me soon, then turned round and cycled the sixteen miles back to his base, ten miles the other side of Marham.

Timothy must have weaved some kind of magic over me that night, because from that moment on I was hooked. He came to see me every opportunity he got. If there wasn't much time, we'd grab a flask of tea and some home-baked sausage rolls and sit in the fields near Wallington, or if there was more time we'd head to the pictures. We never had more than a few hours together, but the snatched moments we did have were so precious. His base was sixteen miles away and he got about the same amount of time off as me, so being alone together was rare, which made it all the more enjoyable.

Suddenly I started baking like crazy. I knew from

years of working in kitchens that the way to a man's heart was through his stomach, so on one occasion I presented him with a steamed suet pudding with apples and cream, sneaked out of the back door when no one was looking.

'Heaven,' he moaned when he tasted it. 'I'd bike to the ends of the earth for this.'

The suet pudding was swiftly followed by a steak and kidney pie, then bread and butter pudding and, his favourite, sausage rolls. The kitchen was constantly full of the warm smell of baking and I skipped around the place like a giddy sixteen-year-old, a faraway smile plastered on my face.

No matter that by the time he'd biked over to me it was almost time to turn round and head back for base. He did it for the same reason I started baking like a domestic goddess, because we were falling in love, and love, as we all know, makes you do some very strange things!

He wasn't controlling like Alan or a bigot like my Blackshirt. I quickly learnt he had a bit of a temper all right, but he was strong, confident and ambitious. Above all, he was a man happy in his own skin. I was totally entranced by my handsome airman.

Tom the chauffeur noticed. 'I daresay someone's had their head turned,' he joked one morning as I whistled away, lost in a daydream. Even Mrs Luddington smiled knowingly when we chatted at our morning meeting.

My sausage-roll offensive worked. Hint: if you ever want a man to fall in love with you, start baking!

One evening, four months after we'd met, on a warm

spring evening in May, we were on a bike ride when Timothy stopped straight ahead of me.

'Sit next to me,' he said, dismounting and leaning against an old oak tree. 'I think I may be getting posted to a new station soon,' he confessed. 'I can't bear to think we'll never see each other again.'

'What'll we do?' I cried.

He turned to look at me and tenderly clutched my face in his hands.

'There is a way,' he said breathlessly. 'I know it's soon but . . . will you marry me, Mollie Browne?'

My heart started to thump in my chest. I hesitated. If I said yes, I knew I'd have to leave my job. There was no other way in them days. No married woman in her right mind worked if she didn't have to. I was twenty-one and, what's more, I'd worked hard to make a cook's position so young.

All those hours spent toiling, for what?

But then I looked at those intense cornflower-blue eyes. They seemed to burn right into my soul. A deep wave of contentment spread through my chest. Being with Timothy felt right.

I started to laugh, caught up in the sheer thrill of the moment.

'Well, I'll have to see what my father thinks and it is very soon, but . . .'

Oh, what the hell.

'Yes!' I shouted. 'Yes, I will marry you.'

We laughed like maniacs as we got back on our bikes and cycled down the country lanes back to Wallington Hall. A mad rush of spontaneity gripped me and I took my feet off the pedals like I used to all those years before as a child and whooped into the wind.

'I'm going to get married!'

Back at Mother's house two days later, one look from my father was all it took to pop my bubble of joy.

'It's too soon, Mollie,' he croaked. 'Why do you want to do that?'

Mother shifted uncomfortably beside him. 'Hear her out, love,' she said.

'He's in the RAF,' my father stormed. 'War's in the air, I tell you, and when it breaks out, then what?' On and on he went. 'He'll be all over the place. You'll never see him. He's a fly-by-night.'

Indignant rage boiled up inside me. No one told me what to do.

'Well, I'm marrying him,' I snapped. 'I'm twenty-one now. I can do what I like.'

As I stormed out of the door, Father's words chased after me –

'You can't build a marriage on dreams!'

I'd show him. I'd show them all. Timothy Moran was going places and he was going there with me right by his side. War or no war! So I ignored them all. *I* was master of my own destiny, nobody but me. I hadn't let anyone push me into working in a dull seamstress shop aged fourteen and I wasn't going to be told what to do now.

So the marriage date was set for six months' time, Saturday 5 November 1938. In the event, Timothy wasn't posted away, but with war brewing we knew time was of the essence. Besides, I reasoned, why wait?

A Catholic church was booked in King's Lynn and Granny Esther bought me a beautiful slinky silk wedding dress cut on the bias from Downham Market for twenty shillings. Ordinary folk didn't have big receptions back then, so we planned to invite guests back to Mother's for salmon sandwiches and cake. It wasn't going to be anywhere near as grand as Anna Luddington's wedding had been, but I didn't give two hoots for marquees and champagne. At long last I was marrying a man I loved.

Mrs Luddington wasn't best pleased to be losing her cook, but I think ever since Timothy and I had started courting she'd half-expected it and was ever so nice to me despite me handing in my notice.

As I cooked I found my mind wandering to how handsome my tall fiancé would look all done up in a smart suit, those piercing blue eyes on mine as I was pronounced Mrs Moran.

Cooking and dreaming, dreaming and cooking.

But as I dreamed and schemed, events elsewhere were moving at a rapid pace. Events that were to alter my own destiny and the fortunes of all around me, forever . . . For just as I was planning my wedding, Hitler began his ruthless plan of expansion.

He had pressured Austria into joining forces with Germany and after the Allies agreed in 1938 to allow him to annex Sudetenland, the German-speaking part of Czechoslovakia, German troops had taken the land by autumn of that year. Next, Nazi troops and supporters began destroying Jewish shops in German towns and cities. The Third Reich had openly begun its anti-Semitic operations. War wasn't just brewing, it was imminent. One man who was determined to avoid war and keep the peace at all costs was the British Ambassador to Berlin, Nevile Henderson, one of the most maligned diplomats the UK has ever had.

During his posting to Berlin in the two-year run-up to war, he cabled the Foreign Office to tell them: 'If we handle him [Hitler] right, my belief is that he will become gradually more pacific. But if we treat him as a pariah or mad dog, we shall turn him finally and irrevocably into one.'

Apparently Nevile Henderson was also very sick with cancer during this time and returned to Britain for treatment. It must have been on one such occasion that he was invited to Wallington Hall by Mr Luddington to partake in a shoot. As he headed down to the peace and beauty of Wallington, I was taking my leave of it.

On my last day, Mrs Luddington summoned me to her office and presented me with an exquisite silver tea service.

'Just a little token of our appreciation and to wish you well in your new life,' she smiled.

I was at a loss for words.

'This is just so . . . so generous, Mrs Luddington,' I stuttered.

I could have wrapped her in a big hug. Instead we shook hands politely and said our goodbyes.

I was to stay with Mother in the two-week run-up to my wedding. It was safe to say she was as excited as me about the big day and soon we had filled the kitchen with delicious baking smells and laughter as we cooked up a storm for the reception. I even baked and iced my own three-tier wedding cake.

Six days before, I was just trying on my wedding dress to show Mother, when there was a knock at the door. There stood the flushed face of Tom Jackson, the chauffeur. He looked like he'd been running and was as red as a beetroot.

'Tom,' I said, 'whatever's wrong? Come in and sit down.'

'You've got to come back, Mollie,' he gasped, gripping the back of the chair as he tried to catch his breath. 'Mrs Luddington's in a right pickle. You look lovely, by the way.'

'Whatever for?' I asked, pulling Tom up a chair and lighting a fire on the stove for tea.

'They've got a big shooting party arriving tomorrow and staying for five days and the new chef has just left them in the lurch. He reckons the kitchen's not smart enough and he can't possibly cook for twenty people on an Aga. What's more, he says he can't do it all with just one kitchen boy for help.'

'What rubbish,' I scoffed. 'I've managed perfectly well this past two years.'

'Exactly! Mollie, please say you'll come back! Mrs Luddington's tearing her hair out. The shooting party's full of VIPs, including the British Ambassador to Berlin, Nevile Henderson.'

'But, Tom,' I said, shaking my head. 'Politician or no politician, it's the week before my wedding. Brides should be making themselves beautiful. Not slaving in a hot kitchen.'

'I know, Mollie,' Tom pleaded, suddenly looking overcome with tiredness. 'We wouldn't ask if we weren't desperate. You're our only hope.'

I glanced over at Mother.

'It's your choice, Mollie,' she shrugged.

I thought of lovely Mrs Luddington and how badly it would look on her if she couldn't supply food to her important guests. She'd been so kind to me, I really couldn't let her down. Perhaps the years I'd spent in the service of the gentry had engrained in me a total devotion, but I knew there was no way on earth I could say no.

'I'll be along as soon as I can,' I sighed. 'Mother, can you help me out of this dress?'

So much for relaxing before my big day. Already my mind was whirring with menus to serve up to Mrs Luddington's VIPs. I didn't know much about Nevile Henderson, other than he had his work cut out trying to negotiate peace with Hitler.

Over the coming days I churned out meal after meal, but on the very last day of the shoot I got to wondering about what I could make for the guns and my final dinner at Wallington Hall.

Fish? Not restorative enough. Pork? Too common. No, Nevile Henderson needed something to put fire in his belly.

Then it came to me. I figured that what that politician needed was a nice hearty bowl of Mollie's Irish stew. That would make him forget his troubles with Hitler all right!

I made a beautiful one by slow-cooking a neck of mutton in the Aga with button onions, potatoes, stock and parsley. The meat was so tender by the time it was ready it looked like it might melt to the touch. I even baked a couple of loaves of crusty bread to mop up the juices with. A great hunk of that served with some fresh salted butter and a piping hot bowl of stew and Hitler would be a distant memory.

By the time the kitchen boy and butler had taken it through to the dining room on a silver tray, I felt quite happy with myself. That poor man had God knows what on his plate when he returned to Berlin. Least I could do was put a good meal in his tummy and fortify him for tough times ahead. I even followed it up with Mr Luddington's favourite – sticky, sweet bread and butter pudding and a jug of fresh cream big enough to drown a German battleship.

Later on I was just clearing away and getting ready to take my leave when Mrs Luddington burst into the kitchen.

'I don't know what you put in that stew, Mollie, but the gentlemen of the shooting party were most impressed and have asked to meet you.'

'Certainly,' I smiled, wiping my hands on my apron and following her through the green baize door into the corridor that led to the dining room. I was never usually invited into these parts!

Mrs Luddington ushered me into the beautiful wood-panelled dining room where ten or so men in tuxedos with their wives sat around an enormous mahogany table. I felt like I should take a curtsey.

Mr Luddington was seated at the head of the table with Nevile Henderson to his right. He was a tall, thin man with a hook nose and bushy moustache. He smiled right at me, an empty plate in front of him.

'Meet Mollie,' said Mrs Luddington. 'She's come to our rescue by cooking for you all and she's getting married tomorrow. Above and beyond the call of duty, wouldn't you say?'

The men clapped politely and smiled at me.

And just like that I was ushered out again.

Back in the kitchen, Mrs Luddington pressed a brown envelope into my hand. 'A tip from our guests,' she whispered.

I had a sneaky look and was stunned to see two large crisp five-pound notes. Ten pounds! Bearing in mind I earned a pound a week, this tip was the equivalent of ten weeks' wages. Perhaps it was down to the high calibre of the guns on the shoot, but I'd never had a tip as generous as this before.

'That's a fortune!' I shrieked. 'I can't accept this.'

'You can and you will,' insisted Mrs Luddington.

Along with the tip was a card signed by all the guns, including Nevile Henderson, expressing their warmest wishes and thanks.

'Well,' she said. 'You deserve it.' She placed her hand on my shoulder and smiled sadly. 'Good luck, Mollie. I hope you are very happy in your new life. Make sure to visit, won't you?'

'I will and good luck to you too, Mrs Luddington.' I smiled back.

We may have come from opposite ends of the social spectrum, but for that brief moment I felt genuine affection and kinship towards her. She was a proper lady through and through.

When I left Wallington Hall that day, on the eve of my new life, I realized something – I may never have discovered Sir Francis's hoard of hidden treasure, but I was still leaving with a fortune.

*

The wedding ceremony went like a dream and afterwards my new husband and I, and all our guests, returned to Mother's for tea.

I was just chatting to a guest when out of the corner of my eye I saw my father sink into a seat. His face had gone

Me and Timothy on our wedding day, Saturday 5 November 1938. We're outside my mother's farmhouse, where we held the reception. Only the day before I'd been cooking for politicians and VIPs.

a deathly grey and I knew a coughing fit was imminent. Rushing to his side, I started to rub his back, when all of a sudden he began to cough uncontrollably and a fountain of blood gushed from his mouth all over my cream wedding dress. A haemorrhage I think they'd call it now, but my poor, poor father – imagine the mortification and pain he must have been in.

'Mollie,' he gasped, horrified, when he spotted my dress. 'It doesn't matter,' I soothed. And it didn't, not in the

This is me, a newly-wed, just before the outbreak of the Second World War. Every so often my husband would take me out to dances and I'd dress up beautifully, always in a hat and pearls.

grand scheme of things. I saw my mother's stricken face and a horrible feeling of doom settled in my stomach. As we raced ever closer to a second world war, the terrible legacy of the first was finally catching up with my father.

I settled down to married life in a cottage near Timothy's new base in Saffron Walden in Essex. Cooking for just one man was certainly a whole lot easier than cooking for an entire household of the gentry. Dare I say it, my life even became one of ease. Rising late, doing a few chores and a bit of housework before cooking Timothy his favourite dinner and a pudding ready to have on the table, piping hot, when he finished work.

Life as a newly-wed was like easing myself into a hot bubble bath and soon I had slipped into a warm and comfortable routine.

In April 1939, five months after our wedding, I even discovered I was pregnant. And I suppose that would have been that, the end of the story. Except life has a funny way of pulling the rug from under your feet when you least expect it.

In some ways we all knew it was about to happen, but it was still a shock when, on 3 September 1939, Prime Minister Neville Chamberlain announced the news that we were at war with Germany. Seems the Irish stew I cooked for our ambassador to Germany, Nevile Henderson, wasn't enough to help him negotiate peace with Hitler.

Life changed in an instant. Timothy was summoned to stay on base where he would remain for the foreseeable future and I packed my bags and returned home to live with Mother. She and Father were in a state of shock and sat glued to the wireless, just as I'm sure everyone did that day.

As I sat stroking my blossoming baby bump, the king's hesitant voice crackled out of the wireless:

'In this grave hour, perhaps the most fateful in our history, I send to every household of my peoples, both at home and overseas, this message, spoken with the same depth of feeling for each one of you as if I were able to cross your threshold and speak to you myself. For the second time in the lives of most of us, we are at war.

The man of my dreams, Timothy, on active service in India, where he was stationed for most of the war. I worried about him out there more than I did about the threat of invasion.

'Over and over again, we have tried to find a peaceful way out of the differences between ourselves and those who are now our enemies; but it has been in vain. We have been forced into a conflict, for we are called, with our allies, to meet the challenge of a principle which, if it were to prevail, would be fatal to any civilized order in the

349

world. It is a principle which permits a state, in the selfish pursuit of power, to disregard its treaties and its solemn pledges, which sanctions the use of force or threat of force against the sovereignty and independence of other states.

'Such a principle, stripped of all disguise, is surely the mere primitive doctrine that might is right, and if this principle were established through the world, the freedom of our own country and of the whole British Commonwealth of Nations would be in danger. But far more than this, the peoples of the world would be kept in bondage of fear, and all hopes of settled peace and of the security, of justice and liberty, among nations, would be ended. This is the ultimate issue which confronts us.

'For the sake of all that we ourselves hold dear, and of the world order and peace, it is unthinkable that we should refuse to meet the challenge. It is to this high purpose that I now call my people at home, and my peoples across the seas, who will make our cause their own. I ask them to stand calm and firm and united in this time of trial. The task will be hard. There may be dark days ahead, and war can no longer be confined to the battlefield, but we can only do the right as we see the right, and reverently commit our cause to God. If one and all we keep resolutely faithful to it, ready for whatever service or sacrifice it may demand, then with God's help, we shall prevail. May he bless and keep us all.'

My father, God bless him, looked exhausted by the end and retired to his hut. Mother had never said as much, but I knew how she worried about him. He'd already survived one war and had witnessed unimaginable loss of life and

horrors in those muddy trenches in France. The poisonous gas he'd inhaled had left him a shadow of the man he'd
once been. Now we were at war with Germany again and
this time it looked like it might be right on our doorstep.

There was a real fear that the Germans would drop
poison gas bombs on us civilians and the government had
already issued thirty-eight million gas masks.

The big question for us was: could my father survive
another war?

Four months after war broke out, in January 1940, I gave
birth to a little girl, Ruth.

She was the sweetest little thing you can ever imagine,
with copper-coloured hair and her daddy's bright blue
eyes. I was utterly entranced from the first time her tiny
fingers curled round mine. When I kissed her musky little
head and breathed in the sweet smell, it didn't matter
to me that we were at war and facing God knows what
dangers. I felt an overwhelming rush of love for this tiny
little soul. Protecting her was all that mattered.

'You'll be safe with Mummy,' I whispered as she slept
in my arms.

Sadly, her daddy didn't get to see her that much. From
the moment war was announced he was informed he was
to wear his uniform at all times and he barely got to leave
base, apart from the odd visit. The RAF was gearing up
for the fight of its life. In some ways my father had been
right when he'd said I'd barely see Timothy. As a corporal
in the RAF during the war, his first loyalty had to be to
king and country.

As little Ruth started to wake up to the world and open

those magical blue eyes, my father took his leave of it. His death, shortly after her birth, hadn't been a surprise. Ever since his haemorrhage on my wedding day he'd been in and out of a sanatorium and seemed to shrink with every passing hour.

That brave man had fought for so long, but the prospect of another war in his lifetime had just been too much for him.

My mother was heartbroken. She'd lost her soulmate.

'How many more good men need to die before we see peace?' she sobbed.

I only thank God her granddaughter gave her a new focus to detract from her grief.

By the time Ruth was two, Timothy had been posted to India and Mother and I had moved to a rented flat in Wisbech, Cambridgeshire. It was nice, but it wasn't Norfolk.

'I'm going to visit friends in Downham,' Mother announced one day. 'Why don't you and Ruth come too?'

It was the perfect opportunity to pay a visit to Mrs Luddington. It had been over two years since we'd last seen each other, but I'd never forgotten her kindness to me. Besides, I couldn't wait to show her my little girl.

Ruth had blossomed into the most adorable little toddler. Her cheeky face and bright blue eyes were topped with a mop of shiny copper curls.

'We're going to a very grand house indeed,' I said as I dressed her in a lemon-yellow Viyella dress I'd made. Lacing her into a little pair of white boots, I stood back to admire her.

'There,' I grinned. 'You look just like Shirley Temple.'

We got the train to Downham and I picked up my old bike from our cottage for the last leg of the journey. By the time I popped Ruth in my wicker basket ready to cycle to Wallington Hall, I was bursting with pride and was looking forward to showing her off to Mrs Luddington.

As I cycled, I reflected on the hugely different times in which we were all living. Everything my former employers cherished was now under threat – no more glittering parties, presentations at court, five-course dinners on a silver service and front steps so clean you could eat your dinner off them. Now we all had to ration and stretch, substitute and make do. Preparing a lavish five-course meal for one man dining alone would be viewed as an extravagant and wasteful habit – selfish, even.

The ways of the old world were changing. A new life was being thrust upon us all. But even I was surprised at the life that had been thrust upon Mrs Luddington.

As I cycled across the fields I was startled to see army vehicles parked outside the magnificent hall. And when I dismounted, I was stunned to see Mrs Luddington frantically waving at me from outside a small workers' cottage on the estate.

'Mollie!' she cried. 'We're over here now. The army have requisitioned the Hall so we're living here.'

As I stared at her I realized with a jolt how different she looked – less groomed and definitely a lot more frazzled. Her three children tore round the garden looking, dare I say it, a little scruffy. The cottage was cramped for all those children and wet clothes were hanging over every surface to dry.

She turned to face me, despair etched over her beautiful face.

'It's gone, Mollie,' she whispered. 'It's all gone.'

'What do you mean?' I asked, shocked.

'This war is terrible. Connie the nanny's been called up to do war work, Mr Luddington is working elsewhere. All the staff have gone. It's just me, on my own, in this little cottage with the children.' Her voice trailed off. 'I'm not really sure I know how I'm coping. It's quite tough, I confess.'

My heart went out to her and, as we sipped tea together, I felt for her, desperately. It wasn't her fault she'd been brought up in a life of privilege and ease. She'd been born with a silver spoon in her mouth and, sadly, it hadn't prepared her for the demands and rigours of this new life. No more nannies, under nannies, champagne, cooks or servants to summon up at the ringing of a bell. Now, for the first time in her life, she had to do it all, alone.

I felt quite guilty as I left.

'You take care of yourself, won't you?' I said.

On the cycle home I was struck by the irony. Working for Mrs Luddington and others like her had prepared me well for this new life. A life of rationing, of stretching and making do and hard, hard work. Oh yes, I knew a thing or two about that. Watching what you ordered and managing food rations was second nature to me, as was making my own clothes. Life was tough, but so was I.

And, as the sun set and Hitler's bombs began to rain down on our once-peaceful land, I knew this was the end of an era.

Something told me I was going to be all right.

TIPS FROM A 1930S KITCHEN

...

Steamed Suet Pudding

The way to a man's heart is through pudding! Men cannot get enough of them. No man, from chimney sweep to lord of the manor, can resist. Give 'em something sticky, sweet, oozing with jam, covered in custard and piping hot and they'll love you forever. My husband's favourite was steamed suet pudding with apples and cream. You can replace the apples with jam, blackberries, raspberries or whatever you fancy.

8 oz (225 g) self-raising flour
4 oz (110 g) shredded suet (you can buy this in packets)
6 large cooking apples
2 tablespoonfuls sugar

Mix flour and suet with a little water to form a firm dough, roll out thinly on a floured board to under half an inch thick and line a pudding basin with it.

Use the scraps and roll out again to make a lid for the pudding.

Cut the apples very finely and lay inside the bowl. Keep layering the apples until the basin is full. Sprinkle with two tablespoonfuls of sugar. Wet the edges of the pastry round the basin and then stick the lid on and seal over. Trim the edges.

Cover with foil or greaseproof paper secured with string, and cook in a saucepan half-filled with boiling water. Keep it simmering for two hours. Once cooked, shake the basin and then carefully turn it out on a plate. Serve with warm custard or cream.

Household Tip

Don't spend a fortune on products designed to tackle limescale. To remove limescale on the end of taps, put two lemon halves on them overnight. Hey presto, sparkly new taps!

Afterword

Today I am ninety-six years old. I may not climb trees or shin down the side of Tudor halls any more, but I've still got a fair bit of life in me. I walk my poodle, Rodney, on the beach and compete in a Scrabble group every Monday. I'm not bad either – I won the Scrabble tournament in December 2011. Ruth, my daughter, says I exhaust her!

I still cook too and I get enormous pleasure from it.

Whenever I host the Scrabble club I cook for thirty people. Some of them worry it's too much for a ninety-six-year-old woman but I love it. It's all in the planning and I make big curries, shepherd's pies and apple crumbles. Old habits die hard!

My 'carrot-top' red hair has long since faded to grey, but the dreams and memories of a long and happy life have yet to fade. I'm very grateful for the adventures I got to experience and the laughter I shared below stairs. And it's not over yet! My mind's still buzzing with plans and I'm forever plotting new adventures, like my next get-together with my dear old friend, Flo Wadlow.

Flo is now one hundred years old and would you believe we're determined to meet up soon for a cup of tea and a chat about old times. Until that happens, we talk regularly on the phone, and boy do we have a laugh! We cackle until the tears are streaming down our faces when we remember climbing out of the servants' quarters at Woodhall to sneak out to the dance that time or the memorable occasion the runaway pheasant burst through the kitchen window, showering glass in the soup!

They really were the best of times and I feel so honoured to have shared them with Flo. She is the most kind-hearted person I know. She's talented too. Do you know, she went on to make cook too, in her twenties. She worked for the Marquess of Lothian at a grand old home called Blickling Hall in Norfolk, where she cooked for, amongst others, the Prime Minister Stanley Baldwin during the abdication crisis and Queen Mary, George V's widow.

Between us we've cooked for royalty, politicians and the gentry. They truly were remarkable times. We could tell the writers of *Downton Abbey* a thing or two, that's for sure!

Here we are, 196 years of experience between us, and still got our wits about us. I put our remarkable good health down to the fact that we have eaten well all our lives. No vegetables stuffed with chemicals or nasty processed food. We've worked hard and never sat down on our bums for long.

Granny Esther lasted until 1953 and the ripe old age of eighty-five, and my mother didn't die until 1985 when she was ninety, so I suppose you could say the women in my family are battlers.

More than anything – and I passionately believe this to be true – I've enjoyed my life and tried to find the fun in any situation. That's why I'm still here to tell the tale. More than can be said for most of my old employers, I'm sad to say.

Kind old Mr Stocks passed away in 1957 and left Wood-hall to his son, Captain Eric. Mr Orchard remained faithfully by his side until the day Captain Eric died in the summer of 1974, aged seventy-six. He left Woodhall the minute Captain Eric's wake was finished. Where he went, nobody knows. Loyal to the end, Mr Orchard had devoted

Larking about shortly after the birth of my son, Timothy James, in 1946.

a lifetime to the service of the Stocks family, unshakable in his belief that what he was doing was worthwhile, that he was born to serve them. Every day for over forty-four years he tended to his master's every need, carefully pla-cing the silver-framed menu on the table, faithfully sounding the gong to announce dinner at seven thirty p.m.

The sound of a chiming dinner gong may well have died out in the hallways of upper-class houses in Britain, a symbol of a bygone age, but I like to think Mr Orchard's legacy lives on. He certainly taught me a thing or two about hard work and devotion to duty.

That butler was one of a dying breed. Once all the rank and deference had collapsed after World War Two and domestic service faded away, he clung to the ways of the old world. He couldn't have coped with the new, more democratic, way of life. Flo and I may have been born to serve in the way that Mr Orchard was, but we didn't live to serve. We took our opportunities and we used them to our advantage.

Mrs Jones will long since have died. I don't know where she went to as, sadly, we lost touch, but I'll never forget her. She was fierce, yes, but also fiercely loyal and I have her to thank for turning me from a scullery maid into a cook! I thought I knew it all, but in reality I was just a kid. Sneaking off with that troubled footman and Henry the Blackshirt showed me up for what I was, a rebellious little girl. I thought she was just exerting control over me but now, with the benefit of hindsight and wisdom, I can see she was only looking out for me. She always did. She's probably up there now, sitting on a cloud, giving some cherub hell.

As for lovely gentle George the farmhand, believe it or not we stayed in touch, even after I left Woodhall, and we remained friends for years. He became a proper old bachelor. I got him a job near where I lived years later in

Bournemouth. He was a dear, sweet, kind man and I often wish he'd found the love that eluded him. He died in 1986 in a nursing home, aged seventy. I was with him when he took his last breath. It may sound strange but we became so close that he was almost like family. When he got ill, suffering from cancer of the throat, and we knew the time was near, Timothy and I visited him every day.

On the day of his death a nurse rang. 'George is asking for you, Mollie,' she said. 'Can you get up here now, he's not got long.'

I grabbed my keys and raced up to the hospital. As I burst into the ward I was relieved to see him propped up in bed. When he spotted me, a gentle smile flickered over his face and his eyelids closed.

'Mollie,' he whispered, slowly stretching out his hand across the bed sheet and lacing his fingers through mine. My name was the last word he ever said. Sixty seconds later, he died. I'll never forget my lovely farmhand.

I'm afraid to say that kind Mrs Luddington didn't have quite such a peaceful end. After I visited her that day, during the war, I never did see her again. I was horrified to hear that on 29 February 1960 she was killed in an earthquake in Agadir in Morocco. It was the most destructive and deadly earthquake in Moroccan history and killed around 15,000 people. It lasted just fifteen seconds, but killed one third of the population of Agadir.

Poor Nell. She would have been fifty years old. Such a terrible end for such a gentle woman. My heart went out to her poor husband and children. I don't know what became of her husband, but I understand Wallington was passed down through the generations until it was sold in

2007. The location of the buried treasure remains a mystery to this day, but I've heard the bitter ghost of Elizabeth Coningsby still makes her presence known!

The rest of the gentry that I knew of fared no better than Nell in many ways.

Before and after World War Two Wallis and Edward were suspected by many of being Nazi sympathizers. After the duke's death in 1972, the duchess lived in seclusion and was rarely seen in public.

In May 1940 Oswald Mosley and his wife Diana Mitford were interned. They were released in 1943 but spent the rest of the war under house arrest. The war ended what was left of his political reputation.

As for our beloved King George VI, the stress of the war was believed to have taken its toll on his health and he died in 1952.

I walked over miles of heather from King's Lynn to pay my respects and watch his coffin being placed on the train at Wolferton Station, the official station for Sandringham. What a strange day. I and a group of sombre onlookers bowed our heads in respect as the queen (the Queen Mother as she later became), Elizabeth and Margaret all walked down the platform past us, following the coffin, in long, heavy black veils.

There was no security or burly bodyguards to hustle us back – there simply wasn't the fear that anything bad could happen to them. They were so loved by their people that they accepted us just standing there within touching distance of the coffin.

It may sound strange, my wanting to watch the coffin

go off, but I adored our royal family. Their lives felt so intertwined with my own. In many ways we felt like they were our own family, and so I too wanted to pay homage as the king left his country home for the last time.

Elizabeth would have been just twenty-five as she followed her father's coffin up the platform, aware of the

Me and my son, Timothy James, aged two. We had our photos taken at Selfridges for half a crown. The war was over but rationing was still biting, so photos like this were a small, affordable pleasure.

enormity of the task ahead of her. I'd seen her playing as a little girl in her garden and, nineteen years later, on the threshold of being made our queen. What an enormous responsibility for one so young! How incredible I find it that sixty years on we have just celebrated her Diamond

Jubilee. Not since I witnessed her grandfather King George V's Silver Jubilee back in 1935 have I seen such a total outpouring of patriotism and love.

The end of World War Two brought about many changes, not just the demise of our king and accession of his daughter Elizabeth. It was also the end of the domestic servant as we had known it.

Many trends that began the decline in service from the First World War were accelerated by the Second World War, but in a more pronounced and permanent way. For the first time, after World War Two, domestic appliances such as cookers, Hoovers and electric irons became available. Time-consuming tasks that would have required housemaids like Irene suddenly became easier and quicker, meaning servants weren't needed.

Huge employment opportunities, like clerical work, became available to young women as a result of the war. What young woman wanted to work long hours as a scullery or kitchen maid when she could get paid more and work fewer hours in an office? The rise in the school-leaving age meant that girls like me, who would have started as a scullery maid aged fourteen, now had more educational opportunities open to them. Thanks to the war, people viewed domestic service differently too. Doing things for yourself became popular and the idea of the 'housewife' as an identity also took off.

Although many households did still employ servants, it was on nowhere near the scale that I had witnessed. Usually it was confined to just one or two servants, such as a cleaner or a charwoman who lived out. It's impossible, really, to overstate how much the war changed the lives and homes of Britons from every single class background.

It was all change for me too. In 1953, soon after the death of King George VI, with two young children in tow – Ruth and a son, Timothy James – I finally departed British shores. My husband rose through the ranks to become an officer and was posted to the Far East and we went with him.

I may not have made it to Spain but I did make it to Singapore, Malaysia, Hong Kong and Yemen to name but a few.

As an officer's wife I had an incredible time and saw some amazing sights. I saw Singapore before there was even a single high-rise building built, travelled over developing countries in an eight-seater Commodore plane, watched native burning ceremonies in Kuala Lumpur and drank gin and tonic on a troopship from Singapore to England. What a trip that was. It took us a month to get home, sailing through the Suez Canal, stopping at Yemen and then Gibraltar. Every night there were fancy-dress parties, card games and drinks for the officers' wives and we all dressed up to the nines. I even had a man assigned to my cabin who ran my bath for me every night and brought me whatever I wanted. They virtually wiped your bottom for you. It was a high old time!

The kids and I once travelled through the Malay jungle under armed guard, clutching a Sten gun for fear of kidnap by communist terrorists. But after facing Mrs Jones in the kitchen, nothing fazed me. Like I say, nothing frightened me much when I was young.

The ultimate irony to my mind is that as my husband

rose through the ranks and we grew in so-called social prominence, we began to have staff of our own. Suddenly I found myself in charge of a household of staff. In Singapore we had no end of servants to help cook, clean and look after the children. As a commissioned officer in the RAF, my husband even had his own airman-come-personal-servant, known as a batman, who would come

On board HMS *Clyde* in 1954, sailing back from Singapore. I'm sat to the right wearing a scoop-neck dress. Timothy was on board another ship that had set sail weeks earlier. As an officer's wife you were given first-class service, and had servants to run your bath, warm up your toilet seat and pour your gin and tonic.

to the house to do our cleaning and sort out his uniform. I hated it. How would you feel having a strange bloke in your home doing your housework? Maybe it was the years of cooking and cleaning I did for the gentry, but I knew just how I wanted things doing and it felt wrong to sit back and let other people do it for me.

I suppose you could say I've been in the unique position of having been on both ends of the social scale, downstairs and upstairs, but believe me, I'm in no doubt which was the more fun place to be. The ten years I spent in domestic service were some of the happiest times of my life and have made me the woman I am today.

Starting as a scullery maid and working up to cook instilled in me confidence, a good work ethic, self-esteem and pride in my work. How many other professions today give young people those feelings?

It taught me to think on my feet, not to be reliant on anyone and not to be afraid of hard work or finding fun.

I can cook and I can count and those two skills, along with a willingness to work hard and the love of a good man, have carried me through my whole life. Service may seem like a class struggle to some and slavery to others, but to me it represented adventure and freedom beyond my wildest dreams.

From my humble beginnings as a scullery maid to my dream job as a cook, I owe domestic service a debt of gratitude. I'll keep on believing that until the final gong sounds.

Photographs

p. 7 Here's me at the ripe old age of ninety-six. My face may be wrinkled and my hair faded to silver, but I think you can tell by the twinkle in my eye that I still find the fun in life.

p. 11 Me as a baby being held by my indomitable Granny Esther. I was always her favourite.

p. 27 That's me on the far right, aged ten, being awarded first prize at school sports day in 1926. I was the fastest runner and the highest jumper in the whole area – I always thought I was better than anyone else back then!

p. 41 Downham Market Baptist Church members on a day out in the 1920s. I'm in the middle, behind the boy in the white shorts.

p. 57 Number 24 Cadogan Square, Knightsbridge, Mr Stocks's London house. We'd come up here every year for the London season.

p. 67 A very desirable postcode – all the gentry had a London house for the season.

p. 87 My dear friend Flo Wadlow, the kitchen maid I

worked with at Woodhall and Cadogan Square, in her uniform in a previous job. She was my partner in crime and a gentle, kind and loyal friend. We met in 1931 and we're still friends to this day.

p. 97 On the left is Louis Thornton (in the white apron), Mr Stocks's second chauffeur. A good deal of time was spent lusting after this handsome man. On the right is Ernie Bratton, Captain Eric's valet, a lovely fella who took me to the Chelsea Arts Ball.

p. 117 A plaque in Woodhall's church graveyard to commemorate Captain Manby, previous occupant of Woodhall and inventor of a rocket device used to save the crews of shipwrecked ships.

p. 127 Mr Stocks, my boss and the owner of Woodhall. A finer gentleman you'd be hard-pressed to find. Unlike some of the gentry, he was kind and generous and a real old-fashioned gent. We didn't have much to do with him, mind you, but whenever I did see him he would be striding about the place in his plus fours, flat cap on his head and a Labrador trotting by his side.

p. 156 This is the back of Woodhall. Can you see the fire-escape ladder Flo and I used to sneak out of the servants' quarters to go to the dance?

p. 174 Magnificent Woodhall, a beautiful listed Tudor home in the Norfolk countryside.

p. 199 Here's Flo again. She always had a smile on her face, no matter how hard we worked or how tired we got.

p. 212 The young lad in the back row, far left, is loyal farm-hand George Thornton, Louis's younger brother, aged about seventeen. I fear I broke that poor man's heart.

p. 249 Mr Orchard, the snooty butler who kept a watchful eye on me and my shenanigans. He was always giving me a telling-off but, looking back, I probably deserved it!

p. 282 Me in the grounds of Woodhall, in a rare moment off duty, aged about eighteen.

p. 303 This is beautiful Wallington Hall where I worked as a cook. The ancient shooting lodge, set in 600 acres of private grounds, is mentioned in the Domesday Book. It even had its own resident ghost.

p. 322 Here I am, a fresh-faced cook, aged about twenty-two.

p. 346 Me and Timothy on our wedding day, Saturday 5 November 1938. We're outside my mother's farmhouse, where we held the reception. Only the day before I'd been cooking for politicians and VIPs.

p. 347 This is me, a newly-wed, just before the outbreak of the Second World War. Every so often my husband

would take me out to dances and I'd dress up beautifully, always in a hat and pearls.

p. 349 The man of my dreams, Timothy, on active service
in India, where he was stationed for most of the war. I
worried about him out there more than I did about the
threat of invasion.

p. 359 Larking about shortly after the birth of my son,
Timothy James, in 1946.

p. 363 Me and my son, Timothy James, aged two. We had
our photos taken at Selfridges for half a crown. The
war was over but rationing was still biting, so photos
like this were a small, affordable pleasure.

p. 366 On board HMS *Clyde* in 1954, sailing back from
Singapore. I'm sat to the right wearing a scoop-neck
dress. Timothy was on board another ship that had set
sail weeks earlier. As an officer's wife you were given
first-class service, and had servants to run your bath,
warm up your toilet seat and pour your gin and tonic.

Acknowledgements

With grateful thanks to:

Orion Books for allowing reproduction of recipes and excerpts from *Mrs Beeton's Book of Household Management*.

Universal Media for the reproduction of excerpts from the film *Frankenstein*.

Friends of Mosley (FOM) and Mr Max Mosley for allowing reproduction of Oswald Mosley's speeches.

Andrew Luddington, Mr and Mrs Charlesworth of Woodhall, Tian and John Plaxton of Wallington Hall, Flo Wadlow (author of *Over a Hot Stove*, Mousehold Press, 2007) and Alan Childs (editor of *Over a Hot Stove*) for their help in the history, research and photography of Woodhall, Wallington Hall, Norfolk, and Cadogan Square, Knightsbridge.

Katherine Stone, PhD student, War Studies Department, King's College London.

He just wanted a decent book to read ...

Not too much to ask, is it? It was in 1935 when Allen Lane, Managing Director of Bodley Head Publishers, stood on a platform at Exeter railway station looking for something good to read on his journey back to London. His choice was limited to popular magazines and poor-quality paperbacks – the same choice faced every day by the vast majority of readers, few of whom could afford hardbacks. Lane's disappointment and subsequent anger at the range of books generally available led him to found a company – and change the world.

'We believed in the existence in this country of a vast reading public for intelligent books at a low price, and staked everything on it'
Sir Allen Lane, 1902–1970, founder of Penguin Books

The quality paperback had arrived – and not just in bookshops. Lane was adamant that his Penguins should appear in chain stores and tobacconists, and should cost no more than a packet of cigarettes.

Reading habits (and cigarette prices) have changed since 1935, but Penguin still believes in publishing the best books for everybody to enjoy. We still believe that good design costs no more than bad design, and we still believe that quality books published passionately and responsibly make the world a better place.

So wherever you see the little bird – whether it's on a piece of prize-winning literary fiction or a celebrity autobiography, political tour de force or historical masterpiece, a serial-killer thriller, reference book, world classic or a piece of pure escapism – you can bet that it represents the very best that the genre has to offer.

Whatever you like to read – trust Penguin.